ALL ELSE
FAILED

ALL ELSE FAILED

THE UNLIKELY VOLUNTEERS
at the HEART *of*
THE MIGRANT AID CRISIS

DANA SACHS

BELLEVUE LITERARY PRESS
New York

First published in the United States in 2023
by Bellevue Literary Press, New York

For information, contact:
Bellevue Literary Press
90 Broad Street
Suite 2100
New York, NY 10004
www.blpress.org

Cover photograph by punghi/Shutterstock.com

Library of Congress Cataloging-in-Publication Data
Names: Sachs, Dana, author.
Title: All else failed : the unlikely volunteers at the heart of the migrant aid crisis / Dana Sachs.
Description: New York : Bellevue Literary Press, 2023.
Identifiers: LCCN 2022021758 | ISBN 9781954276093 (paperback) |
ISBN 9781954276109 (epub)
Subjects: LCSH: Humanitarian aid workers--Greece. | Humanitarian assistance--Greece. |
Political refugees. | Refugees. | Refugees, Arab.
Classification: LCC HV640 .S23 2023 | DDC 362.8709495--dc23/eng/20220805
LC record available at https://lccn.loc.gov/2022021758

Bellevue Literary Press would like to thank all its generous donors—individuals and
foundations—for their support.

 The publication of this book is made possible by the support of
Le Korsa and the Josef and Anni Albers Foundation.

 This publication is made possible by the New York State
Council on the Arts with the support of the Office of
the Governor and the New York State Legislature.

This project is supported in part by an award from
the National Endowment for the Arts.

Book design and composition by Mulberry Tree Press, Inc.

Bellevue Literary Press is committed to ecological stewardship in our book production practices,
working to reduce our impact on the natural environment.

♾ This book is printed on acid-free paper.

Manufactured in the United States of America.

First Edition
10 9 8 7 6 5 4 3 2 1

paperback ISBN: 978-1-954276-09-3
ebook ISBN: 978-1-954276-10-9

For Todd, and for all the volunteers—
those who have homes and those who do not.

*". . . are we beholden to each other,
must we take care of each other,
or is it every man for himself?"*

—Rebecca Solnit

*"I don't know how we'll do it,
but everything is feasible somehow."*

—volunteer on Lesvos Island

Contents

Individuals

*Individuals whose stories unfold in this book**

TRACEY MYERS: An English community activist, born in 1977, who began volunteering on Lesvos Island in the summer of 2015.

JENNI JAMES: A jill-of-all-trades New Zealander, born in 1967, who began volunteering on Lesvos Island in the summer of 2015.

THE KHALIL FAMILY: Ali Khalil (known as Abu Omar Khalil following the birth of his son, Omar) born in 1977 in Damascus; his wife, Salma, born in 1986 in Damascus; daughters Layla (2004) and Nura (2007) and son Omar (2015), all born in Damascus; daughter Zahra, born in Germany in 2017.

KANWAL MALIK: Born in 1981, a social worker from Nottingham, England, who began volunteering in Greece in the fall of 2015.

IBRAHIM KHOURY: A Syrian humanitarian relief professional, born in 1987, who arrived in Greece as a refugee in the fall of 2015.

RIMA HALABI AND HER CHILDREN: A Syrian mother of six, born in 1979, who had to get her children from suburban Aleppo to Germany on her own.

SAMI MALOUF: Born in 1990, a Syrian from the coastal region of Latakia who arrived in Greece in the fall of 2015.

---

* I've changed the names of the refugees as well as certain identifying details in order to protect their safety and privacy.

Prologue

O N SUMMER DAYS IN 2016, THE WEATHERED BUILDING in Athens looked like any other abandoned school. Greece had endured years of financial crisis, and a lack of funds had shuttered many municipal facilities. With its vacant playground and locked front gate, the place would seem deserted to a passerby. But anyone staring at the building would have noticed signs of life: open windows, clothes drying on lines, and, on the balcony overlooking Acharnon Street, tiny curious faces staring down at passing cars.

In fact, four hundred people lived inside. When the sun finally set, bringing relief from the day's scorching heat, dozens emerged on the courtyard playground to enjoy the evening air. The residents, the vast majority Syrian refugees, had become stranded in Athens that summer. With nowhere else to go, they had taken shelter in the abandoned building, sleeping in tents in the former classrooms upstairs.

They called the place the Second School. Earlier that summer, local solidarity activists had broken in, implemented a few cheap and minor upgrades, then reopened the building as an illegal housing facility, known as a "squat." By mid-July, it was full of displaced people. On those summer evenings, children raced like freed prisoners across the asphalt playground. Young mothers pushed strollers in slow loops around the perimeter. Beside a crumbling stone wall, preteen girls gathered in gossipy clusters while, next to the main entrance, a "security team" of young men stood guard, ostensibly protecting the inhabitants from riffraff but mostly just horsing around. Because few of the residents would have eaten much, if anything, over the course of the day, they kept their eyes on Rima. She was a refugee, too, and the squat's volunteer cook, and a mother alone in Greece with five children. Every day, Rima parked her infant daughter in a stroller, stepped into the cramped shed that served as her kitchen, then proceeded to prepare dinner for four hundred. When the smell of onions with cinnamon, cardamom, and nutmeg—the triumvirate of Middle Eastern cooking—began wafting through the air, everyone at the Second School knew they'd eat that night.

To a large extent, the squat's occupants kept the facility running. They engaged in endless meetings, made schedules, created work teams to clean the bathrooms and sweep the stairs. In addition to Rima, there was Harun, a dewy-eyed teen who managed the supplies in the storeroom and slept on a mat on its floor. Graying, brawny Ali Khalil, whom everyone called Abu Omar, was a former taxi driver who often roamed the building, haranguing all the people who'd shirked their chores.

The refugee residents of the Second School faced countless obstacles. They lacked money, tools, supplies, foreign language skills, and basic expertise in operating a large housing facility in Athens. For help, they relied on a network of nonrefugee supporters, whom everyone called "the volunteers." Neighbors and solidarity activists offered advice, administrative support, and supplies. A team of young people from Spain was spending the summer providing activities for children. Rando, a flight attendant from London, regularly pulled up in a rental car and unloaded things like diapers, toilet paper, and eggplant, all bought with funds he'd raised online. A middle-aged Syrian leftist émigré named Castro had helped establish the squat. When things went wrong or people argued, he became the go-to problem solver and, often to his dismay, the disciplinarian. That summer, too, a British social worker named Kanwal came to Athens to help with the relief effort, and she ended up as the squat's day-to-day manager. Every morning, Kanwal showed up wearing the building's keys on a cord around her neck, then proceeded to do everything from organizing language classes to negotiating prices for cooking oil and shampoo. By midsummer, the squat had attained a kind of normalcy, but nothing could be normal in a place where four hundred vulnerable people were sleeping in tents.

How did all these asylum seekers end up living in an abandoned school in Athens, aided by volunteers, not by the European Union, the United Nations, or the world's vast network of nongovernmental aid organizations? The answer lies in an extraordinary geopolitical drama that had begun to rage in Europe the previous year. As violence swept across much of the Middle East, hundreds of thousands of refugees fled their homelands, reached Turkey, and crossed the Aegean Sea into Greece. Once there, almost all continued north through the Balkans, then fanned out across Europe. By the end of 2015, some 800,000 had taken this route. It was the largest movement of displaced people in Europe since World War II.

In the early months of this emergency, traditional relief networks proved themselves incapable of delivering a productive response. Most of the refugees had made the dangerous trip to Greece on flimsy boats, arriving hungry, traumatized, and, in many cases, injured and ill. They needed help, but Greece, buried in debt, did not have resources to address the crisis. The European Union, for its part, allocated millions of euros in aid but failed to disburse the funds effectively. Part of the problem lay in the stumbles of the world's major humanitarian actors—groups like the United Nations High Commissioner for Refugees (UNHCR), the International Committee of the Red Cross (ICRC), and the International Rescue Committee (IRC)—which talked about helping but offered only limited support on the ground. UNHCR, for example, had decades of experience addressing emergencies in regions like Sub-Saharan Africa and South Asia, but almost none in providing assistance in Europe. Again and again, world leaders and humanitarian professionals announced plans to deliver relief, then failed to follow through successfully. In crises of human suffering, a gap always exists between need and available services, but in Greece, in 2015, displaced people received almost no official aid at all.

And that's when something surprising happened. Thousands of individuals—Greek villagers, Swedish college students, Irish retirees, Italian lifeguards, and, eventually, refugees themselves—stepped forward to fill the gaps. Some had expertise. Others had no idea what they were doing. They had very little money. Working together, however, they supplied dry clothes, hot meals, and basic medical care. They never had enough, and an awful lot went wrong, but the grassroots volunteer effort eased suffering. Over the months that followed, and even after the world's large humanitarian actors began to shoulder a larger share of the burden, these individual Good Samaritans worked together and, again and again, averted disaster.

IN EARLY 2016, THE CONDITIONS OF THE CRISIS SHIFTED. The European Union and Turkey signed a deal to close Greece's northern border, preventing asylum seekers from continuing north across Europe. The goal was to staunch the flow of refugees, but the border agreement ended up trapping tens of thousands who had already entered Greece. With no way to leave the country, and no desire to return to their shattered homelands, they became stuck in a nation with very little capacity to provide for them. Thousands ended up in remote vermin-infested camps run by the Greek military. Others fled to Greece's cities, creating the enormous need for housing that was (illegally) addressed by the squats. The volunteer movement had gotten its start by handing out warm blankets to people stepping ashore from boats. A year later, amateur aid teams were providing shelter, meals, and education. Within a few weeks of opening, the Second School had reached full capacity, as had other squats across the country.

I spent time in Greece that summer, not only to conduct research for this book. Earlier that year, several friends and I had become involved in the grassroots effort. Our role was fairly simple: We raised funds in the United States, then took that money to Greece and spent it on low-cost initiatives providing basic supplies like underwear, sanitary pads, and fruit. Over the years since then, on every visit to Greece, I have witnessed the urgent need for strong global aid mechanisms, the ongoing failure of the international community to provide comprehensive help, and the essential role that grassroots volunteers have come to play in addressing humanitarian needs.

The grassroots movement in Greece may be more extensive than others, but it has much in common with such efforts around the world. While one volunteer helped refugees out of boats on Lesvos Island in

2015, another distributed rain ponchos to displaced people in Serbia. Someone knit winter caps for Syrian babies in London. And someone else handed out cups of tea at a migrant camp in France. More recently, as people have fled their homes in Central America, volunteer groups along the Mexico–United States border have provided food and clothing to thousands of migrants and asylum seekers there. Many of these volunteers become confounded at some point over the insufficiency of official assistance. "Shouldn't they have the Red Cross or somebody over here?" one volunteer in Matamoros, Mexico, mused to the *Los Angeles Times*. He was posing a question I've asked myself many times, and he came to a similar conclusion: "[If] we don't do it, they go hungry."

This is a book about a humanitarian emergency and the volunteers who stepped forward to address it. The narrative follows seven individuals (or, in two cases, families) who played roles in this effort, and it illustrates how their lives became intertwined in Greece as they came together and formed a new community. I also hope to illuminate a fundamental but often overlooked fact about the events in Greece in recent years: Whereas the word *volunteer* might conjure images of Good Samaritans from wealthy countries, refugees themselves have actually formed the backbone of the volunteer movement. All of them lost their homes, their possessions, their livelihood, and their homeland, and many also lost loved ones. They arrived in Greece after having traveled across continents. They'd been cheated and robbed. They'd endured violence and constant uncertainty about the future. And yet, in the depths of their suffering and deprivation, many stepped forward to help. Often that effort brought dignity back to their lives.

ON SUMMER NIGHTS AT THE SECOND SCHOOL, after Rima had finished serving dinner, people lingered in the courtyard to socialize. They were an unlikely community—foreigners and Greeks, the homeless and the housed—and they would likely never have met if circumstances had not thrown them together in this strange way. Kanwal, the British social worker and site manager, liked to end her day sitting near the kitchen shed, playing with Rima's baby. The Spanish volunteers, laughing and silly, kicked soccer balls around with the kids. Abu Omar Khalil, the former cabbie, smoked cigarettes and chatted with new friends while keeping an eye on his children. Often, after dinner, some of the younger guys would disappear inside the building, then reappear moments later holding hand drums. Soon this makeshift ensemble began singing and beating out the rhythms of the *dabke,* beloved music of the Middle East. Everyone in the courtyard gathered close at that moment to listen, dance, chant, and clap hands. Here and there, the pale glow of cell phones dotted the darkness as people made recordings to send to faraway family and friends. They didn't need to type words. The video alone said it: Look—I'm okay.

This book tells that story.

ALL ELSE
FAILED

PART I

Lost

CHAPTER 1

The Escape Corridor

To best understand what happened in Greece, we need to go back to a beach on Lesvos Island one day in August 2015, when two women stood looking out across the Aegean. Tracey Myers was a quiet Brit, thirty-eight years old, a coal miner's daughter with bright orange hair. Jenni James, a forty-eight-year-old New Zealander, was a small platinum blonde, and stronger than she looked. From where they stood, only a few short miles separated Lesvos from the Turkish coast. Most days, a person standing on this beach could easily see Turkey.

Jenni had shoved her black wraparound sunglasses up into her hair, and she held a pair of binoculars to her eyes. She never left her hotel room without them these days. Out in the water, not far offshore, a boat foundered and started taking on water. As the women watched, it began to sink. They could see passengers in the sea, their red or yellow life jackets bobbing in the waves.

Tracey and Jenni pulled off their clothes, ran down to the water, and jumped in.

Later, Tracey described herself as wearing nothing but "knickers nicked from my sister and a lacy bra." She was a strong swimmer, though, and she quickly rescued an Afghan man who could no longer keep his head above the water. Jenni pulled in someone, too, and then, back on the beach, performed CPR on both of them. The women had come to Greece to help, but neither had expected to save lives quite so literally. "I don't think I'm the person to be a lifeguard," Tracey remarked later, posting about the day on Facebook. "I'm a heavy smoker. I'm a bit overweight. I certainly wasn't thinking like a lifeguard."

She also realized that the experience had put her own concerns into proper perspective. "Bikini phobia gone," she noted.

The women had come to Lesvos only a month before, heeding an online call for volunteers. By the end of July, 124,000 displaced people had arrived by boat in Greece in 2015, an increase of 750 percent from the previous year, according to the United Nations. Many landed on Lesvos, overwhelming the local population of only 85,000. Back home in New Zealand, Jenni had taught sustainable resource management, but she had long wanted to join a humanitarian relief effort. When she saw the callout for volunteers, she headed to Lesvos. Tracey had merely flown over from England to help her friend get settled. After she saw the extent of the need, she stayed.

During their first weeks on the island, Jenni and Tracey struggled to get their bearings. Volunteers took turns standing with binoculars, scanning the sea for incoming boats. As the dinghies approached, arrival teams stepped into the water, guided them in, then helped the passengers to shore. A safe landing signaled success, but what would happen next? Lesvos had almost no relief infrastructure, no systematic distribution of food, no dry clothing, no transportation. Most boats came ashore on the north side of the island, which meant the new arrivals would then have to travel sixty kilometers south, to the city of Mitilini, to board ferries to mainland Greece. During the early days of the emergency, Greece's antismuggling laws forbade private vehicles and commercial buses from carrying migrants. Volunteers handed out donated clothes, bottled water, sandwiches and fruit, but the travelers were essentially on their own. After a rest, they began to walk. Everyone walked, even small children, pregnant women, the elderly, amputees. The narrow rural roads had no public toilets. People who had fled war-torn countries, traversed Turkey, and survived the crossing by boat now found themselves facing one more indignity—having to relieve themselves in roadside ditches in Europe. Volunteers, both local and foreign, drove by, handing out bottled water, trying to keep people from passing out in the heat.

Day by day, a makeshift aid network began to take shape. Teams of Spanish lifeguards joined local fishermen and the Hellenic Coast Guard in rescuing people from sinking boats. Greek villagers offered food from their own kitchens. Midsummer in Lesvos meant high season for vacationers from all over Europe. Suddenly, the tourists were witnessing a humanitarian emergency as they made their way from the breakfast buffet to the beach. An article in Britain's *Daily Mail* described travelers' resentment over the situation. "We don't like it," said one of them. "We won't be coming back if it's like a refugee camp again next year."

Tracey observed something very different. She had spent eighteen years—almost her entire professional life—working for social justice causes, and she expected nothing from the wealthy vacationers who filled the island's fancy hotels. But then they joined in to help. Their efforts didn't always go smoothly. Maybe they were giants of industry back in London or Stockholm, because they often bossed others around. Tracey heard a lot of "Take this" and "Go there," but not a lot of "I'll do that." The situation made her laugh. "Everyone was a manager and no one was a doer," she recalled later. But as days passed, she found herself moved by their determination. They weren't like volunteers she'd ever seen, but they got the job done.

As the crisis unfolded that summer, in fact, it was locals and tourists—not the Greek government, not the United Nations, not the European Union, not the Red Cross—who shouldered the burden of care. On Lesvos Island, locals took in vulnerable refugees at a volunteer-run camp. Along the island's northern coast, they organized aid teams to meet boats and help exhausted people make it to shore. One village restaurateur, Melinda McRostie, who founded the grassroots Starfish Foundation, later described "the enormous, bewildering gap created by Greece's lack of resources and the failure of nations and aid agencies to recognize the emergency here early on." The volunteers tried to fill that gap themselves. When it became clear that they couldn't address the situation on their own, they turned to the internet and put out more calls for help.

WHEN TRACEY AND JENNI STOOD ON THE BEACHES of Lesvos, scanning the water for boats, they were at the midpoint of a migration highway—an "escape corridor," some called it—that started in war-torn Middle Eastern and African countries, moved up through Turkey, crossed into

Greece, then continued on toward Northern Europe. Scholars and aid professionals call this highway "the Western Balkan Route" or just "the Balkan Route," and it dates back millennia, to the time when humans first figured out how to cross the narrow straits between Turkey and Greece. Over the centuries, migrants have traveled in all directions, but recent instability had turned this highway into a one-way route, propelling more and more people toward Europe. By the summer of 2015, the line of displaced stretched all along the Balkan Route.

The Syrian city of Idlib had fallen to the Islamic extremist al-Nusra Front only a few months before. António Guterres, then head of UNHCR, called Syria's civil war "the worst humanitarian crisis of our generation." At the same time, tens of thousands of Afghans, Iraqis, and citizens of other tortured nations were fleeing violence and collapsed economies. Migrant numbers spiked. Boats arrived on Lesvos every day. By August, people were sleeping on the streets, by the sides of roads, outside the ferry terminal in the town of Mitilini.

TRACEY MYERS HAD PLANNED TO SPEND ONLY A WEEK OR TWO volunteering. As time passed, however, she found herself unable to stop. She kept imagining that the well-established international aid organizations would "swoop in and sort it out." Occasionally, professional teams did arrive on the island. Their staff saw the piles of discarded life jackets, the refugees trudging up the road. They took notes—"assessments," she heard officials call them—and then disappeared again.

Meanwhile, boats kept coming.

It was in the midst of this chaos, and lack of institutional support, that Tracey had pulled the drowning man from the water. In the moment itself, she simply dived into the sea without thinking. In the days that followed, though, she experienced what she called "a trauma reaction." She couldn't stop mulling over the fact that if she hadn't been standing on that beach, another human being would have drowned. Suddenly, it no longer seemed possible to leave a scene of such overwhelming need. She had to stand on the shore, scanning the waves for flashes of red and yellow. She had to pass out sandwiches and bottled water. She had to remain on Lesvos until the professionals, with their skills and money, finally stepped in. That would happen, she told herself, anytime now. Until then, she'd keep volunteering.

WHAT MAKES SOMEONE LEAVE BEHIND THEIR OWN LIFE in order to help strangers? Altruism plays a role, as does political or spiritual commitment, but people also have very specific personal reasons that spur them forward.

I once asked Tracey what propelled her and Jenni toward Lesvos. "We'd had our own shit," she replied.

The two women first met in 2013. Tracey, who had been working as a youth health educator in England, had left her job to travel, stuffing a few possessions into a backpack. She ended up in New Zealand, where she spent her days hiking, kayaking, and playing pickup games of Scrabble in little country towns. Then, in Auckland, she and Jenni both ended up at a lesbian comedy night called Dykes on Mics.

In Auckland's insular queer community, everyone noticed a new face. Jenni thought Tracey was beautiful. Normally reserved, she surprised herself by walking over to Tracey's table and sitting down.

Tracey thought, Here's somebody who's trying to enter my life with some gusto.

Jenni, a single mom, had recently dropped her son at college, and she, too, was looking for adventure. She had invested a small inheritance in the purchase of a Volkswagen Kombi van she named "Blue Moon" and outfitted for long-distance travel. Pretty soon, the two were tooling around New Zealand together. Eventually, they traveled to North America and Continental Europe, then decided to head to England and visit Tracey's hometown. That's when things went wrong.

It was 2014, and debates about immigration and Britain's relationship with the rest of Europe—always controversial—were becoming increasingly fraught. Jenni had no problem entering the UK the first time, but after she left for a few days to attend a women's festival in Spain, authorities balked at letting her back in. They saw on her passport that she'd been out of New Zealand for three months already, then asked her to explain why she hadn't made a single return trip home.

"You're kidding me," Jenni responded. "I'm on a year's holiday around the world. I'm not going to pop back to New Zealand."

But the border agents saw Jenni as a risk for overstaying her visa. They took away her passport and detained her at Tracey's house, threatening to expel her from the country and place a red stamp on her passport that would impede her travel for the rest of her life.

Jenni hunkered down, panicked, while Tracey researched immigration law and human rights. She realized that Jenni was lucky that she was white. A person of color might have ended up in a detention center instead of a private home. The two women decided to fight the decision, embarking on what Tracey called "a humongous immigration battle with the UK." Tracey wrote letter after letter to immigration rights attorneys and rallied her own local community—veterans of marches for gay pride and human rights—to speak up on Jenni's behalf.

Ultimately, the British Home Office agreed to a compromise. Jenni would not be *forcibly* removed, but she had to leave. If she ever wanted to return to the UK, she'd need proof that she had a full-time job and owned a house in New Zealand.

"That," said Jenni, "ain't ever going to happen."

The stress took its toll on their relationship. Their life as a couple ended, but somehow the friendship survived. So, in the summer of 2015, when they heard that thousands of asylum seekers were risking their lives to reach Europe, the crisis felt personal to them. As Tracey put it, "We'd started to understand what borders felt like." They went to Greece.

BY THE END OF AUGUST, TRACEY AND JENNI HAD BEEN ON LESVOS for nearly two months. Tracey, who still had a job in England, hurtled back and forth between the two countries, while Jenni stayed on the island, assisting with sea rescues and overseeing construction, infrastructure, and distribution projects. The sea rescue effort did not come naturally for Jenni, who could barely swim. When boats approached the shore, she felt terror as she waded into the water, suppressing panic while trying to keep her head above the waves. Sometimes, in the confusion of an arrival, boat passengers tumbled on top of her, nearly pushing her under. Few of them could swim, either; plus, they carried the added weight of backpacks, trauma, and fear. Jenni had to stay calm to keep both herself and them from drowning.

On land, things went better. The daughter of a horse trainer, Jenni had grown up on remote farms in New Zealand where, if a toilet broke, you had to fix it yourself. By her early twenties, she had become so mechanically adept that she rebuilt an entire car. In Lesvos, her practical skills became central to her efforts. "I'll put my hand to anything," she would say, and if she didn't know how to build something, fix something, or jury-rig something, she'd turn to Google to figure it out.

One day, Jenni drove a truck to the airport on the southern end of the island to pick up the first load of a huge aid shipment from Slovenia. The boxes, which amounted to two and a half tons of goods arriving over several days, included tents, clothing, shoes, and personal hygiene supplies. Most came from individuals, but donations also came from pharmaceutical companies and the Slovenian Red Cross. There was some irony in the fact that a national Red Cross was shipping aid to a fledgling volunteer team in Greece. Wasn't the system supposed to work the other way around, with donations from individuals or small organizations going to the Red Cross for distribution? In Lesvos, the system regularly ran backward.

Volunteering could put a person through the whole range of emotions—the whole *bloody* range of emotions, as Jenni might put it—in a single day. Recently, for example, she'd met a pregnant Syrian, a university professor, who had just arrived by boat. The woman hadn't felt her fetus kick in days, so Jenni's team called an ambulance. While they waited, the woman's family spread their soaking wet documents out to dry. Hours passed. The ambulance never arrived. Jenni found a car and they rushed to the hospital. The doctors declared the fetus healthy, but the family's joy turned to panic when they realized they'd left their documents drying in the sun. By the time Jenni returned to the spot, all their papers—birth certificates, university diplomas, records of employment—had disappeared, making it almost impossible for them to relaunch their professional careers. The record of their lives had vanished.

Maybe it was the regular experience of sadness that compelled Jenni to relish any moments of joy. When the Slovenian shipment arrived at the airport and the volunteers transferred the boxes to their truck, Jenni paused for a moment and created a short video to thank donors on social media. Wearing a bright red SLOVENIA T-shirt and carrying a handmade THANK YOU SLOVENIA sign, she yelled like a cheerleader: "Thank you, Slovenia! Awesome, Slovenia!"

THE VOLUNTEERS' ONLINE UPDATES CONNECTED the aid movement with concerned observers around the world. The communications had real practical value in terms of bolstering support. Once, when Tracey returned briefly to England, she appealed for donations by requesting specific items on Facebook: "Men. I need your trousers and trainers. Want to fill a case with them by Friday for folk who really need them. Can you help?"

Sometimes, too, the internet gave an unfiltered view of the situation as it unfolded in Greece. In a video that a volunteer named Adam Rosser posted on YouTube, an overloaded dinghy approached the Lesvos shore. The video showed a dozen or so aid workers in bright yellow vests wading into the surf to meet the boat, then doing the same as many other boats followed. Quickly, and with practiced efficiency, the helpers lifted babies and small children, then carried them over the rocky beach while parents disembarked. When an elderly woman, a gray scarf neatly covering her head, teetered as she moved through the surf, an aid worker held her arm.

In the video, many voices spoke many languages. A little girl smiled. A boy, pale and shivering, perched on a rock. A volunteer held a baby, and when a man approached and reached for the child, the volunteer asked, "Are you the father?" The man responded, "Baba," and the volunteer set the child into his arms.

At the end of the video, the camera panned the shore. By now, the new arrivals had left the beach and begun their trek to the reception centers across the island. Only a few volunteers remained, plus piles of neon-colored life jackets and the carcasses of deflated dinghies.

In the final seconds, the narrator of the video said, "We're in this bucolic little fishing village. Looks like there were twenty or thirty boats today so far. And we are told that there are sixteen on the way tonight."

I didn't see this video until a year or so later, after I'd walked through the teeming border camp at Idomeni and visited the crowded squat residences of Athens. The thing that surprised me most was not the overwhelming number of people on the boats, or even the fear and exhaustion in their eyes (sadly, there was no longer anything surprising about that). No, it was the evidence that, even in the earliest months of this crisis, absent any effective official aid, a community of strangers had already organized a fledgling response. When boats reached Greece, volunteers stood ready to help.

CHAPTER 2

War Zone

IN THE SUMMER OF 2015, MANY PEOPLE who would later become volunteers were far from Greece. They remained in their homelands, trying to survive.

Among those were the Khalil family of Damascus—a father, a mother, and two young daughters—who had already endured four years of civil war. Bombs had driven them from their home in the Yarmouk district to rented rooms in Jaramana, a Druze enclave that was comparatively safe and, therefore, teeming with the displaced. Nothing completely mitigated the fear of living in a war zone, however. As the conflict dragged on, one question plagued them: Should they stay in Syria or flee?

Ali Khalil earned his living—barely—by driving a cab that summer. Over his lifetime, the thirty-eight-year-old had cycled through a number of jobs. He'd run a falafel stall, sold cars, worked as a print-shop technician, and hauled goods as a cross-country truck driver. Now, with the war in full swing, he just wanted to make enough to pay the rent, a difficult task when he had so few passengers. He couldn't travel far from home because if a bomb dropped near his daughters' elementary school, he would have to rush over to save them. Even when the girls were home with their mother, he limited his driving range to a small geographical area. The Assad regime had instituted a military draft for men between the ages of eighteen and forty-five. Given the violence of the war, Syrians considered conscription a death sentence and used various means to avoid it. Military checkpoints, scattered around the city, became sites of danger, where officials interrogated men trying to cross. "Why aren't you serving?" they would ask. If a man lacked a convincing reply, he could be drafted then and there. Ali avoided checkpoints.

It helped, too, that he looked older than his age, making him less tempting as a potential conscript. He had spent his youth gambling, drinking, and chasing women. The hard living had left its marks, giving him the gray hair and fleshy jowls of a much older man and the crooked nose of a second-rate boxer (the nose was not, actually, the result of a brawl, but of a car accident during a night of carousing). His parents, hoping to see him settle down, pressured him to marry. He chose Salma, who was small-boned, fragile-looking, and only sixteen. He thought of her more like a kid sister than a wife, but they both did what was expected. Within a few years, Salma gave birth to two daughters, Layla and Nura.

During the early years of their marriage, Ali cheated on Salma secretly. After she discovered his philandering, he cheated in the open. For a long time, she suffered, but eventually something in her began to change. Much later, she told me that she had "arrived in that place like a blind kitten, and then I started knowing things." She left him in 2012, moving back to her father's house.

That decision changed everything. Syria's laws favored husbands in terms of custody, so Salma had left her kids behind. Now, suddenly shouldering complete responsibility for his family, Ali realized how much he valued his wife. Desperate to win her back, he called her day and night to express his love.

It wasn't her husband's pleas that finally convinced Salma to come home. She missed her daughters. When Ali begged her to return, she listened. He promised to be faithful. "If you come back," he told Salma, "I will change completely."

The surprising thing about this story is not that the philandering husband vowed to change but that he did change—completely. Salma returned to Damascus. Ali remained faithful and they turned their focus to creating a stable family life. Much later, Salma would remember the subsequent years as the happiest of her life, even though, by that point, war was raging all around them.

Bombs came very, very close. Once, a rocket shattered windows at their daughters' school. Layla, the elder, was in her classroom when the teacher yelled, "Run downstairs as fast as you can or you'll die." The students ran. They had learned the school's emergency plan, and within seconds they huddled together in a downstairs hallway. Teachers, standing at both ends of the crowd of children, worked the phones, calling families to let them know what had happened. The parents who lived closest got there first. The second rocket hit just as they arrived.

Syrians did not trust their government to provide accurate information, so the Khalils never knew how many died that day. The official number was three—two children and an adult. Down in the hallway, students and teachers waited until school administrators declared the emergency over. Later, as Layla and Nura left the building, they saw red stains on the playground. "It's not blood," one teacher told them; "it's just tomatoes."

The next day, the girls returned to school. The administration implemented a few changes. Students no longer spent recess outside. When rockets fell, they hid under their desks. Girls cried. Boys cried. Teachers said, "Don't worry. It's nothing."

Why did parents endanger their children by sending them to school? Because the risk was greater at home. One day, while the Khalil girls were playing outside, a rocket hit the street, landing inside the blade of a bulldozer parked on the road. Otherwise, their father realized, his girls would have died. By his reasoning, for every ten rockets that might hit the school, a hundred could hit the house in Jaramana. Ali had completed his military service as a young man. He knew the rules of war. Weren't opposing factions supposed to avoid shelling a school? At some point, parents began to notice that the worst fighting near the school took place on Thursdays, so the Khalils kept their girls home that day. Otherwise, Layla and Nura went to school every morning. Layla had a cell phone now. In emergencies, she could call her parents.

Time passed. The family muddled through. One day, a bomb gravely wounded Ali's younger brother, Anwar, who had merely gone to pick up something at the store. The incident shattered his leg. With Syria's medical system wrecked by war, the family arranged to smuggle Anwar out of the country so that he could get the care he needed. In time, he reached Germany and received treatment, but he was now completely isolated in a foreign land.

The Khalils considered leaving, too. Sometimes, it seemed like practically the whole nation was on the move. Out of a prewar population of 21 million, some 7.6 million had joined the ranks of the country's "internally displaced" by finding shelter in safer locations within Syria's borders. Another four million had left the country altogether. By the summer of 2015, fully half of Syria's prewar population had fled their homes.

Life felt very fragile, especially once the Khalils found out Salma was expecting another child. But they did not want to leave their home. They did not want to become refugees.

Layla, age ten, could still remember the days when her biggest anxiety centered around the question "What if I do badly on my exams?" Nura, who was seven, could barely remember a time before the bombs. At night, the girls curled close to each other in bed. They couldn't fall asleep unless they held hands.

In a different part of Syria, the town of al-Dana, near Aleppo, another family also faced an agonizing situation. Rima and Musa Halabi had five children, plus one more on the way. Only four years had passed since they'd moved to this region from Damascus, leaving the capital for safety's sake, so that Musa could avoid the draft, and joining the ranks of Syria's internally displaced. They had no desire to leave Syria.

They had moved for other reasons, too. After living for a decade in a single room in Musa's parents' house, Rima had become fed up with her in-laws. For the past four years, she and Musa had managed to live an ordinary life in a region of olive groves and almonds. Rima was thirty-six years old, elated to have escaped her husband's bossy parents. I hold my own key in my own hand, she told herself with glee. The Halabis had a roomy modern house with an American-style kitchen, granite floors, and solid doors, a particular point of pride for Rima. They'd settled in a fine location, too. Al-Dana was far from the bustle of central Aleppo, but close enough that forty-one-year-old Musa, who owned a small taxi van—*service*, Syrians called it—could find work shuttling passengers between Aleppo, Idlib, and the Turkish border.

Rima ran the home while Musa zipped across the region. His absences seemed like nothing compared to an earlier time in their marriage. For seven years, Musa had worked as a laborer in nearby countries, returning to Syria for only fifteen days a year. You could see the result in the pattern of their children's births, even if Rima and Musa didn't pay much attention to exact dates. They had two daughters, Shakira and Malika, around 2002 and 2003, respectively, and then no children for seven years. After Musa returned to Syria, the family began to grow again. Around 2010, Rima gave birth to a son, Yusuf, and another son, Hassan, a year or so later. Their daughter Lina arrived around 2014. By the spring of 2015, Rima was pregnant with their sixth child.

If years earlier someone had told Rima that she would end up as a wife and mother of many children, the news might have surprised her. Her father had died when she was thirteen, leaving the family without a patriarch. Over time, she developed a dislike of men, and that feeling turned to hate when a cousin, forced into an arranged marriage, suffered brain damage after her husband threw her against a wall. Rima had vowed never to marry. When her brothers proposed an engagement, she refused. And then she met Musa. She liked the guy and decided to marry him. She hadn't regretted it.

In appearance, Rima was more handsome than pretty. Her well-chiseled features made her look like someone you didn't want to cross, but she was actually lighthearted and social. She valued her own comforts, too. "I have to take care of my family," she'd say, "but I'm not going to neglect myself." She bought high-end, natural cosmetics and avoided chemicals that might damage the skin. At home, she mixed yogurt, cornstarch, rose water, and fresh fruit into homemade face creams and masks, which she used on herself and also slathered on her children. In this rowdy household, Musa relished his role as father, too. The youngest Halabi child, Lina, considered her dad the center of the universe, trailing him everywhere around the house.

In al-Dana, Rima was known as the neighborhood *mukhtar,* or "chosen one," a sign of real respect for her, as the word was usually reserved for a man. Neighbors gathered at the Halabi home to visit, celebrate the Muslim holidays, and share heaping platters of food. Rima could not know then that she would soon have to flee this life and become a refugee in Europe, but the qualities that eventually led her to become the Second School Squat's volunteer cook were already fully developed back in al-Dana, where she took so much joy and pride from feeding her community.

This life of tranquillity ended in March 2015, when the al-Qaeda-affiliated al-Nusra Front swept through al-Dana while taking Idlib Governorate. The Islamic fundamentalists imposed a strict form of Sharia. Rima could no longer leave her house without a male escort. Al-Nusra rounded up opponents, jailing some and executing others. Down the street from the Halabis' home, the new regime converted a school into a holding center. "We're caring for displaced people," the leaders announced, but local people knew that half the building had become a prison. Now, al-Nusra's enemies considered the whole neighborhood a target. Bombs exploded in the streets around the Halabis' home. Musa's taxi business dwindled to almost nothing. They didn't know how long their savings would last.

Ramadan began in mid-June that year, and Rima's uncle Kareem arrived in al-Dana. He had hired smugglers to get him across the nearby border into Turkey and he planned to stay with the Halabis until he got word that he could leave. Now, observing the violence in al-Dana, Uncle Kareem offered blunt advice to Rima and Musa: "You should flee."

Kareem was a worldly man in his sixties who enjoyed the role of family sage. The situation in Syria was deteriorating, he said. "Go now, while you can."

Rima's house looked like a child-care center, with so many kids running around. Their thick shocks of hair made them look zany, especially after they got out of bed in the morning. Rima could count on her eldest, Shakira, to help, but her second daughter, Malika, had a rowdy streak. Sometimes, for fun, Rima put a little lipstick and blush on her girls' faces, wrapped them in head scarves, and showed them how they'd look as young ladies. But they were children. How could this unwieldy crew make the dangerous crossing to Turkey, and with Rima six months pregnant, too?

The bombing continued. Uncle Kareem kept urging them to flee. On some level, both Rima and Musa knew that he was right, but they hesitated. Rima resented her uncle. Years earlier, when his brother—Rima's father—died, leaving Rima's mother to raise her children all alone, Kareem did nothing to help the family financially. The name Kareem means "generous," Rima said to herself, but he's not.

To Kareem, Rima said, "We don't want to leave."

Musa said, "We want to stay in our home."

Kareem had no patience for this thinking. He looked at Musa. "You spent all those years traveling out of the country and now, of all times, you stick to Syria?"

What could they say to that? They lived in the world of lesser evils. They had only bad choices: Walk to the market without an escort and risk arrest, or let the children go hungry? Abandon their home and go to Turkey, where they would have nothing, or stay here, where their house could be flattened by a bomb?

These are questions people ask before they bolt.

CHAPTER 3

No Handbook

On September 2, 2015, a boat full of refugees capsized while trying to cross from Turkey to Greece. A three-year-old Syrian boy named Alan Kurdi drowned. His mother, his brother, and nine other refugees also died, twelve people among the nearly 3,800 that the International Organization for Migration (IOM) would estimate lost their lives in the Mediterranean that year. After this particular catastrophe, a photojournalist snapped a picture of Alan's body lying on a Turkish beach. It was a startling image. The boy didn't look dead so much as asleep, as if he'd paused in the midst of play to take a nap. The peacefulness of the pose, along with the normalcy of his outfit—red T-shirt, shorts, tiny shoes—made the photo wrenching. The image shot across the internet. Soon, world leaders were having to defend policies that forced refugees to imperil themselves to get to safety in the West. French prime minister Manuel Valls tweeted that "a Europe-wide mobilisation is urgent," while his British counterpart, David Cameron, insisted, "We do care."

In Europe's halls of power, not much changed, but the photograph galvanized many members of the public. Migrant Offshore Aid Station, a small boat rescue operation, registered a fifteenfold spike in donations in the first twenty-four hours after the photo went viral, and other charities saw dramatic upticks in donations, as well.

The photo appeared on a computer screen in Nottingham, England, some sixteen hundred miles from where Alan Kurdi drowned. There, a thirty-four-year-old social worker named Kanwal Malik stared at the picture, baffled. This is Europe, she thought. What's going on?

Kanwal, like so many, had been observing the war in Syria with concern. It wasn't until Alan Kurdi died, however, that she made a decision: She would fly to Greece to help. She found a cheap deal—£250 for a week at an all-inclusive resort on Kos, an island that had, like Lesvos, seen a crushing number of arrivals. Three friends decided to join her. The women created an online appeal for donations. By the time they left for Greece a few weeks later, they had filled their suitcases with warm fleeces, medicine, and clothes. They had a lot of money, too. Their fund-raising campaign, which began with a goal of three thousand pounds, quickly shot past thirteen thousand pounds.

What made Kanwal decide to help? In a sense, she'd been raised for this kind of effort. She was born in England to Pakistani immigrant parents. Her father abandoned the family, leaving Kanwal's mother, Robina, to raise her two small children alone. Robina responded with fierce competence. She put herself through college, became a kindergarten teacher, tutored neighborhood children in Urdu and the Qur'an, took in foster kids, and pulled herself out of bed at six every morning to spend an hour making the famous Nottingham lace that local souvenir shops sold to tourists. If anyone mentioned the man who had left her, Robina declared that she was her children's mother and father both. "My blood overrides his blood," she said.

Robina's passion lay in study and working to improve the world. "Humanity makes us who we are," she'd told her children. She wasn't exactly shocked, then, when Kanwal announced her plan to help refugees.

It was not a convenient time to drop everything and fly to Greece. Kanwal not only had a busy career but she and her boyfriend, Asad, were also planning to marry that November. Kanwal insisted that she could manage it all. She would stay two weeks, help as much as she could, then return in time for the wedding.

That October, the little team flew to Kos. The scene confused them at first. Walking to town from their beachside resort, they saw only peaceful beauty, no hint of disaster. "There're no refugees," they said to one another other, looking around. "Where are they?"

Then they turned a corner and the harbor came into view. In front of them lay a scene that defied imagination. The entire waterfront was lined with tents. "Families were just *there*," Kanwal later recalled. "Kids were just *there*." Everywhere she looked, she saw weary-looking people.

Kanwal's group felt a huge responsibility to spend their donation money wisely. "Okay," they said. "Let's take two days to assess. Let's see what the gaps are and see what we can do to fill them."

WHAT IS A REFUGEE? ACCORDING TO THE UNITED NATIONS, "Refugees are persons who are outside their country of origin for reasons of feared persecution, conflict, generalized violence, or other circumstances that have seriously disturbed public order and, as a result, require international protection."

What is a migrant? That's a bit trickier. "While there is no formal legal definition of an international migrant," says the UN, "most experts agree that an international migrant is someone who changes his or her country of usual residence, irrespective of the reason for migration or legal status."

And what's an asylum seeker? The UN defines an asylum seeker as "someone who says he or she is a refugee and seeks international protection from persecution or serious harm in their home country."

In other words, displaced people are considered asylum seekers while a state processes their claim. If the state accepts the claim, they're refugees. If it rejects the claim, they're migrants. All of which can seem like an unjust and overly simplistic way of defining the supremely complicated experience of fleeing one's homeland. "Who is a true refugee?" the writer Dina Nayeri has asked. "It makes me chuckle, this notion that 'refugee' is a sacred category, a people hallowed by evading hell. Thus, they can't acknowledge a shred of joy left behind or they risk becoming migrants again."

The world insists on defining the displaced, however. For decades it has fallen to UNHCR to stand on the front lines during humanitarian disasters, helping governments distribute aid to desperate people. But that did not happen in the early weeks and months of the crisis in Greece. In fact, neither UNHCR nor the Greek government played major humanitarian roles during that initial period. The humanitarian response faltered, in part, because bureaucrats across Europe couldn't agree on whose job it was to help.

UNHCR serves at the invitation of governments. Except for a brief and fairly limited effort on behalf of Syrian refugees in Bulgaria in 2013 and 2014, the agency had never provided humanitarian aid within the European Union. It showed little interest in jumping in, either. The European Union had plenty of money and seemed capable of managing without UN assistance in Greece. UNHCR's leadership, in fact, expressed concern that allocating staff and resources to a relief effort in Europe would divert support from other critical regions—in Africa, for example, where needs remained acute. Greece was enduring a severe economic crisis, but it belonged to the European Union. Couldn't the EU take care of its own?

For most of 2015, the Greek government also took a narrow view of its responsibility. Because 90 percent of arrivals wanted to continue to other parts of Europe, Greece was known as a "transit country." Like a crossing guard ushering pedestrians from one side of an intersection to the other, the government focused on facilitating people on their journey north through Europe. In terms of emergency relief, the Hellenic Coast Guard did an extraordinary job saving lives, but many other government institutions did little more than stand back and watch the masses moving through.

By late summer of 2015, when the need for a more robust response became unavoidable, Greece and the European Union formally invited UNHCR to ramp up its operation there. Three years earlier, the agency had employed fewer than two dozen people in Greece. Now, the UNHCR workforce would surpass six hundred, and the agency, which spent eight million euros in the country in 2014, spent twenty million a year later.

That was a lot of money, but considerable time would pass before the mobilization made an impact on the ground. In the meantime, refugees went hungry, and volunteer teams trying to shelter new arrivals had nothing more substantial to offer than tents. The fledgling grassroots system, powered by local citizens and volunteers from around the globe, remained the main source of comfort for displaced people.

In 2017, the Greek Ombudsman would issue a scathing report on the response in Greece, calling out the European Union, in particular, for failing to recognize the looming crisis even as war and unrest swept across the Middle East. "The signs were evident long ago, and the time was adequate for formulating an integrated and cohesive plan for addressing it," the report noted, adding that European member states "were late in grasping the magnitude of the issue, and when they actually did, they reacted in a piecemeal manner." In particular, the Ombudsman seemed flabbergasted at the EU's "unjustified bewilderment" when more and more boats arrived on its shores.

TINY RELIEF TEAMS WERE SPRINGING UP ACROSS GREECE. An academic study published in 2018 would identify forty-one grassroots volunteer groups working on Lesvos Island alone, most of them formed in 2015 in response to the surge in arrivals there. The report's authors called them "AHGOs" (ad hoc grassroots organizations), but the teams themselves preferred more evocative names, like Starfish Foundation, Help Refugees (as of 2021, its name changed to Choose Love), and A Drop in the Ocean. One group dedicated itself to improving conditions at Moria, the crowded registration center. The name of that team's project simultaneously acknowledged the dismal situation and conjured a brighter future: Better Days for Moria.

Meanwhile, many of the more established players, such as the Red Cross and the UN, were still conducting studies. Another, the IRC, declared it was taking "steps to achieve a coordinated response," while also admitting to "significant delays." UNHCR, for its part, produced an assessment of the security situation for women and children, identifying "grave protection risks" and calling for individual governments, the European Union, and established nongovernmental organizations, or NGOs, to step up the response.

Study was necessary to develop a successful plan of action, but refugees needed immediate relief. After locals protested the antismuggling law that prevented citizens from transporting refugees in private cars—"That's also a crime, to let someone die in the street," Greek activist Efi Latsoudi pointed out in *The Guardian*—authorities relented, changing the law. UNHCR and the IRC began providing bus transport from busy arrival spots up north to registration centers in the south. Thousands of people needed transport, however, and grassroots teams shouldered the burden of caring for them while they waited for rides. That September, the volunteer-run Starfish Foundation had transformed the parking lot of the Oxy Discotheque outside the village of Molyvos into a make-shift transit center. Here, volunteers provided food, dry clothes, diapers, and even arts and crafts for children. A system using color-coded tickets helped prevent chaos.

Three months had passed since Tracey Myers and Jenni James had arrived on Lesvos. Tracey had given up her job in England and now, like Jenni, volunteered full-time. On the outskirts of Molyvos, the two women rented a room in a cheerful hotel overlooking the sea. The spike in refugee arrivals had decimated tourism, and the hotel now scraped together income by renting rooms to volunteers. The pretty gardens and swimming pools were mostly wasted on these guests. Tracey and Jenni had no time to bask in the sun. On top of their work responsibilities, they were also caring for a menagerie of stray animals, at one point sharing their accommodations with three dogs and six cats.

Jenni put in regular shifts with the water rescue teams. By now, the situation on Lesvos had become a global story, so the media was out in full force. One day, Jenni's team had to shove through a clutch of reporters in order to help new arrivals out of boats.

"Stop pushing us!" one of the journalists snapped.

Jenni shot back, "You're putting my life in danger. You're putting these people's lives in danger."

It was a bizarre scene. Refugees found themselves surrounded by cameras as they stepped off boats. Some hid their faces or shielded their children. "I think that means they don't want their photos taken," Jenni said, but the journalists kept snapping pictures.

Later, talking with me about that episode, she still fumed. "I hated the media. I hated them."

But media coverage also had a positive effect on the grassroots movement, serving to marshal resources from all over the world. "That was how the money came in, too," I reminded her.

Jenni sighed. "Yeah, I know. Tracey would keep telling me that. But it hindered what we were doing."

The media attention brought an increase in volunteers, but that was a mixed blessing. Jenni considered some of them "tourist volunteers" because they took so many selfies documenting their adventures. A few lacked basic sensitivity, as well. Jenni described how, after boats landed, she'd sometimes see distraught parents running along the beach, searching for their kids. It would turn out that some volunteer had blithely carried a child to a car to keep the boy or girl warm—without telling anybody. "There was no concept," she said, "that there were parents there."

Jenni could perform like a peppy cheerleader for an online thank-you video but couldn't always control her temper. "I didn't have time for good words, for being calm and stuff," she told me. "I was working seventeen, eighteen, nineteen hours a day, sometimes twenty-one hours a day, seven days a week. We were working on adrenaline and working on 'If we're not there, these people are going to die.' That's reality. That wasn't, 'I've got an ego—If I'm not there, it's all going to collapse.' If we weren't there, it *was* going to collapse."

Not surprisingly, volunteers struggled to keep themselves in balance. Stress led to conflict. Two people might share a concern for refugees, but that didn't necessarily mean they got along. On Lesvos during those months, Tracey worked closely with another volunteer, with whom she was barely on speaking terms. There's a bigger thing at play, Tracey continually told herself. Try and make it work.

Much later, when Jenni talked with me about those early months of volunteering, she spoke of the experience with horror and shock—horror over the disaster itself and shock that so many disconnected individuals ended up managing an aid movement. "We had no handbook," Jenni told me. "There was nobody there to lead the way. We had to just do it."

Some 175 miles south, on the island of Kos, Kanwal Malik and her friends worked shifts with Kos Solidarity, a team of local and foreign volunteers.

On her first night, Kanwal settled in at the harborside "reception point," where refugees first made contact with grassroots teams. Before long, dozens of people began to appear. They had just stepped off boats. "More people are coming. More people are coming," someone shouted. The volunteers had boxes of dry clothing—donations from all over Europe—and they handed out items quickly. Later, looking back on that night, Kanwal remembered the expressions on the faces of these new arrivals. "The relief. The trauma. The anxiety: 'What's going to happen now?' They came to Europe thinking that they would be coming into hotels, that people would be here as reception, that the UN would be cradling them. And they were literally just looking around, thinking, Well, what are we supposed to do?"

The relief teams distributed bottled water and energy bars. Refugees changed into the dry clothes, men holding up chadors as privacy screens for their wives. "Where are these people going to go?" Kanwal asked the more experienced volunteers.

"They have to go around the camp, check the tents, and if there's an empty tent, they sleep inside."

"But what about blankets?"

"The UN won't distribute any new blankets. The old blankets that are in the tents, that other people left, they have to use those."

All through the night, boats arrived. People approached the aid teams, wet and shivering. Volunteers handed out more clothes, more energy bars, more bottled water. After the newcomers received the rations, they wandered off in search of empty tents.

At one point during that night, a father showed up with three little boys. In the midst of all that chaos, Kanwal was struck by his composure. "My boys need trousers," he said calmly. "They need jumpers. One boy's underpants are wet." Kanwal's team gave him clothes.

"And we need a place to stay," he told her.

She tried to explain the shelter situation, suggesting that he scavenge for blankets. "You'll have to check inside the tents."

A look of astonishment crossed the man's face as he realized that his family would not be sleeping indoors. He said nothing, however. He led the boys away, found a space in a tent, helped his children get settled, then stepped out again and lit a cigarette. He smoked for some minutes, then leaned back inside and checked on the boys. Satisfied that they were safe, he walked a few feet away from the tent and started to cry.

Later, Kanwal would learn that the man's wife had died in a bombing. Somehow, he had gotten the children out of the war zone, through Turkey, and safely across the Aegean. That night in Kos, he gave himself a couple of minutes to grieve.

Kanwal walked over and handed him a bottle of water. She might have hugged a woman, or even a man from her own culture, but she couldn't do that here. "Are you okay?" she asked.

"Yes," he said. He walked back to his tent. Then he stood there, staring out at the harbor.

TRACEY AND JENNI BOTH TOOK ON LEADERSHIP ROLES at Oxy Camp on Lesvos. Jenni supervised construction of the infrastructure, which meant bulldozing a gravel tract and erecting physical shelters, including portable plastic sheds and two UNHCR-donated warehouse tents, each of which could hold hundreds of people. After the facility began operations, Tracey coordinated the volunteer staff. The Starfish Foundation, which ran Oxy, didn't actually have an office. The team had been founded by local restaurateur Melinda McRostie, so Tracey operated out of Melinda's restaurant, the Captain's Table, which overlooked Molyvos Harbor. Every morning around 9:00 A.M., Tracey plunked herself down at a table outside on the piazza, and she stayed until well past dark. Sitting in that scenic spot all day, she probably looked like an extremely unadventurous tourist. In truth, she was frantically creating schedules, organizing work shifts, training volunteers, and meeting with other aid groups to streamline activities.

Some mornings, Tracey would run three separate orientation sessions, each for twenty or thirty new volunteers. "Sometimes," she later told me, "I thought I might cry if one person asked me one more question." But she needed every pair of hands. For Oxy Camp to function well, teams had to distribute food, provide security, watch the shore for incoming boats, and care for recent arrivals, many of whom were sick and weak. In the coming months and years, displaced people themselves would take on such responsibilities, but at that time few stayed longer than several hours. The operation relied, then, on volunteers from stable countries, many of whom could devote only a few days or weeks to the effort. This labor shortage meant that Tracey constantly had to recruit and train new people. Her roster typically had ninety open shifts. She never had that many volunteers.

Again and again, Tracey appealed for help from people who had already worked sixteen or eighteen hours straight. Again and again, she saw volunteers push themselves beyond what seemed humanly possible. And yet they kept going. The youngest, often eighteen or nineteen years old, touched her most deeply. Back home in England, Tracey had worked in youth communities, and she knew their potential. But still, these kids amazed her. "No one would ever have given them a job in [aid work]," she remembered later, still marveling at their dedication. "No one would ever have trusted that they could take this responsibility." Watching them, she thought, They're going to change the world.

Ultimately, the burden of the grassroots effort weighed most heavily on local people and long-term international volunteers, like Tracey and Jenni, who remained in Greece for extended periods. The demands of the situation pushed them to their limits. Professional aid organizations had systems in place—like the five-day workweek—that helped prevent burnout by mandating time off. The grassroots movement had no such rules.

Later, when I listened to Tracey or Jenni talk about that period, I wondered how they kept themselves sane. Once, I asked Tracey, "What did you guys do to take a break?"

She struggled to find an answer. "I mean, in retrospect, we could have taken a break," she said. "But, in reality, I worked every waking hour." Structurally, the grassroots effort functioned like a pyramid turned upside down. At the top, hundreds of inexperienced volunteers worked short stints on aid teams. At the bottom, a small group of veterans held up the whole operation. If Tracey took a day off and failed to schedule staff, who would hand out sandwiches? Who would distribute blankets? "I perpetually and always had urgent tasks," she explained. "If I didn't do them, then [the volunteers] wouldn't be there."

They carried enormous responsibility, particularly because failure could generate tragedy or extreme distress. Plenty of volunteers turned to drugs and alcohol to cope with the burden. "People lost their shit, and it was a mess," Tracey told me. Back in Leeds, she had been a social person, a music fan who loved evenings in pubs with friends. Here on Lesvos, she hardly socialized at all. She became a recluse to preserve her sanity.

MANY REFUGEES HAD UNREALISTIC EXPECTATIONS about what they would find in wealthy, peaceful Europe. At first, they were just relieved to have gotten there alive. The IOM's Missing Migrants Project collects information on drownings at sea, and in September of 2015 alone, the group reported, some 269 people had died trying to cross the Mediterranean. Survivors sent selfies to loved ones to show they'd made it. Then, after a brief rest on the beach, they pulled on their backpacks, picked up their children, and looked around at Greece.

That was the moment when many realized that the relief effort had major problems. International aid organizations were largely absent. Volunteers, struggling to address the needs, lacked resources. Kirk Day, the emergency field director for the IRC, told *The New Yorker* that the last time he had witnessed conditions as bad as those on Lesvos was back in the 1990s, during Zaire's civil war. "The system is just not working," he said. It didn't demand any specialized knowledge to recognize a botched aid effort; any refugee could see it, too.

That autumn, yet another boat arrived on a Lesvos beach. This time, stepping ashore among the rattled grandmas and shivering babies, a tall, wiry twenty-eight-year-old from Damascus paused and looked around. Ibrahim Khoury—blunt, observant, and somewhat ascetic—took in the situation with expert attention. Like others coming off the boat, Ibrahim had fled conflict in his homeland. Unlike most others, he was also a trained humanitarian professional, having worked with local NGOs in Syria. Ibrahim soon realized that a major international response was being managed, to a large extent, by European college students, local Good Samaritans, and tourists on vacation. He knew he could help.

Most members of Ibrahim's family had left Syria years before. He was a single man without any dependents and he could do as he pleased. He also came from a wealthy family, so he didn't have to worry about running out of funds. ("Life is easy when you have money," he told me later.) Like most asylum seekers, Ibrahim had planned to follow the Balkan Route, heading north through Greece, then farther into Europe. But looking around Lesvos, he realized that he could put his skills to good use here. He telephoned his family, who had expected him to continue north. "I'll stay a few days," he told them.

Then he approached one of the aid teams and offered the assistance that seemed, at that moment, most necessary. "Do you need a translator?" he asked in excellent English.

CHAPTER 4

Beautiful People

ONE DAY THAT FALL OF 2015, A HUGE EXPLOSION rocked the home of Musa and Rima Halabi. The windows rattled and the good doors shook. Pregnant Rima began to bleed, then started to panic that she'd miscarry. "We've got to go back to Damascus!" she cried. "We can't stay in this situation! We should go to Turkey!"

"What will we do in Turkey?" her husband asked. "There's no life for us there."

Rima didn't care anymore. Even after the bleeding stopped, she continued to insist that they leave. That was when Uncle Kareem proposed a plan. Musa and one child should travel to Turkey, then cross to Greece and continue north toward Germany. Once there, the presence of a child would expedite an application for resettlement. Within a few months, father and daughter could successfully establish themselves in Europe, then apply for family reunification. Meanwhile, Rima would give birth, recover, and prepare the rest of the family to flee. Soon, Kareem promised, the Halabis would all be together in Germany. Six months, max.

Rima and Musa listened. The plan sounded reasonable. Musa and one child could lay the foundation for a new life. Rima could stay behind with the others and have her baby in familiar surroundings. But which child should go first? Their attention turned to Malika. While Shakira, the eldest, was shy and helpful with the little ones, Malika loved adventure. She'd do well on the road.

The family sold the house, then rented it back so they'd have a place to stay until they left. With cash from the sale, they hired smugglers. But then, on the day that Musa and Malika planned to leave, more bombs fell. Musa, consumed with worry, hadn't eaten for days. Now his face filled with anxiety. He looked at his wife. "I'm not going to leave you alone like this."

What choice did they have, though? "We've already spent the money," Rima reminded him.

Uncle Kareem, the know-it-all, said, "A few months from now, you'll all be together in Germany."

That day, Rima and four of her children stood on the balcony waving good-bye as the travelers got into the car down below. She was not a romantic. She had seen too many disastrous marriages. But she had spent the best years of her life with Musa. Now he and Malika were leaving. Rima wanted to believe Uncle Kareem's promises that the family would quickly reunite, but the risks terrified her. Uncle Kareem could not guarantee that everything would go as planned.

On their balcony in al-Dana, the four remaining Halabi children crowded around their mother, watching the car drive away. Rima, her belly swelling, tried to keep the little ones calm. She had to be strong for Shakira, who was only thirteen; for the baby, who hadn't even emerged into the world; for the little boys without their father. But it was Lina, the toddler, whom she worried about the most. The child didn't understand why her dad had disappeared. Over the weeks that followed, it was all Rima could do to get the little girl to eat.

In Damascus, the Khalil family made no plan to leave. Salma gave birth to their first son, Omar, in September. In keeping with Muslim tradition, friends and family began calling Ali by a new name, Abu Omar, or Omar's Father. After years of unhappiness together, nothing demonstrated the rebirth of their marriage better than the arrival of this boy. But now they had one more child to keep from dying.

Abu Omar was hardly a vibrant young dad. He looked robust, but he suffered from middle-age ailments and heart problems. Despite that, he also continued to worry about conscription. Whenever he had to cross a checkpoint, he brought along his wife or a child to signal that his family responsibilities made it impossible for him to join the military.

In fact, Abu Omar's "family responsibility" extended far beyond his wife and children. The Assad regime had arrested Abu Omar's father and tortured him in prison. When they finally released him, the once powerful patriarch emerged severely diminished. Abu Omar, as the eldest son, had to lead the family now, taking charge of everything, from keeping everyone safe to supervising matchmaking for his younger sisters. One sister, Nashwa, had chosen a groom for herself already, but how could the family afford a celebration when the war had made their finances so precarious? How could they keep the groom out of the military? Plus, Abu Omar pondered a more mundane problem: No one in the family liked Nashwa's boyfriend. Should he support the match? Should he condemn it and risk the possibility that she'd elope? And, always, the overriding question loomed: Should they stay in Syria or flee?

MOST MORNINGS THAT FALL, JENNI JAMES ROLLED OUT OF BED early, picked up the binoculars she kept by the window, and looked out toward the rough stretch of sea that separated Turkey from Lesvos Island. With the sun coming up, she could count the smugglers' boats already making their way toward Greece.

With the arrival of autumn, Jenni had noticed a change in the type of craft used to transport people across the Aegean. Increasingly, large wooden boats carried hundreds of passengers. Unlike the inflatable dinghies that had become the iconic symbol of refugee journeys, these wooden vessels looked substantial and seaworthy. For human traffickers, the size and apparent safety of the boats allowed them to charge higher fees; plus, they earned more by cramming aboard so many passengers. Typically, women and children descended into the hold, while men sat on the open decks above. For Jenni, the risk of these vessels soon became clear. Because they were big, they easily ran aground near the coast, sending passengers into panic and trapping women and children inside.

Boat groundings occurred regularly. Beach rescue operations could succeed if one occurred close to shore, because rescue teams created a human chain, each volunteer gripping a safety rope that led from the beach to the boat. After they helped passengers off, they gently guided them along the rope line, through waves and over slippery rocks, until they reached dry land. After four months spent doing sea rescue, Jenni's confidence had increased significantly. She no longer panicked when she had to enter the water.

One morning, Jenni stood on a hill with a group of volunteers. They were tracking the approach of another large wooden boat.

Then it vanished.

Jenni stared through her binoculars. "Where did the boat go?" she asked. She turned to another volunteer. "Eric, the boat's disappeared."

Everyone surveyed the water, passing the binoculars back and forth. Soon they began to spot life jackets bobbing in the waves. They called the Hellenic Coast Guard.

On any given day, thirty or forty refugee boats could arrive on Lesvos from Turkey, and some days would see as many as two hundred. The Hellenic Coast Guard regularly pulled people from the sea. Its fleet was small, however, designed for the typical emergencies of a fishing community. These days, the crews sometimes had more people drowning than they could save. In recent weeks, the rescue effort had gotten a significant lift with the arrival of a team of lifeguards from Spain—Tracey Myers, who watched them admiringly from shore, called them "the Spanish Baywatch dudes." While the coast guard performed rescues on boats, the Spaniards used Jet Skis. Together, the combined teams could save dozens of people at a time.

Even this united rescue operation was overwhelmed, however, when a boat carrying several hundred people sank in deep water, with women and children trapped inside.

That day, rescuers raced out to the wreck from the shore. The sinking boat was too far out for a human chain. Local fishermen and Frontex, the European border guard, joined the effort, everyone pulling people out of the sea. In the village of Molyvos, Tracey's Starfish team got a call from the coast guard asking volunteers to prepare a receiving station as quickly as possible. "This is going to be bad," the caller said. Soon the volunteers transformed the village's picturesque restaurant-lined cove into a setting for disaster response. They fashioned UNHCR's signature gray wool blankets into makeshift stretchers and laid them out along the waterfront.

Rescue boats began to arrive in the harbor, staying long enough to unload victims before heading back to the wreck. The first run brought twenty or more children, their bodies turning blue. Emergency workers tried to get them breathing again. More boats appeared with more children, women, the elderly, teenagers, men. On the shore, survivors sobbed, searched for missing loved ones, and wandered around in shock.

In the end, at least twenty-nine people died in that disaster alone. Three days of shipwrecks increased the number of dead to fifty. Criticism of the slow response—of the Greek government, the European Union, and traditional aid organizations—rose to a roar. "What we don't need in the wake of this tragedy is another 'extraordinary' meeting that leads to a dead end," an apparently fed-up Gauri van Gulik of Amnesty International told Reuters. "What would be truly out of the ordinary—but completely necessary—is real and concerted action."

Jenni and Tracey went back to their hotel exhausted and grieving. Both turned to Facebook to share their pain. "When will the real help come?" Jenni asked, calling on the world's most prominent NGOs to step forward so that "these people fleeing war have a safe road to travel."

Tracey made no effort to temper her rage. "Trigger warning," she wrote. "We have lines of children half dead waiting to be hung upside down so we can pound the water out of their tiny lungs. boat after boat. We have ambulances, wailing soaked terrified people who have been fucked by this world and forced onto a boat in storms. We have separated kids, families, bleeding people, bereaved and broken people. We dont have enough clothes or blankets. these are beautiful people. The people helping them are beautiful people. The whole thing is an abomination against humanity."

A few years later, Jenni tried to describe for me the scene at the harbor that night. We were talking over Skype and suddenly I couldn't hear her. The connection had been dropping out throughout our conversation, so I assumed I'd lost her again. "Are you there?" I asked.

Silence. And then I realized she was crying. "It's really hard," she finally said. "I never want to see anything like that again."

CHAPTER 5

The Watchtower

A T A SUMMIT IN BRUSSELS IN THE FALL OF 2015, the European Union announced a quota system to resettle 120,000 refugees from the frontline nations of Greece and Italy in other parts of Europe. The agreement's viability was questionable from the start. Four times that many people had arrived illegally in the first nine months of the year. "The relocation plan in itself will not be sufficient to solve the crisis," UNHCR spokeswoman Carlotta Sami told *The Guardian*. But the loudest complaint was not that Europe was taking too few people; it was that Europe was taking too many. Four Central European nations—the Czech Republic, Hungary, Slovakia, and Romania—all voted against the plan. "As long as I am prime minister, mandatory quotas will not be implemented on Slovak territory," that country's prime minister asserted.

In Greece, nothing changed at all.

Ibrahim Khoury, the Syrian humanitarian worker, was only a few weeks off the boat himself. He had lingered in the village of Skala Sikamineas, where cafés lined a stone-paved plaza, their tables neatly arranged for optimal views of the harbor. Cats lazed in the sun. Colorful fishing boats bobbed in the water. Two roads reached the village, a narrow track that descended steeply from the hills and another that meandered along the shore. Most days, one could easily see Turkey across the narrow strait, which explained why, in the summer and fall of 2015, Skala Sikamineas and the stretch of nearby coast became ground zero for refugee arrivals in Greece.

In conversation, Ibrahim identified himself as a refugee, but his skills were so obvious that other volunteers immediately recognized his value to their teams. Soon after his arrival, he was already playing a significant role in the relief effort. The dearth of professional aid workers deeply bothered him. Back in Syria, Ibrahim had always relied on *The Sphere Handbook*, which set forth a widely recognized set of principles and standards for humanitarian response. First introduced in the 1990s by a consortium of aid organizations, the Sphere Project was meant to improve results and hold governments and NGOs accountable for their disaster relief efforts. Did you need to erect a shelter for refugees? Sphere had specs: "The internal floor-to-ceiling height should be a minimum of two metres at the highest point." What about the most practical way to provide drinking water? "Don't allow queuing time at a water source to exceed 30 minutes." There was nothing random about Sphere's recommendations. Why a maximum wait of thirty minutes? "Excessive round-trip and queuing times indicate an inadequate number of water points or inadequate yields at water sources." Sphere dug into the details. Without this kind of guidance, aid teams were just winging it. In Greece, however, such metrics often served a different purpose, which was to underscore that the relief effort was faltering comprehensively.

In a viral video titled *Disgusting Aid Agencies!* Eric Kempson, a British resident of Lesvos and active volunteer, described the situation as "nine months of people suffering, and they're still suffering." The problem, he added, "is not as though the money's not there; the money is there. It's just the will's not there. And that's wrong."

Established aid professionals agreed. "What you see [on Lesvos] is ugly," Ron Redmond, a spokesperson for UNHCR, told *The New York Times*. "What these volunteers are seeing is shocking and extremely distressing." The agency, he went on to explain, was hampered by the peculiar situation in Europe. Unlike in a war zone, where the United Nations might have full control of relief operations, in Greece the agency had to follow the government's lead. "We are trying to get the support that Greece needs, but they run this, not us." Redmond added that funding was not as plentiful as volunteers might expect. "We can't even get funding for our operations in Syria."

Still, some volunteers suspected that established agencies showed up only for media events and claimed to be more effective than they actually were. Eric Kempson, creator of the *Disgusting Aid Agencies!* video, told

The New York Times that Red Cross volunteers, who should have been well supplied by their own operation, had appealed to him for blankets and children's clothing. "These aid agencies," he said, "have got to step up their pace here." On the Red Cross website, the organization focused on accomplishment. An article entitled "Red Cross Helps as Refugees Flee Homelands" stated that "[b]etween 1,500 and 2,000 people arrive every day on [Lesvos]," then added that a "Red Cross reception center is there, providing assistance to the refugees."

One day, Ibrahim and several other volunteers decided to call the Red Cross. "Where are you?" they asked, without identifying themselves.

"Lesvos," the person on the other end of the line responded.

"Well, we are here. We never see you."

Pause, and then: "Sorry, that's a different department. We don't know exactly where they are on the ground."

THE LARGE WOODEN BOAT HAD SUNK ON WEDNESDAY, October 28, 2015. Later, speaking among themselves, volunteers just called the event "Wednesday."

Wednesday changed Jenni. For months, she had been working to mitigate tragedy. Now she committed herself to preventing it, even though she was just a volunteer. To do that, she decided to build a "watchtower," an observation system capable of visually following boats for their entire journey across the Aegean. If watchtower volunteers spotted trouble, they could notify the coast guard and quickly get rescue crews to that location.

Jenni wanted her watchtower to have a clear sight line from the embarkation points along the Turkish coast to the landing spots on northern Lesvos Island. She knew just the place for the project, too: Her own hotel sported magnificent views all the way to Turkey. These days, the establishment sat virtually empty except for rooms rented by a few volunteers. Jenni sat down with the hotel management and, after some sweet talk, convinced them to give her team a free room to use for the project.

Within days, the observation post began operations. Jenni used donation money to buy binoculars and telescopes. A British yoga group funded a thermal imager, which allowed the team to follow boats at night and through rain and fog. The equipment was so powerful that volunteers standing in that hotel room on Lesvos could watch migrants climbing into boats on Turkish beaches four miles away. Once a boat set off, the team gave it a number, wrote the number on a wall chart, and began tracking it across the water. To better communicate among themselves, the volunteers created a map that divided the area into four zones. Spots along the Turkish coast received names affiliated with landmarks: the Three Hotels, the Single Hotel, the Mosque, the Tower, Assos Town. Observers watching boats embark could predict each craft's intended destination. At that point, they notified people on the shore. "Boat number seven looks like it's coming in Skala way," someone in the watchtower might announce, and a team near Skala Sikamineas would mobilize to meet that boat when it arrived.

Weeks passed and temperatures dropped. Rescue teams remained on the beaches. Jenni, who still took shifts herself, later remembered the hours as grueling. "It was freezing cold and we'd be out there with our gloves on and our down jackets and absolutely like the abominable snowman." But they couldn't see an alternative.

No, they *could* see an alternative—Wednesday—and they were determined to avoid that. Jenni told me, "I refused to lose another boat."

Reporting to friends and family about the situation on Lesvos, Ibrahim Khoury said that people in war zones lived under better conditions than the refugees in Greece. Even countries at war could produce electricity sometimes. Here, people shivered in unheated tents.

Day after day, boats continued to arrive. When Ibrahim slept at all, it was on a sofa at the Goji Cafe on Skala Sikamineas's main square. The refugee situation had shattered the local tourism economy, but the café's owners kept their establishment open twenty-four hours a day, not merely to feed customers but also to hand out dry clothes and give tired refugees the use of the restaurant's Wi-Fi and toilets. When Ibrahim's own cash ran low, he asked the owners if he could eat other patrons' leftovers. They didn't mind, but they brought him food anyway. They just stopped charging him for it.

The chaos increased the chance that volunteers would panic and make mistakes. For advice, then, Ibrahim often called his former mentor back in Damascus, who offered a salient principle for the younger man to follow: Don't provide first aid until you've pulled the accident victim out of the road. In other words, consider everything before you act. "Listen, understand, think, decide, do." Every day, the mentor recommended, Ibrahim should get himself a cup of coffee and just *sit*.

Despite everything, the Syrian was falling in love with Greece. He abandoned his plan to travel farther north in Europe and instead decided to settle there. Somehow, the place suited him. "Everyone is happy, but everything's a problem," he would say, finding the contradiction appealing. Besides, Ibrahim was addicted to tobacco. "You can smoke anywhere."

In time, the loose associations of international volunteers began to coalesce. One night, Gunnar Björkland, a Swedish military veteran with extensive disaster relief experience, invited Ibrahim and a few others to meet over dinner and talk about ways to formalize their activities. The discussions led to the establishment of Lighthouse Relief, an organized aid team that registered itself in both Sweden and Greece and went on to build a transit camp right beside the village beach. There, new arrivals could change into clean clothes, eat, sleep, and receive medical care before being transported to the registration centers farther south.

Amid all the complaining about the larger aid organizations, volunteers often singled out one agency for praise and admiration—Doctors Without Borders, known in Greece by its French name, Médecins Sans Frontières, or MSF. "They were utterly brilliant the whole time," one volunteer later told me. When Ibrahim and his colleagues at Lighthouse Relief started to build their transit camp, they turned to MSF for advice about installing toilets. "You are the experts," they said. "Can you help us with this?"

At that time, MSF was running its own emergency transit center in the north of Lesvos and also fielding a team at Moria Camp in the south. "We're busy right now," they said. "Can you give us two hours?"

Over the next four days, MSF staff members spent two to three hours every day advising the Lighthouse team about toilets. Installing portable toilets in an outdoor camp is actually no simple thing, and the Lighthouse folks had all kinds of questions: Where do you buy the components? What kinds of problems might occur? What do you do about rain? Or flooding? Other large NGOs, Ibrahim realized, might have dismissed a call for help on a project with which they had no affiliation, but MSF "didn't even think about it." They seemed to see themselves not as an isolated organization but as part of a united effort to address a major crisis.

They are not angels, Ibrahim told himself, but they are really good human beings.

AS MIGRANT NUMBERS CONTINUED TO RISE that autumn of 2015—over 200,000 people reached Greece in October alone—debate intensified over who qualified as a refugee and who did not. The European Union devised a three-tiered registration system that separated people into different camps, expediting the paperwork of Syrians over that of people from other countries. In an interview with *The Guardian,* the manager of one of the camps called the mostly Afghan, Iraqi, and Pakistani residents of the lowest-tier facility "economic migrants" and said that the populations at the higher-tier camps were "people who come from countries with a refugee profile." This minimizing of national tragedies might have caused resentment among residents of the low-tier camp. After all, Afghanistan had endured violent conflict since 1978, and Iraq since 2003. Pakistanis had lived with terrorism and drone strikes for over a decade.

Asylum questions became increasingly politicized, and volunteers took sides. Some supported a "no borders" ideology, which advocated for a universal right of free movement. Others believed in borders but felt that prioritizing some nationalities over others made a difficult situation more fraught.

That fall, the debate over migration took a grim turn. On Friday, November 13, a series of coordinated terrorist attacks on Paris left 130 people dead. When authorities discovered that one of the terrorists had posed as a refugee and traveled through Europe on a fake Syrian passport, the news raised questions about immigration policies across the Continent. An official in Germany, the country that had accepted the most asylum seekers, declared, "The days of uncontrolled immigration and illegal entry can't continue just like that. Paris changes everything."

Within days, Greece's northern border was closed to all migrants except Syrians, Afghans, and Iraqis. The move effectively divided displaced people into those lucky enough to continue north and those who were stalled. Suddenly, the fields around the small farming village of Idomeni, right on the border with Macedonia (the country would officially change its name to North Macedonia in 2019), filled with stranded people, many of them Iranian, Moroccan, and Pakistani. As more arrived, the atmosphere deteriorated.

On a regional and political level, the decision to limit crossings from Greece signified an important development. "Two decades into Europe's open border project," reporter Malcolm Brabant said on the PBS *NewsHour*, "razor wire now separates some countries."

The policy change also immediately provoked criticism. "Everyone has a right to claim asylum . . . and then there should be a decision whether these people are refugees or not," George Kosmopoulos, director of Amnesty International in Greece, told the *NewsHour*. "What we are actually seeing here is just people being divided according to nationality and nothing else. And that's discrimination."

The population of the makeshift camp at Idomeni grew and grew. Farther south, on Lesvos, volunteers followed the development up north with concern. Lighthouse Relief decided to send someone to the border to assess the situation. They had just the guy to do it, too: a fluent speaker of Arabic who understood the needs of refugees because, well, he was a refugee himself. Ibrahim Khoury headed to Idomeni.

CHAPTER 6

Blankets as Much as Possible

WHEN KANWAL MALIK RETURNED TO ENGLAND after ten days on Kos, she had a difficult reentry. Walking through her local supermarket, she felt shocked by the abundance of fresh produce, the supersize packs of diapers and bottles of shampoo. At home, her full refrigerator seemed slightly obscene. Why did people here have *so much* while refugees had *so little*? She kept thinking of the boats arriving in Greece, each one full of needy people.

Meanwhile, Kanwal had a wedding to get through, and that had its own complications. Kanwal had known her fiancé, Asad, for years. In fact—and her face filled with sheepish regret when she eventually told me this story—she and Asad had married and divorced once already. They both came from Britain's close-knit Pakistani community. Before she met Asad, she'd doubted she'd ever meet someone she liked enough to marry, sometimes joking that she'd passed her "sell-by date." But she was still in her twenties, hardly geriatric. Notably pretty, with large, luminous eyes and a warm smile, Kanwal had a sweet manner that partially obscured her adventurous spirit. Asad, a telecom engineer from London, had fallen for her quickly.

The two had first met at a club, and Kanwal, a traditional girl, urged him not to get the wrong impression. "I'm only looking for a halal relationship," she told him.

He obliged with an old-fashioned courtship. Like a movie hero, he swept her off her feet, charming her friends and family, too. "He's like from Bollywood," one friend gushed. Kanwal had never had a serious boyfriend. She met Asad in July 2006. The following April, they married.

He changed instantly. Later, looking back at her wedding night, Kanwal felt that she went to bed with one husband and woke up with another. The couple lived with his mother and brother. Anger became the prevailing force in the household, most of it directed toward the young bride. Asad took control of everything. He didn't allow Kanwal to use the phone, watch television, or even touch the remote. As she learned more about his family, she realized that he was mirroring his parents' marriage.

Kanwal was a social worker who counseled victims of sex trafficking and domestic violence. At work, she advised clients to leave controlling husbands, but she couldn't leave her own. She had inherited her mother's determination. "I'm a fixer," she told herself. "I can heal the family."

She stayed with him for five years. When she finally asked for a divorce, in 2012, her mother supported her completely. "You have nothing to be ashamed of," Robina said, then helped her daughter buy a house—a substantial brick two-story one with bay windows and a garden on a quiet Nottingham street. Now Kanwal would have her own home, no matter what happened.

Two years passed and she began dating again. "You need to stop seeing men as people you can fix," friends told her. "You need to see them as companions, rather than projects." Kanwal tried to move out of "fix-it" mode. When one boyfriend exhibited controlling behavior, she immediately broke up with him. But her high standards had an unexpected effect. In comparison to other guys, Asad didn't seem so bad, actually. The story she told herself about her marriage began to change. We lost that love, she thought, but we became healers for each other as well.

Then, in June of 2014, Asad contacted Kanwal, and her affection welled up again. I've missed all the good things about him, she realized. When they met in person, he apologized for his behavior during the marriage, acknowledged his faults, and told her that he'd changed. Kanwal had changed, too. Her own attempts at self-improvement had made her optimistic about the future. Soon they were seeing each other again, then asking themselves, Why not give marriage another shot?

In September 2015, Kanwal told her mother that she planned to remarry Asad. Robina, furious, said, "I'm not having anything to do with it." The couple set their wedding date for November.

Then Kanwal read the news about little Alan Kurdi's drowning and decided to volunteer in Greece. By the time she got back to Nottingham, only days remained before her wedding. She had no time to reflect on her experience. Asad seemed uninterested. He didn't dismiss what she'd done, but he didn't want to know much, either.

Volunteering had sparked something in Kanwal, however. After her wedding, she constantly monitored the news from Greece. Eventually, she made a decision. "Asad," she told her husband, "I have to go back." He didn't argue. She believed she could return to Greece and also make her marriage work. I'll just put closure on it, she told herself. She'd volunteer one more time, then settle down to married life.

BY NOVEMBER 2015, IBRAHIM KHOURY HAD LIVED in Greece for two months. Now, doing reconnaissance for Lighthouse Relief, the Syrian asylum seeker had traveled two hundred miles to the country's northern border so that he could report on conditions for his colleagues in the grassroots movement down south.

Camp is too tidy a word for what he found at the border. A reporter for *The Guardian* described a scene where "[t]ens of thousands, including the very young and the very old, find themselves trapped in the open as the skies darken and the first night frosts take hold." UNHCR had distributed some survival gear, like sleeping bags and rain ponchos, but the agency couldn't meet the needs of so many people. Such was the case all along the Balkan Route. Peter Bouckaert of Human Rights Watch lamented that "there is virtually no humanitarian response from European institutions, and those in need rely on the good will of volunteers for shelter, food, clothes, and medical assistance." But the situation was growing desperate at Idomeni.

The village of Idomeni, a five-minute walk from the border itself, was a quiet hamlet of red-tiled roofs, backyard orchards, and tractor sheds. Idomeni Camp, meanwhile, spread across the outlying fields, stretching on either side of the north-south railway line just before it crossed from Greece into Macedonia. To reach the camp, volunteers parked their cars on the village road, then walked in, passing hundreds of tiny colored pup tents erected on the fallow ground.

Ibrahim quickly recognized that he'd need to stay for a while, so he found a new sofa on which to sleep, this one in the lobby of the Park Hotel in Polykastro, a town about fifteen miles from Idomeni. Over the next few months, the Park Hotel, an unassuming roadside inn, would become the primary staging ground for the grassroots effort in the region. Volunteers filled the rooms upstairs, while others slept in scattered rental apartments, hastily organized dormitories, tents in the hotel's backyard, and vans and cars parked nearby. Downstairs, the restaurant became the site for meetings and meals on the go. The hotel management—whether for profit or philanthropic reasons, or both—eventually allowed volunteers to convert a room off the lobby into an administrative office. For now, Ibrahim operated out of the lobby itself, setting up his computer at a table and, once again, making a bedroom out of a public place.

On the islands, the volunteer movement had begun to mature into a more sophisticated relief system. One small group—they simply called themselves the "admin team"—had published an online guide called "Information for Volunteers on Lesvos," which offered advice on many things, including how to buy a bike, find hotel accommodations, and plan a trip from home ("Contact your 'regional volunteer advisor.' That's a fancy-sounding term. It really means 'nice person in your area who has been to Lesvos and can answer your questions.'") The admin team had also created a dedicated Facebook group, which, by the end of 2015, had nearly five thousand members. At the same time, individual teams had established their own social media platforms. In late fall, for example, Ibrahim's colleagues at Lighthouse Relief posted photos of their Lesvos reception facility that showed "a new ramp for the clinic . . . washing basins under roof and . . . wooden floors in our new tents." Though the post was meant to update the general public on Lighthouse's activities on Lesvos, it also served as a thank-you note to the group's financial supporters: "Your donations made it possible!"

As the grassroots aid effort shifted its attention to Northern Greece, volunteers had to create a new distribution system from scratch. This time, though, they enjoyed a significant advantage. Many, like Ibrahim, had experience gained on the islands. They could efficiently assess the situation and formulate plans to help. On November 24, for example, after walking with several volunteer colleagues through Idomeni Camp,

Ibrahim posted their findings on Facebook. "Basic report about the situation here," he began, "(all based on a group opinion and only few hours observing and gathering info of the camp)." What followed was an initial impression, summarizing both good news about what the government or mainstream aid organizations had provided ("toilets and water are great and no need for them") and bad ("I've been told there are doctors but after 3 hours walking around didn't see even 1.")

As a relief worker in Syria, Ibrahim had spent years in the field. He had developed expertise in the areas of first aid and disaster management, but Idomeni demanded skills he lacked. His knowledge of finance, he later told me, was "zero," and he had never played a leadership role in a situation as complicated as the one unfolding along the border. Now, despite his inexperience, he tried to create a concrete plan for aid. On his Facebook page, then, he began by listing dozens of needs, among them:

- Blankets as much as possible

- Woods [to use as fuel] (for fires instead of garbage) as much as possible

- Raincoats as much as possible

- Rain boots as much as possible

- Mattress (to put it under the sleeping bags to sleep) as much as possible

- Gloves as much as possible

- Pallets 40

- Hats (witch [sic] cover the ears) as much as possible

- Sleeping bags as much as possible

All he could do was post the information and hope that people would respond.

IN DECEMBER, ONLY WEEKS AFTER KANWAL'S WEDDING, she and her friend Iram flew to Greece for a second time. Now they headed to the island of Leros, where the situation had turned critical. Sixteen miles off Leros's shore lay an even smaller island, Farmakonisi, an uninhabited Greek military outcrop near the Turkish coast. Smugglers dropped their human cargo at Farmakonisi, fulfilling their promise of getting people to "Europe" without traveling more than a dozen miles from Turkey. Passengers could remain stranded there for days, war-weary Robinson Crusoes without shelter or supplies. Sometimes, volunteers flashed past in boats. Greek law forbade landing, so they tossed water bottles to the shore. Every so often, naval vessels arrived and ferried people to Leros.

On Leros, new arrivals slept beside the harbor. Shelter, in this case, amounted to tin huts without electricity or running water, and too few of those. MSF attended to medical needs. The Greek military provided prepackaged rations, but only until people completed the registration process, at which point they were expected to board ferries to the mainland. If ferries were delayed—strikes were not unusual—volunteers tried to bridge the gap by offering food.

The aid teams followed a routine. In the mornings, they handed out bread, then distributed supplies—clothing, shoes, diapers, milk for babies—from a tiny free "boutique." Kanwal often walked around on "milk runs," taking supplies directly to the new moms so that they didn't have to wait in line. In the afternoon, the team prepared a meal.

A young Lebanese named Farez had become the volunteers' go-to leader. As a boy, Farez had fled his own country's civil war, followed the Balkan Route north, and settled in Denmark. In 2015, he'd joined the volunteer movement in Greece. On Leros, he distributed meals with the help of any volunteers who showed up. If his team had money, he served chicken. If it didn't, he prepared vegetarian food. Most days, Farez's team fed between eight hundred and fourteen hundred people.

In this atmosphere of extreme challenge, relief workers often called themselves or others "robots." Sometimes they were complimenting a person who could work nonstop. But the word also spoke to the emotional toll that the situation could take. How would you survive? Become a robot. Farez seemed never to sleep or take a break. Kanwal and Iram, exhausted, would whisper to each other, "He's a machine." But they respected him, and they came to trust him even more when, in December, the Greek ferry system went on strike, stranding migrants on the island, while more arrived every day. During a ferry strike the previous month, UNHCR had counted 3,400 displaced people on Leros, where the local population was only 8,000. Now, with ferry service suspended again, the number of stranded began to climb from fifteen hundred to sixteen hundred and then to eighteen hundred people. How could the cash-poor volunteers feed so many?

"Falafel," Farez said. The Middle Eastern patties were cheap and filling but demanded a lot of work. The team would have to mix chickpeas with garlic, onions, and spices, grind the mixture, form it into thousands of balls, and then fry each one. Kanwal and Iram were Pakistani Brits and had never made falafel, so their little camp kitchen became a makeshift cooking school. Farez unloaded cases of ingredients and began guiding his team members as they chopped, mixed, formed patties, and fried them. Later, when Kanwal looked back on that day, it seemed like she'd fried falafel for twenty-four hours straight. As she cooked, people began to gather and watch.

The refugees—worn-out, grieving, and worried for the future—brightened almost instantly. "Can we just have a taste?" they asked. Joking, they nicknamed Kanwal "Falafel Girl," because she stood by the stove for so long.

Glancing up every so often as she tossed wet patties into hot oil, she noticed a change in the atmosphere of the camp. As the smell of falafel wafted through the air, refugees started chatting among themselves. They became happier and more social. All it took was the fragrance of a familiar dish.

Since he'd arrived in Greece, Ibrahim had developed a wide circle of acquaintances. Word spread quickly as people read his posts. Day by day, donations poured in, mostly in the form of cash from fellow volunteers and wire transfers through Western Union. Over the next two months, in fact, Ibrahim would end up collecting and distributing some sixty thousand euros in donations. The funds didn't come close to fulfilling the need, but it was a massive sum, particularly for a man who, as a refugee himself, couldn't even open a bank account in Greece.

Ibrahim was handling so much cash that, for security reasons, he would eventually stop sleeping in the lobby of the Park Hotel and instead rent a room upstairs with a door that he could lock. For now, though, pretty much anyone entering the lobby saw the harried Syrian—unshaven, sitting with a cigarette and a cup of coffee, staring at his computer screen, looking for the most efficient ways to convert financial donations into relief for thousands of people.

And every day, Ibrahim's Facebook account pinged with requests for information. Media reports continued to convince volunteers to come to Greece, but they needed instruction. "I've booked my flight and hotels to go to Lesvos" was typical of the messages Ibrahim received. "Should I come to Idomeni?" These people lacked the most fundamental information for planning travel: what their destination was to be. But Ibrahim had no answer. One day, people heard that the Greek government planned to bus refugees to Athens. Another day, rumors spread that the border would reopen. Ibrahim's reply to potential volunteers amounted to an honest assessment of the entire situation: "I don't know."

He was completely alone, far from home, displaced himself, and searching for a route through chaos. The stress of the situation sometimes overwhelmed him. Most days, he used Facebook to communicate practical information, but sometimes it became his confessional, too. "Apologize," he wrote one day. "I have made un acceptable number of mistakes and i'm not hiding it, unfortunately its a huge amount of work for me (logestic , finicial , etc) i will continue to do this mistake which i will try as much as i can to stop." Another day, Ibrahim found himself able to manage only eleven words: "In every single cell in my body, I hate this life!" The online reaction to that statement dominated his page for days, amounting to an outpouring of emoji hearts, comments like "Stay strong, brother!!" and a single plaintive plea in Arabic from a worried aunt: "I wish you would communicate with me directly."

In time, Ibrahim would teach himself finance and accounting. Once, he shut himself in a room for four days to learn a computer program that tracked funds. Still, when he later looked back on those final months of 2015, Ibrahim would describe the state of affairs with a single word:

"lost." Everyone was lost: refugees, volunteers, the Greek government, international aid organizations. No one seemed to know what to do or how to handle the fact that a tent city full of refugees kept growing on Greece's northern border. In the face of such misery, the grassroots effort helped in only the most immediate way. Ibrahim had no illusions about the effect of distributing fresh fruit, for example, amid such squalor. "It's a piece of orange," he told me once, "for someone who is sleeping in the mud [with a] sick child."

As the situation in the camps deteriorated, frustrated residents sometimes turned violent, and that seemed understandable to Ibrahim, too. "Imagine that you are one of these families and you can see that your child is drowning from the snow and the rain," he said. "You will kill for a blanket." The camp became "a jungle." The strongest survived and the weak became weaker. Volunteers, then, faced a dilemma: How could they distribute supplies without creating more chaos?

They adopted a stealth approach. At 2:00 or 2:30 A.M., a volunteer van would pull up near the camp while people lay sleeping. Silently, the team broke into small groups of two or three, carrying only what people could hold in their arms. In the dark, they looked like refugees hauling their meager possessions, not volunteers with supplies. For hours, they slipped through the camp, looking for the most vulnerable—young children, the elderly, pregnant women. Ibrahim thought of his team as fearful—"We didn't even have the courage to do distribution during the day," he later recalled. "Sometimes, a solution is not 'a solution.' It's just reducing the damage." But this system worked. In the dead of night, volunteers found the people most desperate for help. They spread blankets across sleeping bodies and hurried away in the dark.

IN THE EVENINGS ON LEROS, KANWAL FOLLOWED FAREZ as he spoke in Arabic with people camped around the harbor. Once, they met a Syrian woman, whom Kanwal later remembered as "Abdullah's mother." Four family members had originally left home—mother, father, and two boys, ages three and four. They made it as far as Turkey before their money ran out. With only enough to pay smugglers for one adult and two children, the family split up. The father stayed behind to earn money for his passage, while the wife and children traveled first. Then their boat capsized in the Aegean. Rescuers saved the mother and the three-year-old. Abdullah, the four-year-old, drowned.

Now, sitting with Kanwal and Farez, Abdullah's mother pulled out her phone and played her son's last voice recording, which they had sent to the boys' father before their crossing. "Don't worry," Abdullah said. "I'm just stepping into the boat now. I love the sea. The sea has so many fishes in it, so I might just stay in the water with the fish and eat the fish."

"How can the world be so cruel?" the mother asked Kanwal.

The grieving woman also had to grapple with her surviving son's rage. "Why does Abdullah get to spend his life with the fish?" the boy demanded. "I want to be with him." Whenever he had a chance, he tried to jump in the water.

For some reason, Abdullah's mother insisted that Kanwal have this voice recording. She made a few clicks on her phone and, moments later, Kanwal saw the file pop up on her own screen. She stared at it. During her days on the island, she often became a receptacle for other people's sorrow. Sometimes, she'd ask herself, How can you even figure out what to do with all this information? At such moments, becoming "a robot" seemed a reasonable goal.

Kanwal wasn't a robot, however. She was a social worker unable to process so much catastrophe. Wasn't the world supposed to have plans for dealing with disaster? She wondered about the so-called protectors—the relief agencies and governments, which didn't seem to protect at all. Who is accountable? she wondered.

So when little Abdullah's final voice message appeared on Kanwal's phone, it seemed like evidence that the global aid apparatus had failed completely.

Kanwal asked Farez to translate a question for Abdullah's mom: "Should I play the recording for people?" she asked.

The woman nodded. "I want the world to know."

A few days later, a group of journalists came through Leros and asked Kanwal about the situation. She pulled out her phone. "Let me tell you about Abdullah."

CHAPTER 7

Flight

THE EUROPEAN UNION HAD BEEN NEGOTIATING with Turkey to address the migrant crisis. By November, the terms of a deal had become clearer. The EU would supply Turkey with three billion euros in refugee relief assistance and, in exchange, Turkey would staunch the flow of asylum seekers into Europe.

For the Khalil family in Syria, the details of the agreement mattered. If they fled the war, they'd go to Turkey, but how would they provide for themselves there? Would refugees in Turkey be allowed to work? For now, the agreement remained vague, calling for "measures to further improve the socio-economic situation of the Syrians under temporary protection."

What did that mean?

The Khalils faced a choice: remain in Syria or flee to Turkey without knowing how they'd survive there. In traditional Syrian society, the husband made important decisions for his family, but Abu Omar had come to respect the opinions of his wife and daughters. They discussed their options together. They talked about safety, money, the heartbreak of leaving loved ones behind. But in the end, the decision revolved around education. Months earlier, the war had caused schools in Damascus to close completely. The girls were devastated. Layla, eleven, dreamed of becoming a pharmacist. Her eight-year-old sister, Nura, wanted to be a "doctor for children." Without education, how could they fulfill their dreams?

"If we leave Syria," Layla asked, "can we go to school?"

They couldn't know for sure, but, yes, it seemed that way.

Layla was outspoken and spirited. Nura, more reserved, was also strong-willed. Even at eight, she had perfected the skill of silent rebellion. If the family ever entered a café that had a portrait of President Bashar al-Assad hanging on the wall, the little girl turned around and walked out.

Now both daughters agreed. They wanted to study. "Let's go," they said.

The family saw leaving their country as a temporary plan. They would flee to Turkey and if all went well the girls would go to school. After the war ended, they would return and help to rebuild Syria.

MEANWHILE, RIMA HALABI, IN HER LITTLE TOWN of al-Dana, was also planning an escape. Months had passed since Musa and Malika had left home. They had already reached Germany and begun their new life. The rest of the family, however, remained firmly in the old one. Two months earlier, during days of intense fighting, Rima had given birth to her sixth child, Oma, by cesarean section. Lying in her hospital bed, she heard the roar of bombers overhead. She tried to stay calm, telling herself that the planes would never attack a hospital. Then, two days after her discharge, the facility received a direct hit. Rima had to get her family out of Syria. She wanted to leave immediately, but she was still recovering from major surgery and couldn't go until she'd regained her strength for the journey.

So it was late in the year, cool autumn shifting to cold winter, when Rima piled the family into a taxi and set off for the border. They ended up at a smugglers' safe house on the Syrian side, where they waited for the sun to set. The children curled up on mats and slept. Rima plugged in her cell phone and extra charger. The technology had become her lifeline to Musa. She couldn't let the batteries die.

After dark, the smugglers assembled their group of fifty or sixty people to follow a mountain path across the border. They were a motley crowd of war survivors, but even in that company, the Halabis stood out: frail Rima, her adolescent daughter, two little boys, a toddler, and a newborn. As they set out, Rima slung a bag over her back, hauled the infant into one arm, the toddler into the other, and began walking. Beside her, thirteen-year-old Shakira picked up the rest of the bags, grabbed each little boy by the hand, and followed her mom.

The distance from Syria's largest city, Aleppo, to the Turkish town of Antakya is only about sixty miles. Before the war started, thousands of Syrians crossed the border every day, many on tour buses heading to the picturesque haven known as "Tuscany with minarets." These days, Antakya attracted rebel fighters, exiles, and human traffickers who led fleeing Syrians across the border on foot. A Human Rights Watch report described the perils of the route: "[In] some cases, elderly people fell down steep inclines. One woman said she saw an old man die after such a fall. Some groups used women's veils to create makeshift ropes to pull women and children up particularly steep hills." But Syrians kept crossing.

Rima made the trek postpartum while carrying two sleeping children. Like many along the Balkan Route, she had drugged her little ones to keep them safe during a dangerous leg of the journey. At the border, a crying baby could attract Turkish patrols and put an entire group at risk. Sleeping pills, alcohol, tranquilizers—parents employed many methods. Now the baby dozed. The toddler, Lina, who was usually a fireball, lay slumped in her mother's arms. Rima didn't worry about her boys. They were young, but they understood the seriousness of the situation and tramped quietly along beside their sister. The smugglers grumbled at the family's slow pace.

At last, the group reached the border, just a fence with a ladder leaning against it. A storm had settled over the mountains and the line of refugees huddled in the rain, waiting for their turn to clamber into Turkey. When Rima's family reached the ladder, one of the smugglers told her, "You go first."

Rima stopped. At this moment, her family remained together in one country. As soon as she climbed the fence, however, she would be in Turkey and her children in Syria. What might happen then? The smugglers could drag her forward and leave the kids behind.

"No," she said. "My children go first."

The line stopped moving. The smugglers argued with the Syrian mom. Rima insisted that her children take the lead. Rain fell, soaking everyone. Rima didn't budge.

The smugglers gave in.

One after another, Rima's children climbed the ladder, then dropped into the mud on the other side. Tiny shoes disappeared in the muck. By the time Rima herself climbed into Turkey, her children were a dirty, barefoot mess. She gathered them together, organized everything as best she could, then began to follow the rest of the group, snaking silently along a ditch to avoid the border patrol. The boys whimpered. More shoes disappeared. The family fell farther behind. Rima paused, adjusting her belongings and the children in her arms.

One of the smugglers walked up to the distraught mother and said, "It's either your children or your bags."

Rima went through her things. She kept one bag to hold her documents and extra clothes for the little ones. Then she left everything else by the side of the path. The family trudged forward.

Eventually, the muddy trail emerged onto a road, where taxis waited to carry them the rest of the way to Antakya. Rima, almost broken, got her family into a car. She took a deep breath. They had escaped Syria and survived. Now she gripped the baby and the toddler while Shakira and the boys crowded in beside their mom. Yusuf, the eldest boy, stared out the window at this new land. He was five years old, watchful and serious, the man of the family in his father's absence.

The taxi took a circuitous route through the mountains to the city. Turkish authorities threatened harsh punishment for anyone abetting smugglers, and the driver was skittish. He drove too fast, careening around curves, and when he spotted another set of headlights, he sped up, terrifying his passengers. Rima clutched Lina and the baby. With every turn, Shakira and the little boys lurched from side to side.

Rima was a devout Muslim. She prayed.

Then the car skidded off the road, spun on the shoulder, and hit a wall. Everyone sat in silence. They were alive.

The driver backed up his car and got it back on the road. They continued to Antakya.

IN LATE DECEMBER, ABU OMAR ARRANGED the wedding ceremony for his sister Nashwa, who married her sweetheart even though the family disapproved. After that, he and Salma turned their focus to getting out of Syria. They would travel by bus from Damascus to Beirut, then fly to Istanbul and rent a place there until the war ended. They knew that many Syrians traveled on from Turkey to Europe. People called the boat crossing "the Death Trip," and the Khalils refused to take the risk. They'd stay in Turkey, then go home.

First, they needed cash. They began to sell their possessions, discreetly amassing funds. Almost immediately, they realized they needed more money than they'd expected. Transportation to Istanbul would set them back nearly three thousand dollars. On top of that, passports cost one hundred dollars each, and they knew they'd need cash to survive in Turkey while Abu Omar searched for a job.

The anxiety they felt over money paled in comparison to their fear for their lives. The process of applying for a passport automatically triggered a review of a person's military status. If Abu Omar's name popped up on the list for conscription, the government might force him to serve. They had to take the risk, however.

One day, the family appeared at the passport office and walked to the counter.

"Name?" the clerk asked.

Abu Omar gave his name. The government identification system clicked into gear. They could do nothing now but wait.

As they sat there, Abu Omar felt as if his heart, weak already, had stopped beating. He glanced at his wife, his daughters, his infant son. He wondered if the baby could taste the fear in his mother's milk.

A few feet away, Layla gripped the phone, messaging with worried relatives. "What's happening?" they texted. "Is everything okay?" Layla responded to each frantic ping, her fingers rushing across the keys, reporting as the minutes passed. Abu Omar watched his daughter with admiration. The young girl was competent and calm in the face of danger. "We don't know yet," she'd reply. "We're waiting."

Minutes passed. Abu Omar felt like a convict about to receive a death sentence. And then the clerk lifted the official seal and, with a bang on the desk, stamped approval of their documents. Abu Omar felt his heart beat again, but his fear shamed him.

This is what war teaches you, he thought. It teaches you to be a coward.

ANTIPATHY TOWARD MIGRANTS WAS GROWING in Greece. In December 2015, after the government had forced a thousand or more people away from makeshift border camps and transported them to Athens, a video on the internet showed the buses arriving in the capital. Soon the site's comments section filled with vitriol, some noting the dominant gender among the arriving migrants. "Where are the women and children?" asked one. Another said, "And now go back to Afrika with all."

Ibrahim Khoury followed the buses down to Athens, where Greek authorities opened three large shelters to absorb the influx of people. No one considered this arrangement permanent. Even Greece's minister of migration, Yiannis Mouzalas, seemed baffled about the plan. "I don't know where the migrants will go from here," he told Al Jazeera. "You'll find out when it happens."

Unlike at makeshift camps along the border, the government restricted access to the Athens facilities, which meant that most members of the grassroots movement couldn't get through the front gates without specific permission. But Ibrahim, as an asylum seeker himself, could walk around freely. One day, he visited Elliniko, the site of the former Athens airport, whose buildings had become a "hospitality center" for migrants. Ibrahim found conditions terrible, but not as terrible as at Idomeni. Elliniko, he reported, "[wasn't] heaven, but, still, people weren't sleeping in the mud. It's a place with walls. People had some hot water. Of course, the bathrooms are so much disgusting and ugly, but it's still not a tree that you have to [go] behind."

THAT MONTH, THE HUMANITARIAN SITUATION dominated talks among European leaders gathered in Brussels for their end-of-year summit. Luxembourg, which held the presidency of the Council of Europe at that time, gave an assessment that showed how little the continent had actually accomplished:

- Out of 160,000 people identified for relocation, only 184 had been resettled.

- The 22,000 individuals living in camps in the Middle East had been recognized as needing international protection, but only 600 had been allowed into Europe.

- The EU had proposed opening eleven migrant reception centers in Greece and Italy but had established only two so far.

Such were the results after months of study and debate. In Greece, boats carrying migrants and refugees continued to arrive. The official reception system had certainly evolved, but it was hard to see improvement. On Lesvos Island, Starfish Foundation, the plucky grassroots NGO that had established a transit camp in the parking lot of a disco, closed the camp when the behemoth International Rescue Committee opened its own center, called Apanemo, nearby. The change looked like progress. On its website, the IRC announced that its "much-needed reception center provides crucial services to refugees." In *Learning from Lesbos,* a report published the following year, IRC even touted Apanemo as an example of how "effective stakeholder consultation and participation mitigates potential risks and amplifies positive impacts." But the report didn't say why the transit center—which came with a price tag of one million euros—closed after only a few months of operation. A 2017 *Guardian* investigative report would later refer to Apanemo as "a cautionary tale," and explain that the facility closed after the arrival point for refugee boats shifted to a different part of the island, rendering IRC's facility useless. "The site now stands empty," *The Guardian* noted, "while chaotic conditions elsewhere on the same island have resulted in fatalities among refugees."

That December, around the time that IRC opened its flashy new facility, Ibrahim Khoury arrived on the island of Chios, less than ten nautical miles from Turkey. Chios had a population of just over fifty thousand, but between seven hundred and eight hundred migrants were arriving every day. A grassroots food distribution system on the island was managing to serve meals only three times a week. Ibrahim had sixteen thousand euros in donation money, almost nothing compared to the budgets of big humanitarian organizations, but he believed it would help. He came up with a funding plan and presented it to his donors, who quickly approved. Soon the food distribution system had ramped up to three meals a day. The money wouldn't last forever, but it was feeding people now.

PART II

Foreign Land

CHAPTER 8

Exile

THE YEAR 2015 HAD ENDED WITH AN ACCOUNTING. According to UNHCR, one million refugees and migrants had crossed the Mediterranean into Europe over the past twelve months. Out of this number, some 3,700 were believed to have drowned. UNHCR's Vincent Cochetel said, "If there were more legal avenues for refugees to reach Europe, perhaps some of those who died at sea could have found peace and safety instead."

The high numbers reinvigorated political debate in Europe. January began with anti-immigrant rallies in Germany, the EU country that had absorbed the largest number of displaced persons the year before. (In terms of population, however, Germany didn't even make the top ten globally. In Lebanon, the world leader by far, roughly one million displaced Syrians were living in a nation with a population of only four million.) Germany saw some eighteen thousand people march in Dresden and, though pro-diversity counterrallies took place as well, the Dresden demonstration reflected a sentiment then coursing through the country.

Tension in Germany stemmed from a more immediate cause, too. After a public celebration in Cologne on New Year's Eve in 2015, hundreds of women came forward to say that they'd been assaulted there by foreign men. The episode led to arguments that the assaults were not merely criminal but also a sign of the threat of immigration. Britain's *Telegraph* made a historical connection: "The mass assaults have clear echoes of a phenomenon seen in Egypt during and after the Tahrir Square revolution of 2011 when posses of young men would gather apparently spontaneously around young women and harass them, often violently." In the United States, *The New York Times* columnist Ross Douthat used the New Year's Eve episode to call for "closing Germany's borders to new arrivals for the time being [and] beginning an orderly deportation process for able-bodied young men."

In Germany, anti-immigrant sentiment quickly morphed into what *Der Spiegel* commentator Sascha Lobo termed "racist indignation." Lobo urged Germans "to differentiate between those people who perpetrated crimes in Cologne and those thought to look like the people who perpetrated crimes in Cologne." In Cologne itself, a female activist openly wondered why news stories placed so much focus on *foreign* men. "I'm sorry to break this to you," she told Deutsche Welle, "but German-born men also harass and rape."

UNHCR's statistics broke down by nationality. Some 210,000 Afghans had crossed into Greece between January and December of 2015. Significant numbers of Iraqis and people of other troubled nations had arrived, as well. But most of the arrivals—nearly half a million— came from Syria, and their numbers showed little sign of easing. By the end of 2015, over 20 percent of the country's prewar population had fled. A Syrian diaspora was taking shape around the world.

At 4:00 a.m. on January 6, 2016, the Khalil family slipped out of Damascus and increased the number by five.

They began in a van that hauled the family and over two hundred kilos of luggage through the darkness to the Baramkeh bus station. There, they boarded a bus bound for Beirut airport in Lebanon. Before the war, Syrians regularly used the airport in Beirut, but getting there involved considerable risk now. At checkpoints, security forces halted traffic, requiring long waits and presenting one more hazard for military-age men. At one checkpoint, Assad's security personnel stopped the bus carrying the Khalils, demanding, "Why are you leaving? Why aren't you staying in your country?" They pulled all the men off the bus. Inside, Salma gripped the baby. All the family's savings—$2,500—lay inside his diaper.

Hours ticked by. The men remained on the road, the women and children in the bus. And then, as if they had come to the final act of a play, the bus driver, who knew the script by heart, walked among the passengers, collecting small amounts of cash. When he had enough for an acceptable bribe, he handed it over to the soldiers, who allowed them to pass. Abu Omar climbed back aboard. Well, he thought, that marks the end of the show.

Each checkpoint brought its own drama. At one, a soldier focused his attention on Nura, the younger daughter. Something about the child—maybe her gentle intensity, or the sadness in her eyes—must have distilled for him the poignancy of Syria's tragedy, because he burst into tears. "I haven't seen my own children in three years," he told her. "What's your name?"

"Nura."

The man gazed at the girl. "Listen," he said. "When you get older and you come back, will you come here? Will you look for me? Will you tell me that you're Nura?" The child nodded. Her parents, watching, felt unsettled. The soldier seemed to assume that many years would pass before Nura returned to Syria, while the Khalils were planning to go home as soon as the war ended. Were they being unrealistic about the future? Did this kind soldier understand something about exile that they hadn't learned?

The bus moved on. Salma passed the hours in despair. Abu Omar had relatives scattered around the world, but Salma had left almost her entire family behind. Without children to protect, she would have stayed in Syria despite all danger. As the bus slid past the southern tip of the Anti-Lebanon Mountains, crossing from arid plateau toward fertile valley, she felt her heart break.

The bus passed the final checkpoint and crossed into Lebanon.

The day ended, finally, at the Beirut airport. Never having flown before, the Khalils knew nothing of baggage limits. Now airline staffers refused to allow them to check so much luggage. In the terminal, Salma sorted through their possessions, throwing things away. Layla begged to save some treasures. She could leave her clothes, but she wanted her report cards. "Please, Mom," she said. "Can I take these with me?" She'd worked so hard for those grades.

Salma shook her head. "I'm sorry. We can't go if we take all this stuff."

Layla stopped arguing. She watched the papers disappear into the waste bin. This is what I have left from my school, she thought, and I can't ever get it back.

Little Nura didn't have many report cards, but she had a precious doll that her parents had given her for doing well in school. Maybe she could keep the doll?

Looking down at her daughters, Salma began to cry. She allowed herself one long minute of grief, then threw the doll into the trash.

Late that night, a storm came through. It was 3:00 A.M. before their flight departed for Turkey, nearly twenty-four hours after they'd left home. The Khalils saw the land from the sky for the very first time. The girls stared out the window, amazed by Beirut's twinkling lights below. Salma, holding the baby, closed her eyes and fell asleep. Abu Omar, not trusting that a plane could stay aloft, gripped his armrests in terror. He glanced around at the others on the plane. Syrians filled nearly every seat.

CHAPTER 9

The Hurting Hand

THE KHALIL FAMILY ARRIVED IN ISTANBUL in the early morning of January 7, 2016. Abu Omar felt immense relief. They had escaped the war and still had the $2,500 that the Syrian military had failed to discover in the baby's diaper.

At the airport, they hired a van, crammed themselves in with what was left of their luggage, and drove to the home of a cousin. Salma gazed out the window as they moved through the city. The quiet streets looked beautiful in the morning light. The city functioned in a way that she had nearly forgotten was possible. Glancing into homes and shops, she saw bright electric light. They didn't have to stop at checkpoints or show their IDs.

And yet, she felt bereft. I don't like anything as much as I like Syria, she told herself. The farther she traveled, the more she longed for home.

Abu Omar, observing Istanbul, thought, It's nice here. No one's bombing us.

They had just arrived, but their plan had already fallen apart. The Khalils intended to rent an apartment, find work, and wait until peace came to Syria, allowing them to return home. But when they passed through border control at the airport, they did not receive a permit to work. Most Syrians in Turkey found themselves in a similar plight. By early 2016, some 2.3 million people had arrived in the country. The *Guardian* newspaper reported that the Turkish government helped support the ones who lived in official camps, but they accounted for only 9 percent of displaced Syrians. The rest had to rely on the underground economy to survive.

Once the family found a place to rent, the landlord issued a surprising demand, adding substantially to their worries: The girls would have to work. Rather than hiring an adult like Abu Omar, a nearby textile factory would only hire children. Turkey's textile industry had become, by 2016, a major supplier to retailers throughout Europe, with profits fueled in part by child labor. *The Guardian* interviewed a factory supervisor who hired minors and blamed Turkey's government for the practice. "It's not our fault that [children] need to work," he said, "the state failed to provide for them."

Now Abu Omar faced a new humiliation. He had to send his precious, pampered daughters into a factory. *This is the point I've come to,* he told himself.

At the ages of eleven and eight, Layla and Nura joined the workforce of children standing, hour after hour, folding T-shirts. It was painstaking physical labor. Each shirt had to be folded with speed and precision. The air on the factory floor, thick with lint and chemicals, made the girls cough. As they toiled, Turkish floor managers yelled, "Hurry up! It's got to be faster! If you need money, then you need to work hard."

Throughout her life, Nura had suffered from poor health. By evening, the fumes and dust had overcome the little girl. "These people have no heart," Layla told their parents. The next day, Nura stayed home and Layla marched back to the factory by herself. She returned for a third day, then a fourth. Halfway through her fourth day, the supervisor started berating her. Layla couldn't understand the Turkish, but the situation infuriated her. She asked an Arabic-speaking girl on the line to translate for her. "Tell him I don't need to work here anymore," Layla said. "I don't need this." Then she turned around and walked out. The family never received any payment for the days the girls spent in the factory.

It seemed to the Khalils that Turkey had sent them a message: Get on the boat and go to Europe. Seeing no other option, they devised a new plan. They would go to Germany. It seemed the obvious choice. The country had welcomed the largest number of refugees in Europe and thousands of Syrians continued to arrive there every month. Plus, the Khalils had another, more personal incentive to head in that direction. Abu Omar's injured brother, Anwar, had lived in Germany since the family smuggled him from Syria several years before. Disabled and alone, he suffered from intense isolation. If the family went to Germany, they could reunite.

First, though, the Khalils had to survive the Death Trip. With a sense of dread, they borrowed money to hire smugglers. A sister in Syria sold gold and wired them twelve hundred dollars. Another, in Dubai, sent seventeen hundred dollars. "My sisters," Abu Omar told me later, "have practically gone bankrupt for us." On his phone, he researched life jackets. He learned about the cheap fakes stuffed with packing material that, when wet, would sink. He bought the most expensive ones.

Salma and the girls sorted through their belongings one more time. They could take almost nothing on the boat, but Layla tried. She picked up her school uniform. "Mom," she said, "can I just take this?"

Salma shook her head sadly.

Layla held up a small toy. "This?"

"No."

She found a smaller toy. "This?"

"No," Salma said. "Nothing."

The Khalils had discarded practically all their possessions by the time they left for Turkey's coast. Salma felt particular pain in throwing away her clothes. They had no real value, but they connected her to home. Around her head, she wrapped the black-red-and-white-plaid hijab that she had bought just before leaving Damascus. Other than the clothes on their backs, they traveled with their passports and money, their phone, and almost nothing else.

In Izmir, Turkey, Rima Halabi and her five children were preparing to cross, as well. The family had survived their escape from Syria, then traveled by taxi and bus to the coast. Now Rima brooded about the boat. Or, as she put it to me later, "We forgot the problems of the mountains when we began to think about the sea."

The Halabis sat in a safe house and waited. Many times every day, Rima spoke on the phone with Musa in Germany. Her husband's voice calmed her, despite the distance, but she was the one who had to bring her family together. If the Halabis had been wealthy, they might have hired one person or a syndicate to transport them along the entire route. But they economized, like so many other people, by hiring smugglers in each region they crossed. One network had gotten Rima and her children out of Syria. Another conveyed them across Turkey to the coast. Now they were staying in the home of a woman known as Umm Mahmoud, or "Mahmoud's mother." She was the smuggler who promised to get them across the Aegean. Once in Europe, Rima would need to find her way to Germany, but she wasn't thinking about that yet. She was worrying about the Death Trip.

Rima had to rely on people who made their living off the desperation of others. In conversation, Syrians often used the word *mafia* to describe smugglers, but they also depended on these criminals to transport them and keep them safe. In practice, the system ran, to a large extent, on basic capitalism. The 2015 European Commission–funded *Study on Smuggling of Migrants* found that smugglers generally based price on supply and demand, but also on other factors, like the perceived wealth of a potential client. Sometimes, too, special circumstances affected cost. The study noted, for example, that some one thousand migrants benefited from reduced prices during a soccer championship. Smugglers didn't have to work as hard because border authorities were watching the game.

In smuggling, as in any business, certain techniques increased sales. In Turkey, some smugglers agreed to receive their payment via a money transfer. Customers deposited funds into third-party accounts at Western Union or MoneyGram. The third party released the payment only after receiving notice of a safely completed trip. Rima's family employed a different strategy. They paid fees in advance, choosing smugglers recommended by Syrians who had already crossed. So far, no one had cheated her.

Umm Mahmoud, a Syrian from Cyprus, had years of experience in human trafficking and had even smuggled her own children to Europe. She seemed competent and methodical, but time passed. Other refugees arrived in Izmir and set off on boats, while the Halabis remained in Turkey. Rima's phone calls with Musa became a grinding marathon of stress and fear. When would they leave?

Umm Mahmoud kept her eye on the sea. "Not yet," she kept saying.

Why? Rima wondered. Why this delay?

Many worries kept her awake at night. Within the community of refugees and smugglers, she heard vague warnings about sexual predators. "Be careful of your kids," people would say, their eyes resting on Shakira. In recent months, the teenager had grown tall, filled out, and lost her gawkiness. She was pretty, too. Rima had strong, almost intimidating features, but Shakira—delicate and doe-eyed—looked vulnerable. To Rima, the warnings felt like an accusation, as if she had done something shameful by traveling with her children all alone. In English, people speak of "pouring salt on the wound." Rima used the Arabic equivalent: "They squeeze your hurting hand."

Days slipped past. A week. Then two. Rima and her children waited, each hour meaningless except for variations in the light or the weather, a child's complaint of stomach cramps, baby Oma's hungry screams. One day, Rima overheard one of the smugglers ask Umm Mahmoud about the delay. "Why don't you send them on?"

"I promised her husband I'd keep them safe," Umm Mahmoud replied. "When it's safe, I'll send them."

AFTER FIFTEEN DAYS IN IZMIR, RIMA HALABI and her family finally boarded a boat for Greece. Umm Mahmoud had arranged for the Halabis to cross not on a rubber dinghy but on a large wooden vessel. To Rima, it looked impressive. Instead of sitting out in the wind, she and her family descended into the warm hold, where some two dozen children and a few adults spread out on wooden benches. Everything—the assurances of Umm Mahmoud, the sturdiness of the boat, the coziness of the hold—gave Rima confidence. She strapped life jackets onto herself and her kids, then settled down on a bench for the crossing. After some minutes, the engine rumbled to life. The hold had no windows, so Rima couldn't see outside, but she could feel the vibrations of the motor, her body swaying with each soft tuck of the boat against the waves. Good, Rima thought to herself. He's slow. He's a safe captain.

Rima had given Lina and the baby drugs again. They were sleeping soundly in her arms. Minutes passed, then half an hour. Rima relaxed, beginning to ponder the next leg of the journey. Then, suddenly, their bench cracked and collapsed. The family tumbled to the floor. In any other circumstance, Rima might have laughed or merely gotten annoyed. But now, on this voyage that could end in calamity, she panicked, imagining that the boat would break apart. What if they sank? How could she save five children by herself? The little ones remained asleep. Frantically, she tried to rouse them. She could hold the baby, but if the boat sank, little Lina had to be able to scream for help.

The baby woke, but Lina did not. Rima patted the girl, shook her shoulders, cried, "Wake up. Wake up!"

Lina's head rolled back. Her eyes never opened. Rima jiggled her, terrified now that they would end up in the sea and that the sleeping child would drown.

But Umm Mahmoud had done her job. The smuggler really had found a safe boat and a safe captain. While Rima struggled to wake her toddler, that big boat gently landed in Greece.

CHAPTER 10

Death Trip

O N THE NIGHT OF FEBRUARY 17, 2016, the Khalil family arrived at a beach on Turkey's coast, ready to make the crossing to Greece. Vehicles lined the country road, each one full of migrants who had to stumble in the dark toward the water. The Khalils didn't have far to walk, but they heard others left high in the hills, struggling down rocky paths with nothing but moonlight to guide them.

The travelers made very little noise. Everyone knew that Turkish authorities could suddenly appear and stop the boats from departing, or even arrest people as they tried to board. The smugglers seemed unconcerned. Waving guns in the air, they yelled, "No talking! No smoking! Shut off your phone! No mobiles at all, because the government will trace you!"

The boats—if you can use that word to describe these rubber dinghies—sat deflated on the beach. Quickly, the smugglers filled them with air. Within minutes, they were tossing in the waves as people tried to board. If anyone hesitated, the smugglers held guns to their heads and forced them on.

The Khalils quickly became separated. Salma, clutching the baby, ended up on one side of the boat, far from her girls. Abu Omar perched on the outer tubing with the other men. In all, seventy-two people boarded the craft, which had capacity for maybe thirty. The smugglers held the boat's ropes long enough for everyone to climb on, then pulled the chain on the motor and pushed them off. One man volunteered to steer. From all around the boat rose the murmur of people praying.

OF COURSE, THE PEOPLE WHO RAN THIS SYSTEM were breaking all kinds of laws—the laws of Turkey, the laws of Greece, and, more generally, European and international laws that forbade human trafficking. And many people were making money in the process, not just mastermind traffickers but also owners of safe houses, drivers who provided transportation, merchants who sold life jackets and rubber dinghies, and myriad others who played small, key roles in keeping the criminal enterprise humming.

Another group operated within this system, too. They also broke the laws, but their motives weren't financial. They were humanitarian volunteers. When boats left Turkey, they supplied navigational assistance to make the journeys safer.

To protect his identity, I'll call one of them "Marcus." That winter, in his house in Northern Europe, Marcus stayed awake through long nights in front of his computer, his phone by his side. A strong swimmer with vast knowledge of the sea, he had spent much of the autumn of 2015 on the beaches of Lesvos, pulling refugees out of the water. Now, back home, he used technology to save lives.

The calls mostly came in at night. Each caller informed Marcus of a boat launching off the Turkish coast. No one gave their names; he assumed they were smugglers. Maybe they called out of concern for the passengers in their care. Maybe they worried that if customers drowned, they wouldn't get their money. In any case, many boats setting off from Turkey became part of a sea rescue network in which Marcus played a central role. As boats launched, he opened a conversation on WhatsApp and invited individuals from a wide collaborative network to join. They shared a single goal—to prevent drownings.

Marcus always began these conversations in the same way, by asking, "What language?" Arabic? Farsi? Dari? Once he had an answer, he contacted someone from his team of translators scattered around the world. The translator would then join the chat.

Soon he'd have three or four people conversing—Marcus himself, the translator, passengers on the boats, and, in emergencies, members of the Greek and Turkish coast guards. On his computer, he continually checked conditions at sea. "Go north to avoid the swells," he might suggest in English. The translator then communicated the message to people on the boat. GPS coordinates flew back and forth and Marcus transferred them to his map so that he could chart changing locations. With each new set of coordinates, he reentered the information and followed the boat's progress. *Ping. Ping. Ping.* If conditions deteriorated or the boat drifted off course, he notified the coast guard to launch a rescue.

Sometimes, when the weather turned dangerous, Marcus broadcast a warning meant to discourage travel. One, translated into Arabic, read: "Peace be upon you, my brothers and sisters. We are now on the Greek island of Lesvos. We ask that you be careful. From now on and for about a week the sea will be very berserk and we predict waves of four and a half meters. Please stay where you are and do not try to go to Greece or Italy, because no one can help you or save you. We strive to keep you safe. Be safe and stay where you are. Peace, mercy, and the blessings of God be upon you."

THE KHALIL FAMILY'S BOAT DEPARTED THE TURKISH COAST at 3:30 A.M. on February 18. The journey was supposed to take a few hours, but at 6:00 A.M. the weather turned stormy. The man steering the boat typed their location into his phone. "What do we do?" he asked someone on the other end of the line. "Go left? Go right?" The distance to Greece amounted to only a few miles. Most days, one could stand on shore and easily see the other side, but that day the travelers in the boat saw nothing but waves rising all around them.

Messages flew back and forth on the phone. The boat continued moving in the wrong direction. Instead of heading toward the island, they moved toward the open sea. An argument broke out among the men. The pilot, trembling, let go of the rudder. They drifted. Waves crashed over the side of the dinghy. The passengers shifted backward to allow the front of the boat to ascend the rising waves. They tossed their few remaining belongings into the water to lighten the load. Their prayers grew louder.

Abu Omar sat on the edge of the boat. His size and crooked nose gave him a tough authority, but he was just another terrified dad. Across the boat, he could see his daughters, exhausted and seasick. He could see his wife clutching their baby. It seemed that everyone realized the truth at once: They were in mortal danger. Abu Omar no longer cared about Europe.

Dry land. He wanted nothing else.

Crushed amid the women and children, Salma held her wet, shivering son. Once during those hours, she managed to nurse him, but most of the time, amid the press of bodies, she couldn't even get his mouth to her breast. She held his face in the air to keep him from suffocating and tried to keep an eye on her girls. Layla kept vomiting. Nura looked dazed, her head dipping toward the sloshy bilge inside the boat. "Watch out for my kids!" Salma screamed. "Help them." But no one could move.

Layla cried, "Can we go back?"

Nura sat beneath the weight of a large body pushing down on top of her. From nearby, she heard a man say, "Get off her! That's a girl, not a chair."

Abu Omar couldn't reach any of them. Where is death? he thought. In front of us or behind us?

Hours passed. They saw nothing but sea. The battery died on the phone of the guy communicating over WhatsApp. Someone new had to take over. Abu Omar carried their passports, their money, and his phone in a waterproof bag around his neck. He pulled the phone out of the pouch. He had covered it in plastic to keep it dry, so he tried using WhatsApp with a voice message.

A reply flashed back: "We can't hear you. Type it."

The plastic prevented typing, so he kept sending voice recordings. Somehow, the messages got through. The people at the other end were like doctors trying to diagnose the problem: Why was the boat going the wrong way? Abu Omar couldn't answer that basic question, but he figured out how to send his GPS coordinates to the people on the phone. With each reply from them, he conveyed instructions to the guy piloting the boat. Eventually, someone realized that the man at the rudder wasn't steering correctly. To go left, push the rudder to the right, they instructed. But where should they go? They couldn't see land in any direction.

Trapped in the center of the boat, Layla held her breath every time it reached the crest of a wave. She didn't believe they could stay afloat. Again and again, she braced herself to tumble into the sea.

Somehow, the boat stayed upright. Once, in the distance, they saw a ship. A Turkish flag fluttered on the mast, but the vessel didn't approach. Abu Omar continued messaging with the strangers on WhatsApp. Their steady presence offered comfort, but they couldn't save the passengers.

And then the motor died. They floated in silence. Water sloshed through the bottom of the boat. They were seventy-two cold, wet, frightened people, and they were in terrible danger. The men took turns pulling at the chain to get the engine started, but nothing happened. Then one young guy, in a fury, grabbed the chain and jerked as if their lives depended on it. The engine sputtered, then roared.

Gripping his phone, Abu Omar focused on the task in front of him. He pushed aside thoughts of his family.

Eventually, a message came in with new information. "You need the coast guard," it said. "Call 108. In English, say, 'Help me.'"

Abu Omar didn't understand the meaning of those two English words, but he called the number. When someone answered, he yelled, "Help me, help me, help me."

It was just after noon. They had been on the sea for nine hours.

They waited. And then, in the distance, they saw a ship approaching. The man on the rudder began to panic. "They're Turkish," he screamed. "We have to get away."

"No," said Abu Omar. He didn't care if they were Turkish. "Go straight toward it."

The ship was Greek, a vessel from the Hellenic Coast Guard. The sailors on board began pulling off the children, the women, the injured, the men. Then, with everyone on board, they churned toward land. The big rescue vessel moved fast. In thirty-five minutes, they reached Lesvos.

Once they stepped onto solid ground, the grateful passengers snapped photos to send to worried relatives. Abu Omar, looking at the Greek sailors, experienced an almost overwhelming sense of gratitude toward them. He didn't say anything, though. He couldn't speak their language.

AT FIRST GLANCE, LESVOS ISLAND, WITH ITS ARID HILLS and olive trees, looked much like Turkey, which was, after all, only a few miles away. But everything felt different to the Khalil family. They had survived the Death Trip. They had gotten themselves to Europe. Germany, it seemed, lay just ahead.

They stepped ashore on the southern end of Lesvos, near the metropolitan center of Mitilini. Had they landed farther north, they would have encountered more challenging conditions, which Tracey Myers, Jenni James, and Ibrahim Khoury had been working to mitigate for months. Down south, however, the Khalils felt Lesvos embrace them. They quickly found space in a camp. They never knew its name, but it may have been Kara Tepe, which was operated by UNHCR and the Greek government for the benefit of families and vulnerable people. The camp had private tents, decent food, clothing distribution, and hot showers. Their first day on dry land, they slept. Their second day, they completed their official registration, obtaining the documents they would need to transit Greece and proceed to Germany, where Abu Omar's brother was waiting. On their third day in Europe, they boarded a ferry bound for Piraeus.

Often, as refugees told me their stories, the complicated logistics of their journeys led me to ask a basic question: "How did you know how to do all this?" When I asked Abu Omar that question, he laughed. "It's not like you consult with a travel agent," he told me. He explained that he relied on advice from friends and family who'd made the trip already. And he did what we all do when we need information. He googled.

But there were segments of the trip, too, that seemed surprisingly similar to routine travel. One day on Lesvos Island, Abu Omar did actually walk into a tourist office and buy tickets for his family to ride the ferry to the mainland and then travel by bus up the spine of Greece.

By the time the Khalils boarded the ferry, they had very little money left and almost none of the possessions they had carried out of Damascus. But they could see their way to Germany and a new life.

CHAPTER 11

Gas Station Camps

I N TIME, REFUGEES THEMSELVES WOULD POWER much of the grass-roots relief effort, but that winter most asylum seekers were moving too quickly along the Balkan Route to join aid teams. The system relied almost entirely on Greeks and foreigners from stable nations. On Lesvos Island alone, social science researchers identified some eighty NGOs—both long-established humanitarian organizations and brand-new small-scale volunteer teams—providing relief in the winter of 2015–2016. The study estimated that between 2,260 and 4,240 people had volunteered from November 2014 to February 2016.

But volunteers get tired. By early 2016, many foreign ones had returned home, emotionally spent and financially strained. Tracey Myers remained on Lesvos, but Jenni James headed back to New Zealand to run a short-term environmental studies course that she taught every year. She loved the job, but she also needed to take a break and earn some money. When she flew home, she promised to return to Greece in a few months.

The transience of the volunteer labor force had significant effects, compromising productivity and straining everything from boat rescue teams to the provision of emergency medical services. The departures had one positive result, however. Back in their home countries, former volunteers could spread the word about the troubles in Greece. They raised money.

When Kanwal Malik returned to Nottingham from Leros Island that winter, she immediately launched a fund-raiser. "It's me again!" she wrote to friends on Facebook. "I feel like all I have been doing since

October is asking you all for donations. . . . I wouldn't ask if it wasn't needed so please give anything you can xx but most importantly please please share amongst your contacts and direct any questions about any money you donate and how I spend it."

Kanwal was speaking to people already primed to help, her own community of European Muslims. Nottingham's Pakistani community, like Muslims everywhere, followed the practice of regularly offering charity, or *zakat*. Chapter 2, verse 110 of the Qur'an instructs adherents to "establish prayer and give *zakat*, and whatever good you put forward for yourselves—you will find it with Allah." *Zakat*, in fact, is the third of the Five Pillars of Islam, coming after the tenets of faith and prayer and ahead of fasting during Ramadan and making a pilgrimage to Mecca. Islamic practice stipulates that the faithful donate 2.5 percent of their surplus wealth to charity every year.

When Kanwal described what she'd witnessed in Greece, she made it personal. "I just kept thinking this can be me and my family or my loved ones," she would say of refugees she'd met in Greece. People opened their wallets. The thousands Kanwal raised never approached the millions that professional fund-raisers brought in for large NGOs, but she and other volunteers who had returned helped keep the grassroots effort afloat.

Kanwal Malik, thirty-four years old, had found purpose. I'm so broken, she thought. These people are fixing me. On Leros, she had seen how people had joined together for the common good. The system moved her deeply. She wanted to be part of it.

There was only one hitch. Kanwal was also a newlywed and her husband wanted her home.

GREECE'S FERRY SYSTEM WORKED LIKE A FUNNEL, bringing refugees and migrants from distant islands to the mainland port of Piraeus, a 13.5-square-mile swath of piers, storage buildings, and passenger terminals on the outskirts of Athens. In February 2016, *The Guardian* reported on fifteen hundred displaced people camping at the port. One photo showed dozens, mostly women and children, seated on the ground in a cordoned-off area with sleeping bags scattered around them and laundry drying on a fence. Moored nearby was an enormous Minoan Lines ferry with its distinctive red, white, and black markings.

The number of refugees at Piraeus had begun to raise concern among prospective tourists. "What is the situation for embarking a cruise ship and even a taxi from our hotel to the port and is it even safe to stay in Athens?" one worried Australian wrote on Tripadvisor. A number of responses noted that the refugee encampments sat near the ferry terminals, a considerable distance from cruise ships. Some cautioned, too, against equating displaced people with danger. "Refugees are not criminals," one pointed out.

The travelers who faced the greatest danger were, of course, the refugees themselves. Disembarking from the ferries, some managed to transit quickly to buses and trains going north. Others—broke, sick, confused—got stuck at the port. Hunkered down in tents when they could find them and out in the open when they could not, they waited as the winter wind roared in from the sea.

The Khalil family's luck ran out at Piraeus. They had spent 105 euros per person on tickets meant to take them all the way through Greece. The travel agency had promised that a representative of a tour company named Olympia would meet them on the mainland and transfer them to a bus headed north. Now, stepping off the ferry, they looked around in vain for anything with the name Olympia on it.

Abu Omar suspected that he'd been ripped off. He said to Salma, "Wait here," then went searching until he found the Olympia office. "Tomorrow," a staff member said. Abu Omar returned to his family. They spent the night on the floor of a crowded shed.

The Khalils had survived the Death Trip and reached Europe, but they felt a new anxiety now. They had heard rumors that Europe, frantic over the migrant influx, might close the border up north. They had to move quickly. If they didn't cross soon, they could become trapped in Greece.

Despite the assurances of the Olympia agent, more days passed before they even started north. And then, once they began their 340-mile journey, the bus traveled only sixty miles before it pulled into a gas station parking lot and the driver announced, "We'll stay here until further notice."

THE KHALILS DIDN'T KNOW THAT CONDITIONS were deteriorating at the border. The population of the camp at Idomeni had swollen to tens of thousands. In response, Greek authorities diverted northbound buses to gas stations along the highway, trying to ease pressure on the camp. Now thousands waited in a line of gas station parking lots that stretched from Central Greece all the way to the border.

The family sat. Bus after bus pulled into the lot and stopped. Passengers sat inside the building or on the grassy median outside. Typically, a drive from Athens to the border takes five or six hours. Now, days passed. Abu Omar walked among strangers in the parking lot, stopping to talk with other Arabic speakers. "How long have you been here?" he asked.

"Three days."

"Two days."

"Four days."

He returned to his family with a rising sense of dread. Ever since the war in Syria began, in 2011, the Khalils had used cunning and resourcefulness to survive. In their own country, they'd had agency, even if they'd never felt safe. Now, as refugees, they seemed to have lost even that. What could they do, stuck at a highway rest stop in Greece? The weary father looked at his daughters in their donated coats and at his wife sitting on the ground with their infant son. Europe baffled him.

RIMA HALABI NEVER KNEW THE NAME OF THE ISLAND where her family landed in Greece. She and her children quickly transferred by ferry to the mainland, then raced through the port of Piraeus and boarded a bus headed north.

And then, like the Khalils, they stalled. Somewhere in Northern Greece, the bus pulled to a stop at a gas station and parked beside a half dozen other buses. The passengers ended up on the grass, on sidewalks, perched at tables in the facility's restaurant. Some bus drivers abandoned the scene for nearby hotels. The driver of Rima's bus left the door unlocked, allowing passengers to sleep inside.

The gas station remained a gas station, though it was now a tiny refugee camp as well. Motorists continued to pull up to fill their tanks. Rima found the local people very kind. Some brought blankets and homemade food. Some went into the facility's restaurant, placed big orders, then distributed meals. Rima accepted blankets, bottled water, and vegetarian sandwiches, but she avoided meat because her family only ate halal food. For the most part, she and her kids subsisted on these handouts from Good Samaritans, plus the salad, french fries, and cookies that she purchased with her diminishing funds.

As time passed, the stalled travelers became increasingly worried that the border would close before they could cross. Some headed north on foot. A few times, Rima and her children followed. These were weeks when international media regularly published photos of refugees walking along rural roads in Europe—a girl with a teddy bear, two boys pushing a third in a wheelchair. The images captured the strangeness of the situation and, to some extent, its pathos, but not the hours of physical exertion that walking demanded from people who were already hungry and exhausted. With an infant, a toddler, two cranky little boys, and a fed-up teen, Rima's group moved slowly. "My legs hurt. My feet hurt!" the boys would cry. Even though it was winter, the midday sun could turn fierce, making their misery that much worse. Rima's back ached. And then, invariably, a bus pulled up beside them, ordered them to board, and drove them back to where they'd started.

At night, inside the gas station, Rima would dole out french fries and cookies. Sometimes the children would play. Sometimes they'd bicker or whine, utterly bored. Eventually, she'd get them settled on a blanket and they'd fall asleep. Shakira sometimes walked back to the bus to sleep, but it reeked of unwashed bodies and she often returned, complaining of the smell. Rima, too scared for the safety of her children, allowed herself only the occasional intermittent doze. All night long, she sat beside the children on a chair, keeping watch, sending anguished texts to Musa, who could do nothing to help.

Later, looking back on that time, Rima couldn't say how many days she and her children stayed at that gas station. Maybe a week. Maybe two. The time blurred into a haze of anxiety and confusion. At some point, government buses arrived and authorities encouraged the refugees to climb aboard. Finally, Rima thought, they're taking us to the border.

They were not.

THE HALABIS DID END UP CLOSE TO MACEDONIA, but they had no chance to cross. The bus dropped them at Cherso Camp, a facility that Greece's military had recently opened near the small village of Cherso, about ten miles from the border. The camp was little more than an array of white canvas army tents spread across vacant land. The first night, Rima couldn't even find space inside a tent. She did discover a vendor selling supplies out of a truck, and she spent a few of her precious euros on a headlamp so that she could locate the portable toilets. She didn't find the toilets, though. Finally, the family just lay down on the grass to sleep. Rima held her children close.

In the days that followed, the family found an empty tent and settled into an existence that felt like something from the Stone Age. They were middle-class suburbanites now living without electricity or running water. To procure the rations distributed by the military, Rima had to wait in interminable lines, and the meals—often flavorless pasta or rice—had little nutritional value. The camp offered no guidance or services to help people apply for relocation or asylum.

Rima came to look back on her days at the gas station with longing. At least her family had been able to sleep in a building and keep themselves warm. Now they slept inside a canvas tent. When it rained, the earth beneath them turned to mud. Water pooled in puddles and trenches. Their clothes never dried.

CHAPTER 12

Idomeni

Six months had passed since Tracey Myers first traveled to Lesvos to spend a few days helping with the grassroots effort. Now she was one of the more experienced volunteers on the island and her efforts to train and coordinate staff meant she'd had wide influence in the relief community. In public, Tracey knew how to exude cheer. "Anyone super fit, super hearted and super available?" she chirped one day in January 2016 in a Facebook callout for volunteers. She was trying to help staff an outfit called CK Team, which did things like rescue stranded refugees off the sides of cliffs and carry vulnerable people piggyback over long distances. CK's workdays generally lasted sixteen hours and often the weather was awful. Supporting Tracey's Facebook post, former volunteers added enthusiastic comments, some letting people know that you didn't have to be a triathlete to do relief work in Greece. "I have a heart condition," one sixty-eight-year-old commented. "I managed fine for 12 days."

By early 2016, Tracey had turned her main focus to Hope Center, a multifaceted reception facility scheduled to open and operate just steps from a beach where large numbers of people disembarked from boats. Hope Center's organizers wanted to avoid one of the most dehumanizing aspects of refugee life, the endless waits in line. Typically, displaced people had to line up for everything—food, asylum documentation, clothing, shelter. They could spend entire days in line. In winter, they shivered. In summer, they had to sweat in the sun. In rain, they got drenched. Hope Center would operate on a small scale, and with fewer people needing service, the facility might not end up with long lines. If the model succeeded, the organizers thought other teams might duplicate it in other places. Tracey even planned a kitchen garden to supply fresh herbs for the healthy meals the center planned to offer.

Later, looking back on that winter, Tracey remembered feeling optimistic. "The infrastructure, the volunteer movement, everything got very strong and very well resourced," she told me. "Everyone brought money and it was fantastic."

For the first time since Tracey had arrived in Greece, volunteers were creating a response that wasn't merely a short-term fix but also a decent solution to a humanitarian disaster. Established NGOs were now collaborating with volunteers, all of them helping the new facility succeed. A medical team, for example, agreed to help set up a clinic on-site. Once the project opened, new arrivals would only have to walk up a set of stairs from the beach to find dry clothes, medical advice, a warm meal, a lovely garden, a place for their children to play, and a free bus ride to the island's official registration centers. The facility even had its own puppy mascot, Habibi, whose Arabic name meant "my dear."

By early 2016, Ibrahim Khoury had returned to the Park Hotel near Idomeni, where the situation was growing urgent again. Thousands of displaced people now occupied tents along the border. They needed everything—food, clothing, legal advice, medical care. In previous months, when numbers remained small, volunteer teams and larger NGOs had set up kiosks to help people camping in the area. Now, with thousands stuck along the border, the presence of aid teams increased. Larger organizations, like MSF and the Greek NGO Praksis, provided medical care, but volunteers continued to shoulder enormous responsibility. Ibrahim rarely stopped working. At night, he was back on the sofa in the lobby.

Ibrahim had gotten better at his job (he treated it like a job, even though he wasn't paid and remained a refugee in need of asylum). He'd taught himself Excel by watching tutorials on YouTube, and he could handle the accounting that came with distributing funds to small relief teams around the area. In that sense, he'd changed considerably. Back on

Lesvos, Ibrahim had operated in emergency mode, acting as if nothing mattered beyond solving immediate problems. If donors wanted reports or receipts, he would fume, thinking to himself, People are dying, and you want a receipt?

During that awful winter, however, Ibrahim began to see that he was not a single individual battling disaster, but one element of a larger system that functioned best by following standard practices. Now, he criticized himself. Yeah, he thought, they want a receipt. Paperwork needs to be done. A meeting needs to be done. An interview needs to be done. Why not? Be adult enough to accept that.

Over time, the combined efforts of many individuals and teams had strengthened the grassroots effort. Some teams were ramping up food distribution. Volunteer health-care professionals were providing medical, dental, and psychosocial support. Small aid teams gave out firewood in camps as an alternative to burning toxic trash. Many of these teams shared warehouse space, organized joint training sessions, streamlined purchasing, and worked together to tackle complicated problems. For example, to deal with infestations of snakes and rats in camps, Ibrahim researched rat poison on his computer and found a brand that was safe to use near children. He used donation money to purchase the poison, then dispersed it to volunteer teams working directly in the camps. These team members didn't wipe out vermin entirely, but their efforts helped. When they discovered an entire den of snakes, they lit a fire and burned it out.

Ibrahim could never shake the sense that he wasn't doing enough, however. "Within yourself," he once told me, "the feeling of [being] guilty never stops."

Ibrahim belonged to two communities—refugee and volunteer—which meant he often had to negotiate conflicting roles and expectations. As a volunteer, he maintained a presence on Facebook, thanking donors and providing information. As a refugee, however, he occasionally faced criticism from others who were displaced. If he wrote a thank-you post explaining how money had been spent, for example, he might receive snide comments in Arabic: "The really good people, when they help they don't go over the media saying, 'We did this and this.'"

Ibrahim tried to explain. "We're sorry. It's not like we're showing off.

It's just that this is how we receive donations. Without the Facebook post, we can't tell the people what's going on over here."

Once, in talking with me about these tensions, Ibrahim wished he had more clearly explained his actions to the very people he wanted to help. "In a human sense, we should have told them," he said, but he couldn't see a practical way to communicate with the population of an entire camp. "How can you speak with twenty thousand people? Let's say it's one second each. Do the math. It's like, I don't know. Days. A week? Would I spend a week explaining for them why we do this? Or would I be a robot, a rude person, and provide them with three tons of oranges every day?"

Ibrahim became a robot.

THE KHALIL FAMILY, STUCK AT GAS STATION CAMPS, hadn't even *reached* Idomeni. Each time their bus moved north, it traveled only a few dozen miles before pulling off the road again. "Europe" became a series of parking lots.

The Khalils were not a hardy group. Years of war and weeks of displacement had worn them down, and sleeping outside only made things worse. Nura had urinary tract problems. Salma suffered breast infections from nursing the baby. Abu Omar felt responsible for the family, and the stress wasn't good for his heart. At night, the family lay in the sleeping bags they'd acquired on Lesvos. Salma held the baby. Layla and Nura huddled in the cold beside their mom and dad.

Back in Turkey, Abu Omar had worried most about the dangers of the boat. If they survived that journey, he'd believed, they could do well in Germany. His girls could return to school. The Khalils could live in peace. Abu Omar could find a job to provide for his family. He even fantasized about the more distant future, when he would return to Syria and help his country.

"That," he later told me, "was what I was thinking."

But the journey had become interminable. They had at least four more countries to cross before they reached Germany, and they couldn't even get out of Greece. Their funds were running low, too, a fact made more galling when they learned they'd paid twice the going rate for ferry and bus tickets. The Khalils' worldly possessions had dwindled to passports, a bit of cash, and their mobile phone. Abu Omar didn't even have appropriate shoes. He'd stuffed his size-forty-four feet into a donated pair of forty-twos.

And once they reached Idomeni, could they leave Greece? Day after day, they heard rumors of problems there. The European Union was shifting its policy, stopping people from going across the border into Macedonia. The Khalils had registration papers with "Germany" stamped on them. Surely they could continue their journey. Right? *Right?*

Who knew? They only knew that they had to move north fast.

Finally, they abandoned the buses and hired a taxi.

It took just a few hours by car to get from their final gas station to Idomeni. Stepping out of the cab, they could see across the border to the green rolling hills of Macedonia. Closer, they could see the chain-link fence that separated the two nations, and, spread across the fields, hundreds of tents. Over the past few weeks, the makeshift camp had developed into a temporary city. At its center sat trailers of large international NGOs, the police headquarters, medical clinics, and distribution centers. The camp had banks of portable toilets and temporary sinks and showers.

The family picked up their bags and walked up the road, past dozens of tents, and into the center of the camp. It didn't take long to locate the container building where the Greek NGO Praksis coordinated the border crossing. A crowd of people stood in line and the process seemed straightforward. After the Khalils showed their papers, they'd receive a number. When their number came up, they could cross.

Eventually, the family reached the front of the line and presented their passports and the registration documents with "Germany" stamped on them. They received their number, 154. At that moment, people holding number 65 could cross. The Khalils would wait.

They left the Praksis container and looked around, wondering what to do. They were city people, accustomed to electricity, plumbing, washing machines, refrigerators. How could they keep the baby clean and healthy without running water? How could Nura, with her medical issues, manage in dirty portable toilets? That question alone could break a parent's heart.

They had no choices. They had to wait. They felt lucky to find a spot for Salma and the children in a communal tent reserved for women, but men were not allowed inside. That first night, Abu Omar unrolled a sleeping bag and slept on the ground. The next morning, his muscles creaky and chilled from the cold, he walked back to check the number at Praksis. Maybe they could leave that day.

The crossing number was still 65.

After that, Abu Omar watched the crossing number with heightened suspicion. Days passed and it never changed. Were people paying bribes for lower numbers? Each time he checked, his blood pressure rose. Number 65. Number 65.

In Nottingham, Kanwal Malik remained focused on the situation in Greece, and her fledgling marriage suffered. She didn't blame Asad for failing to care about refugees. She appreciated how much he had changed since their divorce. He treated her with respect and no longer tried to control her. But she couldn't ignore the underlying issue: The two were moving in different directions.

Kanwal now wondered if she'd made a mistake in remarrying him. Greece had changed her ideas about what she wanted from life, and she refused to let the marriage hold her back. In February 2016, she set off to volunteer for a third time, knowing that leaving again would widen the fissure at home.

Kanwal and her friend Iram flew back to Leros. The situation had changed considerably since their last visit. A drop in arrivals had decreased the need there, so they devised a new plan for investing their donation money. Knowing that conditions had deteriorated farther north, they teamed up again with the Lebanese volunteer Farez, filled Farez's car with supplies, put it on a ferry to the mainland, then drove north to Idomeni.

Kanwal had seen extreme poverty on family visits to Pakistan and had, of course, witnessed tragedy on Leros and Kos. None of that prepared her, however, for the total breakdown of civilization that she witnessed at Idomeni. Mid-February temperatures routinely dipped into the forties. For warmth, camp occupants burned tree branches, old clothes, and tires, the stench of melting rubber filling the air. All the rain meant that people were, quite literally, sleeping in mud. Kanwal saw an empty wheelchair toppled over on its side. Where has that person gone? she wondered.

And then there was the toilet situation. *The Sphere Handbook* recommends a minimum of one toilet per twenty people. At Idomeni, according to one report, sixty-two people shared a single toilet. Anyone who has used a Johnny on the Job at an outdoor concert knows that the gross factor increases with use, particularly if sanitation services can't keep up with demand. At Idomeni, the effect was predictable: overflowing toilets smeared with feces and urine. Some people refused to use the toilets altogether, opting to go in nearby woods instead. Others relieved themselves randomly, leaving the ground dotted with excrement. Kanwal saw children smeared with feces and mud. She considered the plight of mothers struggling to keep their little ones healthy and safe. You can't even stand in that toilet, she thought to herself, and you've got, say, four children. What are you supposed to do?

At night, the three volunteers slept in the car at the edge of the camp, Iram and Farez in the reclining seats in front and Kanwal curled up in back. The doors and windows were closed, but they still heard wailing—not just from children but from adults, too. Even in daylight, they felt impotent, unable to figure out a way to help. They had a carload of supplies, but they had no way to distribute these without inciting a riot.

Down on the islands, Kanwal had not worried about her own safety, but she did at Idomeni. Walking through camp, she couldn't escape leering men, who seemed to lurk around every corner. She pulled a hood over her head, covered her face with a scarf, but she never felt secure. What would she do, she wondered, if she had to live in this place?

One day, Kanwal ran into a young girl she'd met on Leros Island. The child, like so many others, had traveled north and then become trapped at the border. She showed Kanwal a tiny tube of lip balm that Kanwal had given her all those months before; then she pleaded, "Take me back with you!"

If Kanwal had never returned to Greece after volunteering farther south, she might have known only the beautiful humanity she'd witnessed earlier. But Idomeni revealed absolute wretchedness. "No matter how bad it got on the islands," Kanwal later told me, "these people had hope to move on. The borders were open. Their suffering would result in something." That was not the case in those miserable fields.

Many months later, when Kanwal described to me her experience on the border, she seemed utterly disappointed in her own performance. "I couldn't do it," she said. "I couldn't deal with the screaming at night, with the kids, with the lack of sanitation. I just couldn't cope." It was 2016, and humans were living like animals in Europe.

Kanwal did what refugees could not. She went home.

CHAPTER 13

Tents

Rima Halabi and her children remained in Cherso Camp through the weeks of late winter. Several thousand people, mostly Syrians and Iraqis, lived in the camp. To its credit, the Greek government had so far avoided coercing people to move to these official facilities. *Time* magazine had quoted Greece's alternate defense minister as saying, "The only plan is to persuade them. There is no plan of violence. We will not use force." To persuade, then, authorities planned to offer a rosy picture. Arabic-language leaflets appeared at the makeshift camps, describing "far more comfortable conditions" for refugees who made the move.

But Greece's new official camps were clearly not "far more comfortable." Many of these structures had never been designed for human habitation. The government had converted a tannery, a slaughterhouse, and a factory that formerly produced toilet paper rolls. By April, the activist border-monitoring team Moving Europe would make a fact-finding visit to Cherso and report that the camp's thousands of residents had access to only five showers and ten toilets and that rain had turned the flat terrain into a swamp. As if squalor wasn't depressing enough, residents told the visitors that the Hellenic Army, which ran the place, had announced that occupants should expect to remain there for at least a year. If anyone suffered a breakdown or depression, the camp offered no mental-health services. At Cherso, the Moving Europe report would state, "only basic medical treatment is available."

In time, conditions at Cherso did improve, but not enough to substantially affect the lives of people living there. The UN team would count forty toilets that spring—a significant increase from ten—but the population was also growing, eventually reaching 4,000 in a camp with an official capacity of 2,500. How many toilets do four thousand people need? If you met the standards set by *The Sphere Handbook*—a trusty resource for the European Commission as well as Ibrahim Khoury— you'd have two hundred.

Sixty-eight percent of Cherso's residents were women and children, like Rima and her five kids. Every day the Syrian mom faced challenges she never could have imagined back in al-Dana, like living in a tent without a door to close and lock. How could she keep little ones from slipping out or predators from coming in? She also had to address the eccentricities of her own children. Shakira, the teenager, worried about germs. The girl refused the container rations (beige mounds of rice, beige piles of pasta) that were supposed to count as dinner. On top of all her other struggles, Rima tried to convince Shakira to eat.

TWENTY MILES TO THE WEST, THE KHALILS SAT AT IDOMENI. People who had reached the border the previous fall had crossed quickly. They hadn't needed numbers in order to proceed. But Europe's days of "open borders" had ended.

Every hour that passed added to Abu Omar's fury, but he was also a practical man. He turned his attention to improving his family's living situation. With Salma and the kids in a communal tent and Abu Omar in a sleeping bag on the open ground, they lacked even the comfort of spending nights together. They needed a space of their own.

He decided to approach UNHCR for help. To the extent that Idomeni functioned like a city, the area by the railroad tracks served as its urban center, the spot where many of the aid agencies staffed their offices and clinics. At the UNHCR container one morning, he found a crowd of people already standing in line. He took his place and waited.

It was hot. Winter nights in Northern Greece were cold, but the midday sun could make a furnace of those open fields. Days of worry and nights on the ground had worsened Abu Omar's health. He became light-headed but refused to give up his spot. Finally, he reached the front of the line. He explained his situation. "I need a tent for my family."

But UNHCR wasn't handing out tents. "Go to MSF," an official replied.

He left one office, walked to another, and got in line. The heat had become oppressive, but he was determined to wait. Finally, he reached the front. "I need a tent," he said.

The MSF officials shook their heads. "Go to UNHCR."

Abu Omar had failed to cross the border. Failed to save his money. Failed to keep his family together in the camp. And now, after spending a day in line, he couldn't even acquire a tent.

Everyone has a breaking point. Abu Omar reached his.

He began to yell. He yelled and yelled. All within earshot—people in line, people behind desks—stared at him.

The outburst lasted only a few seconds. Stress and heat had taken their toll, pushing the man's weak heart to its limit. One moment, he was yelling at the world. The next, the world went black. The big man fell to the ground.

He woke inside an ambulance. In time, he would learn that he had collapsed and that someone on the camp's medical staff had given him an injection, then called paramedics. Now they were rushing him to a hospital. Lying on the stretcher, he felt strangely calm. He understood that something bad had happened and that he needed medical attention. But the only pain he experienced was an urgent need to urinate. What will happen to my children? he wondered. To my family? Is this the way I'm going to go? He no longer felt any fury. He surrendered.

No one spoke Arabic with him at the hospital. Immobilized, Abu Omar observed as strangers prodded his body, poked him with needles, rolled machines up to his bed. He listened as they stood beside him, gesturing in his direction, speaking Greek. When they communicated with him at all, they did so through mime. He'd had a heart attack. That much he understood. The doctors kept him in the hospital that night and through the next day. The following evening, they released him. Someone drove him back to Idomeni and dropped him off by the train tracks with a few doses of pills and a prescription he could fill in the MSF clinic—exactly where the drama had started.

Somehow, in the mayhem, he had lost his shoes. Barefoot and weak, he made his way in the dark back to the clinic. Here, at least, someone spoke Arabic. "Get some sleep," the staff members told him.

Now, Abu Omar began to laugh. "Where will I sleep?" he asked. After all that had happened, he had circled back to his original problem: He needed a tent.

It was, by now, well past midnight. The clinic staff gave him a tent and helped him set it up in an empty space outside. He found Salma and the kids. The family gathered in the dark, staring at their new home.

To Abu Omar, the tent represented a superabundance of good fortune. It's like they've given us a house, he thought, a villa.

They didn't have enough blankets. Salma and the kids returned to the communal tent for that night. Abu Omar climbed into his old sleeping bag inside the new tent. Tomorrow, he told himself, begins our struggle for blankets.

CHAPTER 14

Human Resources

Tracey Myers had remained on Lesvos all winter. Working with her sister in England, she had established a nonprofit that supported the general aid effort and offered a stipend for Tracey's living expenses in Greece. Through most of that winter, the stipend allowed her to prepare for the opening of the Hope Center near the village of Molyvos. She finally felt that she was making progress by creating something innovative and humane in Greece.

She could see a change in herself, as well. Throughout Tracey's life, an insect phobia had held her back. It had prevented her from doing humanitarian work in developing countries. It had marred her social life by making her scared and skittish, frustrating family and friends. Even psychotherapy hadn't helped. And then, one day in Greece, Tracey noticed that her phobia had virtually disappeared. In the midst of so much human catastrophe, she later told me, "I felt like I saw what evil is, and what the things to be scared of are. And it's not insects." Working with refugees seemed to have changed her brain chemistry.

At the Hope Center, Tracey dedicated many hours to the herb garden. She had become deeply committed to the idea of humane aid delivery, and providing nutritious food was essential. But she worried, too. Local opposition to the project delayed its opening. Some neighbors supported it, but others condemned the plan to turn a ramshackle beach hotel into a refugee transit facility. Then government officials got involved, threatening the project with legal action. The newly renovated building sat empty while potential clients—just off the boats—slept in tents in nearby fields.

And all along, Tracey had continued reading the grassroots movement's online message boards, which were lighting up with news from Idomeni. Hundreds of refugees were arriving at Greece's northern border every day, and almost none could cross. The camp population was increasing dramatically.

Tracey had put everything she had into the Hope Center and now the entire venture seemed destined to fail. Considering the disaster unfolding along the border, she thought, Shit. There are thousands of people . . . in Idomeni. People are screaming for help, and I'm planting herbs.

She headed north.

ACROSS EUROPE, ALARM BELLS BEGAN RINGING as the population along the border swelled. "We are experiencing the biggest refugee crisis since the Second World War," said Greece's prime minister, Alexis Tsipras. "The problem surpasses the powers of the country, the strength of a government, and the innate weaknesses of the European Union."

Volunteers poured into Northern Greece. Some arrived alone or in small teams from other countries. One from the Czech Republic—they simply called themselves "the Czech Team"—appeared in early March and began to focus on storage and distribution of supplies and donations. Another group of young Europeans, fresh from the migrant camps of France, always needed help at their soup kitchen, Hot Food Idomeni.

While individual teams worked on specific initiatives, Ibrahim focused on the effort as a whole. He received donations, then doled out funds to projects that could use the money efficiently. In February alone, he had managed over seventeen thousand euros in donations. These days, his spreadsheets accounted for everything from the £10 cash given to him by a Dutch volunteer to €2,245 that arrived via bank transfer from the online donation site YouCaring.

Ibrahim wanted to balance survival funding at Idomeni with long-term investment in a humanitarian problem that would continue to challenge Europe in the future. Though he used donation money to fund the purchase of the Syrian flatbread that Hot Food Idomeni handed out with its daily servings of stew, he also wanted to address emerging needs. Now that Greece, with funding help from the European Union, had begun to open official, government-run camps, he had to consider conditions in those places, too. Were they habitable? Government officials would say yes, but they didn't live there. Ibrahim knew, for example, that at one of these camps, Cherso, refugees lived on open ground. When it rained, tents flooded. If he could fund wooden flooring, it would keep people out of the mud. In March, then, Ibrahim made a Facebook appeal to pay for permanent flooring for Cherso. "Let's find a real solution to make it a decent place to live," he wrote.

Strange bedfellows: The Greek government established camps and volunteers installed the flooring. Other unlikely collaborations began to occur, as well. Professional organizations like UNHCR and the Red Cross had money and years of experience, but strict internal regulations and slow-moving bureaucracy left them inflexible at moments of rapid change. If UNHCR, for example, didn't have a line item in its budget for food, then its staff had no recourse, even if children went hungry. Grassroots teams, on the other hand, had flexibility. They could shift funds easily, but a lack of experience could cause dangerous mistakes. A professional aid worker told me that a small aid team had once distributed cans of infant formula printed with instructions in languages unintelligible to refugees. As a result, confused parents ended up feeding milk meant for one-year-olds to newborns, who couldn't digest it.

No single organization oversaw the entire effort at Idomeni, but professional organizations and small aid teams collaborated and also commended one another. After Ibrahim issued his online appeal for flooring, a staff member from a large NGO chimed in with both a supportive response and photo documentation: "For those of you who can not perceive the difference that this flooring makes, [here are] pictures of Cherso on rainy days with tents without flooring." The image showed the opening of a tent, its A-frame spread over an inch of muddy water.

Every day, new volunteers bounded into the Park Hotel and offered a simple "Tell me what to do." They could distribute bananas, haul boxes around a warehouse, or pass out bowls of soup, but they needed guidance. They were musicians, nurses, carpenters, graduate students, and retirees, eager but mostly inexperienced. As their rental cars pulled into the hotel parking lot, grassroots veterans advised them on best practices for aid delivery.

Ibrahim teamed up with two experienced volunteers to lead a crucial HR project. Phoebe, a Canadian, and Cyril, who was Swiss, had been working in Greece for months. They began conducting orientation sessions for new arrivals. What supplies were needed in the camps? They made lists. When did teams require staffing? They posted schedules. Still, with volunteers appearing nearly every hour, the coordinators had trouble keeping up, especially since Ibrahim had to focus on financing. Their tiny team became overwhelmed.

That March, Tracey Myers showed up in Northern Greece. She was shaken by her experience on Lesvos but also anxious to continue to help. She rented a grimy room above a diner across the road from the Park Hotel. Those first few days disoriented her. Without Jenni beside her, and far from the teams she'd come to know down south, she felt out of place, unprepared for the laid-back, hippie vibe of this community up north. She headed straight to Idomeni to find some way to help.

At this point, the makeshift camp had some twelve thousand occupants. Tracey could not solve any of its endemic problems, but she recognized an issue that she could address. All day long, Good Samaritans drove into camp, their cars full of supplies, wanting to hand them out to needy people. In Lesvos, a volunteer handbook had warned against such spontaneous distributions, which could easily spark a riot among desperate refugees. Few of the novice volunteers up north seemed to know this "best practice," so Tracey decided to inform them of the risk.

Every day, she went to camp and stood sentinel at the entrance. While official vehicles drove to the containers in the center, most relief workers parked on the outer road. When Tracey saw private cars heading deeper inside, she assumed they planned a distribution and waved them over. Once they stopped, she offered tips on how to avoid causing a melee when they opened their trunks.

It was only a matter of time before camp residents wanted to know why the orange-haired lady was stopping cars on the road. Tracey wrote out an explanation, then asked Arabic and Farsi speakers to translate it into a statement that she could pull up on her phone when curious people approached. "Hi," it said. "Sometimes people come to camp and try to give things out, but they aren't sure how to do it safely, and sometimes it is dangerous for people, especially children. We are here to try and give advice so people can distribute things in a better way for everyone."

Tracey passed her first week like that. She imagined more efficient methods of educating new volunteers, but at least she was achieving something.

FOR THE KHALILS, SHELTER REMAINED a constant problem at Idomeni. The family had slept for some time in the tent that Abu Omar received from MSF. Then one day, they looked away for a moment and someone snatched their entire tent, their possessions still inside. Two weeks passed. They wandered, sleeping where they could. And then, when Salma was walking through the camp one day, she spotted a tent with a familiar-looking burn mark and the telltale signs of repairs she'd made with orange thread. "That's our tent," she told her husband.

"Are you sure? Because I'm going to make a big deal about it."

"I'm sure."

Abu Omar had a weak heart, but he was still a large guy capable of graphic language. He approached the man inside the tent. "You're a thief," he said, "and I am going to chase you down until the end of your days."

They got their tent back.

It was still a tent, however. And March brought heavy rain. The camp became a sea of mud and muck. Portable toilets overflowed. Pup tents collapsed. Finally, international humanitarian agencies hauled in several large-frame tents, each capable of sleeping scores of people. As it happened, UNHCR decided to erect one of these more substantial structures on the spot where the Khalils had been sleeping. The agency staff brought in supplies, including bunk beds, to furnish the spacious new dwellings. The family sat on one of the beds, watching and talking among themselves about where they'd go inside the tent when the structure was ready.

The agency staffers had their own plan. "Wait," they announced once they'd set it up. "We want to figure out how we're going to arrange people inside."

The agency staffers hadn't even finished saying "Wait," and the Khalils had already grabbed their things, rushed into the tent, and taken over a corner. That's where they stayed. The big canvas shelter with its bunk beds and solid floor was the most comfortable place they'd slept in Greece.

DAY BY DAY, TRACEY ACCLIMATED TO THE GRASSROOTS world along the border. Her rented room in Polykastro—"I never slept in a more disgusting place in my whole life," she later told me, "and I had it good"—lacked even washing facilities. To bathe, she walked across the road to the Park Hotel and stood in line for the paid public shower. As days passed, Tracey came to know Phoebe and Cyril, the volunteer coordinators. She watched as they struggled to put together a viable aid operation. Tracey's months on Lesvos had taught her how to direct volunteer energy in a strategic way. When she spotted Phoebe hunched over her computer one day, she walked over.

"Do you need some help?" she asked.

Tracey's gentle Yorkshire accent caught Phoebe's attention, but Phoebe only grunted and immediately turned her attention back to her screen. She looked like an air traffic controller worried that any distraction might cause a midair collision.

Tracey decided to ask someone else. She had seen Ibrahim Khoury around the Park Hotel, but she knew him only as a shadowy figure in the lobby. Bearded, thin, and disheveled, he didn't even bother to take off the high-visibility—or "hi-vis"—protective jacket that relief workers wore to identify themselves when they walked through a camp. In the mornings, she would see him asleep on a sofa. Midday, he barely stopped moving. By evening, he looked wrecked. After a week sleeping in her own dirty room, Tracey considered herself a mess, but this guy was really filthy—"all mucky in his hi-vis, looking like the walking dead."

But he had an aura, too—"mysterious and omnipotent," Tracey

called him. More than anyone else at the Park Hotel, Ibrahim seemed to understand the situation. He would know how she could help.

It took her a while, though, to pluck up the courage to talk to him. He didn't just seem busy. He actively discouraged conversation. Near his spot in the hotel lobby, he had posted a sign: WHEN YOU HAVE FINISHED YOUR BUSINESS, PLEASE LEAVE IMMEDIATELY.

His gaze was hard as she approached. "Don't waste my time," he said. "Tell me why you are here and what you can do."

Back in the UK, Tracey had managed social welfare projects that involved large teams of people. In Lesvos, she had coordinated volunteers and pulled a drowning man from the surf. She would turn forty soon. Still, she felt like a five-year-old when she talked to him.

IBRAHIM KNEW ABOUT TRACEY MYERS LONG BEFORE she showed up in Polykastro that March. Back in Lesvos, he had heard her name as a member of the volunteer community, but they had never met. Now, with both of them working out of the Park Hotel, Ibrahim couldn't ignore the orange-haired Brit in the combat boots and leather jacket. He noticed, too, that she impressed the other volunteers with her competence and good cheer. Even though Phoebe never had time to talk with Tracey, she'd already suggested to Ibrahim that Tracey join their team. "She's really different," Phoebe told him. "She could be a great help."

But he was not prepared to accept her as a colleague. "No," he told Phoebe.

"Why not?"

"She seems too nice."

"We need her," Phoebe replied.

Ibrahim considered himself a shrewd judge of character. Tracey raised his suspicions. "She's hiding something. She can't be always nice, always agreeing. There's something wrong."

Phoebe stared at Ibrahim. "No. There's only something wrong with you." Then she added a piece of advice. "Trust people."

Ibrahim wasn't ready to do that, but other issues made him waver. A few days earlier, a group of Afghans had tried to cross the river between

Greece and Macedonia. Three drowned, including a pregnant woman and her teenage sister. Later that same day, other refugees pushed down the border fence and crossed. Macedonian police rounded them up, loaded them into buses, and drove them back to Greece. Several foreign volunteers had accompanied the refugees across the border, and they were arrested and jailed overnight. Back at the Park Hotel, Ibrahim steamed. Illegal crossings endangered vulnerable people, and when volunteers got involved, their actions made the grassroots movement look political. Ibrahim wanted volunteers to aid the relief effort, not cause more problems. If Phoebe wanted Tracey Myers to play a role in what they called "Operations Control," Ibrahim wouldn't argue.

So Tracey joined the Park Hotel coordination team. Mornings often found her inside the restaurant, or, on sunny days, out on the terrace, rolling cigarettes, drinking coffee, and trying to guide dozens of enthusiastic and nervous new volunteers. Mostly, she shared a set of principles meant to keep people safe and the aid effort functioning: Park your car facing away from the camp so that, in the event of a riot, you can exit quickly. Don't open the trunk of your car and start handing out stuff randomly. Don't take pictures of people without their permission and then post the photos on the internet; refugees have lost a lot, so don't rob them of their privacy, too.

Among the coterie of long-term volunteers, Tracey felt that she was beginning to prove herself, even to Ibrahim Khoury. She showed up, worked hard, and did her best. One day, she made Ibrahim an offer. He had a habit of scrawling lists and announcements on random pieces of paper, then taping them to the walls in what Tracey called a "crazy, intimidating fashion." When Tracey volunteered to organize everything, he agreed. Over several long nights, she went through every page and translated Ibrahim's iconoclastic English into clear, concise statements that he could post on walls for volunteers to read. Watching her work, he didn't say much, but, little by little, she sensed that he was warming to her. "Maybe because I could be quiet for five hours," she told me later. "Or maybe because he started seeing I wasn't a total idiot."

CHAPTER 15

The Border Closes

EUROPE WANTED TO STOP THE INFLUX of displaced people. With tens of thousands now in camps in Greece, and more arriving every day, the EU had been searching for a solution for months. On March 18, 2016, Europe and Turkey finally signed their long-discussed agreement—later referred to as "the EU-Turkey Deal"—meant "to end the irregular migration from Turkey to the EU and replace it instead with legal channels of resettlement of refugees to the European Union." To achieve these goals, Europe agreed to provide Turkey with three billion euros in aid for refugees in Turkey, to be doled out over several years. In return, Turkey promised to staunch the flow of irregular migration into Europe, both by preventing crossings from Turkey and by accepting the "forced return" of illegal migrants who had reached Europe's shores. For their part, EU member states agreed to increase the number of Syrian refugees accepted for resettlement from Turkey. In early March, Macedonia, Croatia, and Slovenia shut their borders to migrants trying to cross from Greece.

From the beginning, there were questions about the viability, legality, and morality of the agreement. For one thing, Europe had historically placed high value on human rights. A policy of "forced return" of "illegal" migrants could easily undermine that value. Elizabeth Collett, founder of the Migration Policy Institute, noted that to "achieve its self-imposed goal—a significant reduction in arrivals and an increase in returns to Turkey—policymakers will have to drastically cut legal corners, potentially violating EU law on issues such as detention and the right to appeal." Humanitarian organizations expressed concern that the deal would prioritize stopping arrivals over safeguarding refugee rights. UNHCR criticized the agreement and called on Europe to address "the compelling needs of individuals fleeing war and persecution. Refugees need protection, not rejection."

Registering its outrage in a dramatic way, MSF immediately suspended the service it had been providing at Moria Camp on Lesvos Island, declaring that the facility, which had earlier functioned as a protection center, was now becoming a "pre-removal center" meant to process migrants before returning them to Turkey. "MSF," the organization declared, "is appalled by the adoption of this deal that aims at preventing people from seeking asylum in Europe and doesn't want to participate to a cynical agreement that doesn't guarantee that the basic protection and humanitarian needs are covered."

The deal moved forward.

IN THE BACKYARD OF THE PARK HOTEL, dozens of volunteers slept in tents, becoming a parallel community to the one at Idomeni, except that the volunteer campers had access to the hotel's plumbing, electricity, hot meals, and cold beer, and, most important, could go home when they felt ready. A few volunteers actually slept at Idomeni Camp, determined to bear witness to the problems there, but their presence added strain to a system already buckling from the needs of so many displaced.

For the refugee children, like Layla and Nura Khalil, volunteers added sparkle to very dreary days. Some volunteers offered hot tea, others soup and snacks. In the mornings, a team walked through camp, handing out bananas. One young woman volunteer, seeing Layla shivering in the cold, gently wrapped around her neck a red knit scarf, which Layla came to treasure. Not far from where the family slept, a team provided children's programming and art activities out of a couple of repurposed shacks. There, the girls became adept at knitting and making bracelets with brightly colored rubber bands.

Maybe we can learn something, Layla told herself. Maybe they can help us. The girl felt that her family had suffered enough. Europe presented a new life for them. She made a decision to be happy.

More than anything, the presence of volunteers made her feel less alone in the muddy mess of Idomeni. Oh, she thought when she saw them walking through the camp, there are people who think about us.

AS THE WEATHER TURNED WARMER, SNAKES BECAME an increasing problem for people living in camps. One online photo from Cherso Camp showed a snake—presumably dead—that was as long as the height of the man who held it. Another photo showed an English-language sign posted at the camp. In the margins, someone had scrawled Arabic translations. The statement began,

HOW TO STOP THE SNAKES COMING:

SNAKES COME TO EAT THE MICE AND RATS.

THERE ARE MANY MICE AND RATS IN THE CAMP BECAUSE THEY COME TO EAT THE FOOD THAT IS LEFT ON THE FLOOR.

YOU CAN HELP TO KEEP THE SNAKES DOWN IF YOU PUT YOUR FOOD WASTE IN THE BINS.

Who took the time to offer such levelheaded advice? Presumably not one of the mothers in the camp, many of whom were likely too busy fending off reptiles. The statement went on to describe how to address a worst-case scenario, including advice like CUT OPEN THE WOUND OR TRY TO REMOVE THE VENOM and EVEN A VIPER BITE IS NOT ALWAYS SERIOUS.

Rima Halabi, stuck in a tent with five grimy children, cried all the time. She kept her surroundings clean, hoping to deter snakes, but someone killed a huge one right beside her tent. Then Rima learned that Cherso was actually a military camp. She assumed that in the past people had been killed and buried there. Perhaps, she thought, the dead bodies had the effect of forcing the snakes from the ground. She had to get out of this place.

THE BORDER HAD CLOSED, BUT DISPLACED PEOPLE continued to arrive at Idomeni. Tracey Myers wanted to share accurate information with camp residents, the most important piece of which was also the most dispiriting: "These borders aren't going to open." Working with Farsi and Arabic speakers, she created a set of public service statements that she sent out over WhatsApp. Camp volunteers then disseminated them by showing residents the text on their phones. Greek officials simultaneously conveyed information over loudspeakers, encouraging people to board buses that would transport them to official camps farther from the border. Few refugees, however, agreed to go. Over one two-day period, six hundred people took the buses—mostly families with small children who found conditions in the camp impossible to bear. Thousands of others stayed put.

Part of the trouble lay in the lack of trustworthy information. "It was Rumor Land at Idomeni," a professional aid worker told me later. One falsehood, for example, suggested that journalists and the Red Cross would help refugees cross the border illegally. Hearing such information, people felt hope, which made their disappointment more severe once they learned the truth. Day after day, rumors precipitated a repetitive chain of events: Furious camp residents protested, and then, as time passed, protests led to riots and the authorities used tear gas to contain the violence. Eventually, volunteer teams issued a joint statement about the demonstrations, saying, in part, "We have advised our volunteers not to take part in this activity, and are actively trying to de-escalate the situation by both providing accurate information to refugees that the border is not open and discouraging them from joining this potentially dangerous demonstration." Eighteen aid teams signed the statement, many of them represented by people who had witnessed riots at the camp before. They knew that in moments of violence refugees suffered.

Then more riots broke out. As Tracey watched from a distance, angry men pressed toward the Greek police who were blocking the border. Some tipped over trash containers. Some threw rocks. Tear gas filled the air. No one could avoid danger. NGOs had no authority to impose order. That was the responsibility of the police. So the international organizations and volunteers could only stand back and watch—or, at best, try to offer medical assistance—when things went haywire. Tracey heard about tear gas canisters landing on tents, injuring people sitting inside. More than anything else, Idomeni was a residential community. It seemed to Tracey that protesting there was like rioting in somebody's living room.

Day after day, riots flared, children's eyes burned from tear gas, rocks fell on the tents of people eating dinner. But camp residents tried to protect one another, too, and Tracey experienced moments of surprising goodwill. One day she lost her phone in the camp and it later turned up at the Park Hotel. Some honest soul had found and returned it.

Sometime during that ugly week, Ibrahim Khoury approached Phoebe with an apology. "You were right about Tracey," he told her a little sheepishly. "She's really, really, really good."

THE EU-TURKEY DEAL CHANGED NOTHING for the Khalil family, except that they were more anxious than ever about getting out of Greece. Living in the camp made Abu Omar feel like Mowgli in *The Jungle Book*. For a long time, they had slept in tents too small to stand up in. Even now, living in the spacious communal tent, they still had to use the portable toilets. Salma still cooked outside on open ground. Abu Omar still hauled water, hung clotheslines, guarded their possessions from theft.

For Salma, the most physically grueling aspect of life in the camp was her need to hand-wash the family's clothes. Back home, she'd always used a washing machine. Now she spent hours squatting on the ground over plastic buckets, scrubbing. Eventually, her wrists swelled, causing intense pain and damage that she'd eventually need surgery to repair. Later, talking with me about her myriad troubles at Idomeni, she said, "For me, all those things are on one hand and the washing is on the other." Her wrists throbbed.

More weeks passed. The situation on Greece's border had become a major international news story. Journalists flocked to Idomeni as conditions grew worse. Medical professionals in the camp treated pneumonia, fever, septicemia, and, not surprisingly, cases of hysteria and psychosis, as well. Residents were reaching a breaking point, and media reports warned of growing tension. "The situation in Greece should very much worry us all," said Germany's Angela Merkel.

But the hand-wringing did nothing to help.

Every day, Abu Omar looked out across the fence toward the hills of Macedonia. Despite all their setbacks, he had retained hope. When he heard an unexpected noise, he thought it might be the sound of the border opening. He wanted to believe that Europe would see their suffering and let his family through.

But as time passed he began to question his faith in the West as a beacon of light. The morality here made little sense to him. Europeans will put you in jail for hitting your children, he thought, but they have no trouble seeing children dying in the dirt in these camps.

This, he told himself, is a shame on Europe.

CHAPTER 16

Banana Team NEEDS YOU!

Throughout 2015 and into 2016, I had watched events in Europe with concern. Much of my attention focused on Hungary because I'd lived in Budapest for a while a few years before. When, in early September 2015, I read that Hungarian authorities had shut down Budapest's Keleti station and prevented migrants from boarding trains, their actions felt personal to me. I knew Keleti's grand nineteenth-century facade, the hard-to-find ticket windows, the kiosk that sold the best snacks. Now I watched in horror as exhausted people, many, if not most, of them war refugees, huddled together on the sidewalks outside the terminal. Budapest, a city I loved, seemed like a friend who had revealed herself to be very cruel.

I also had professional reasons for following the situation of refugees in Europe. As a writer, I'd focused for many years on issues of war and displacement. In 2010, I published *The Life We Were Given,* a history of Operation Babylift, the U.S.-sponsored evacuation and subsequent overseas adoption of thousands of children from Vietnam at the end of the war there. In some sense, I'd spent the great part of my professional life exploring the traumas of exile, but most of my research focused on events of the past. This humanitarian crisis was unfolding on the daily news right before my eyes.

But I had no plan to volunteer. Like so many others, I assumed that European governments and the large aid organizations I'd supported in the past—groups like the International Committee of the Red Cross and the International Rescue Committee—were handling the crisis. I knew they couldn't solve the problem, but I didn't understand how badly the world's trusted aid apparatus was failing its mission.

Then, in early 2016, my friend Kathryn Winogura, who worked in refugee resettlement in California, told me that she planned to spend ten days volunteering in Greece, where the crisis was most acute.

"You can do that?" I asked. "Just go over there and help?"

"You can." Kathryn explained that thousands were stuck in make-shift camps along Greece's northern border. Small grassroots teams had mobilized to address whatever needs they could.

I decided to go with her.

NEAR THE END OF APRIL, KATHRYN AND I FLEW into Thessaloniki, drove north through sleepy villages and mist-laced farmland, then pulled into the parking lot at the Park Hotel. We had signed up to attend a volunteer orientation session that morning, but a wrong turn had set us back an hour and we'd missed the whole meeting. "No worries," said Tracey Myers, who had led the session. "We'll talk now."

We walked with Tracey into the hotel lobby. Peppy posters on the walls appealed for help: "Banana Team NEEDS YOU! *Volunteers* (+ cars ideally) *needed* every morning!" "INTERVOLVE needs you! Intervolve is doing clothing distribution in both A & B @ Idomeni. They really need extra hands to cover shifts!" In the restaurant, one could hear English mostly, a little Greek, some Spanish, and even some Arabic, too, spoken by refugees who had wandered in for appointments or to look around. At that time of day, a lot of volunteers were holding meetings, their conversations so engrossing that each table looked like its own private planet. Elsewhere, people ate in amiable little groups or sat alone, staring at their laptops, their faces solemn and scrunched. For the most part, it was an antiestablishment crowd heavy on piercings, dreadlocks, and tattoos. Kathryn, Tracey, and I grabbed coffee and headed to the patio.

Tracey's studded leather boots and clunky jewelry made her look like an apricot-haired Joan Jett. "And what made you decide to come to Greece?" she asked, warm as a hostess welcoming guests.

We explained that we'd been watching the situation from afar and wanted to join the grassroots effort because it seemed to make a difference.

Tracey nodded. She pulled a bag of tobacco from her pocket, rolled and lit a cigarette, then proceeded to give a detailed introduction to the workings of the entire volunteer system in Northern Greece. As she spoke, the vague notion of "helping refugees" coalesced into a practical plan of action. Every day, grassroots teams needed volunteers to fill dozens of shifts doing things like handing out food and clothing, sorting donations, and leading art activities for kids.

From where we sat, this region seemed entirely quiet and peaceful. It was hard to fathom that thousands of displaced people were sleeping in squalid camps nearby. When Tracey finished explaining the mechanics of volunteering, Kathryn and I bombarded her with questions: "What, exactly, will we do?" "How can we be most efficient?" "Are we in danger?"

I now know that Tracey had covered these topics countless times—a thousand volunteers completed this orientation over a three-month period—but Tracey responded to every question, even the unanswerable ones, with patience. Turkey and the EU had signed their deal. Greece would shut down makeshift camps, including Idomeni, and move these camps' former residents to official facilities. Rumors flew about when Greece would make that move. Kathryn asked, "Could it happen while we're here?"

Tracey gazed down the rural highway toward the distant hills. "That's the question, isn't it? The official camps aren't ready, but the government is pressuring people to move to them. Meanwhile, they still need clothes. They still need food." For the first time, I saw some strain in her smile. "So here we are!"

We'd completed our orientation, but Kathryn and I hesitated to leave. It was one thing to follow a humanitarian crisis on the internet and quite another to drive into a refugee camp and start to volunteer. And we had another issue that concerned us, too. Each of us had set up crowdfunding pages and we'd amassed thirteen thousand dollars already. "We've got donations from friends," Kathryn told Tracey. "We want to support aid teams financially."

Tracey glanced up from rolling another cigarette. "Oh, super!"

"Do you have any suggestions about who could best use these funds?"

Tracey slid her tongue across the cigarette paper, then nudged her chin toward the hotel's upper floor. "You might want to talk to Ibrahim. He's our finance guy. He works on distribution for the whole region."

The name meant nothing to us. "Should we go see him now?"

Tracey had become Ibrahim's gatekeeper, and she quickly shook her head. "He's quite busy. He likes for us to make appointments for him in advance. Could we set something up for another day?"

JENNI JAMES ALSO BEGAN WORKING AT THE BORDER that spring, although I didn't meet her then. She had completed her teaching assignment in New Zealand, and when she started planning her return to Greece, she faced the same dilemma as other prospective volunteers: Where could she be most useful?

Jenni, however, had a friend with an answer. Tracey, reestablished in the north already, said, "We need you here."

So Jenni headed to the Park Hotel and joined the meal-distribution team Hot Food Idomeni, which operated out of what it called a "camp kitchen," set up in the hotel's backyard. Using rented trailers for refrigeration and storage, professional prep tables shaded by tarps, and a line of gas burners set on the ground, the team cooked enough vegan stews and curries to feed an average of five thousand people a day, all at a cost of thirty-four cents a meal. Every morning, Jenni joined fifteen or twenty others on the kitchen crew to prep. Some stood at the steel tables, chopping enough cucumbers, peppers, and onions to fill large bins. Others sat out in the yard on upturned vegetable crates, rubbing dirt off mountains of potatoes. Once the cooking began, the more experienced chefs positioned themselves at the gas burners, watching over pots nearly half as tall as they were, tossing in a bin of chopped onions here, a cup of cumin there. The concoctions, nutritionally substantial, if not exactly refined, sent clouds of savory fragrance wafting across the backyard. By afternoon, the team loaded the pots into a truck and drove to Idomeni, then reassembled for meal delivery from the back of it.

By three o'clock, lines of refugees had already formed to receive what, for many, constituted the most substantial meal of the day. They waited as this odd food-distribution operation clicked into gear. Inside the truck, a serving area took shape. Plastic spoons and bowls emerged from bags and boxes. Workers pulled the lids off steaming vats of soup. Fifty cardboard boxes of Syrian flatbread were slit open to prepare for distribution. Volunteers moved into position. Someone switched on dance music.

By now, hundreds of people—groups of jumpy, silly boys, men smoking cigarettes, fathers pushing strollers, women wearing head scarves and carrying infants, little girls with ponytails and runny noses—stood in two lines that stretched down the dirt road. Men were in one line, women in another, and children stood in both. When everything was set, a volunteer leader would say, "Okay? Ready? Go."

For three hours, Jenni and the rest of the team distributed food in a systematic whir. They'd dish up the day's meal—sometimes lentils, sometimes curry or stew—then hand out the food with a disk of bread and, if supplies lasted, a pickled pepper. Anyone who wanted another serving could stand in line again. The process didn't go smoothly. Some people cut the line; others begged for extra servings; a few belligerent teen boys shoved their way through the crowds. But people got fed.

THE AFTERNOON OF OUR FIRST DAY IN GREECE, Kathryn and I walked through Idomeni Camp for the first time. The place reminded me of dystopian novels, like Cormac McCarthy's *The Road,* in which a catastrophic event wipes out all modern comforts and survivors make do with almost nothing. Here, tents dotted ground that, in previous seasons, farmers would have tilled. Beside one tent, a displaced family had rigged a baby swing from the branch of a tree. A small child dozed while a woman moved around nearby, sweeping at the earth with a broom. At another tent, the occupants had provided shade for themselves by stretching a blanket between poles. Elderly men sat beneath it, playing cards. We passed a small hexagonal tent stamped with the logo of UNHCR and spray-painted with graffiti that said IF YOU DON'T LIKE

REFUGEES COMING INTO YOUR COUNTRY, THEN STOP VOTING FOR POLI-
TICIANS WHO LOVE TO BOMB THE SHIT OUT OF OTHER COUNTRIES.

Over the next few days, Kathryn and I slipped into the odd routine
of short-term volunteers. We had no responsibilities other than providing extra hands. Some days, we spent mornings peeling potatoes at the
Hot Food Idomeni kitchen and afternoons distributing meals inside the
camp. Other times, we joined the roster at the nearby EKO Gas Station
Camp, filling in at a tent that provided space for moms to wash their
babies. At the cavernous supply warehouse in Polykastro, we sorted boxes
of donated clothes, getting them ready for distribution.

Day by day, we observed the Greek government stepping up its
efforts to persuade camp residents to leave. Driving into Idomeni, we'd
see two or three large tour buses parked by the side of the road. The
buses stayed all day, offering transportation from the makeshift camp
to the new government-run facilities. In the morning, the buses sat
empty. By afternoon, we'd sometimes see small groups of people slid-
ing bags and parcels into the luggage compartments beneath the buses.
They'd chosen to leave, but they moved in such a doleful way that it
looked like surrender.

At the InterVolve clothing distribution center, where we spent some
afternoons, the situation had begun to deteriorate. InterVolve worked
out of a cramped storage container called an IsoBox. Not much bigger
than a typical American walk-in closet, the IsoBox held bins of clothing
organized by size, gender, and garment type—"Boys' Trousers 7–10," for
example, or "Large Women's T-Shirts." For hours every afternoon, six or
seven volunteers moved in and out of the container, searching for a large
sweater for this person, newborn onesies for that one, then delivered the
items to the camp residents waiting in line outside. Generally, the system worked pretty well, though you couldn't ignore the discouragement
on people's faces. They expressed gratitude, but it seemed to crush their
dignity to accept other people's discarded clothes.

InterVolve's most serious problems happened at night. As tension rose
in the camp, vandals regularly attacked the IsoBox. "Container broke
open by refugees," read the WhatsApp message delivered to volunteers
one morning. The text included a photo of empty shelves and a shattered
window. And then, a few minutes later, this addendum: "I spoke [to] a

refugee who told me that a few big guys broke in, stole clothes and [sold] them to refugees. Sad story. I try to seal the isobox."

At such moments, WhatsApp became less of a messaging platform and more of a communal support network for dispirited volunteers. "Yes honey we know how it goes, usually is the same group. Sadly this is routine for the last month and half," wrote one sympathetic veteran. Emoticons zipped back and forth—tearful, angry, and strangely consoling. And then, just like that, the volunteers got back to work. "Hello guys," wrote the team leader, an impish, unflagging young Scandinavian. "As the isobox in A has been raided, we need to spend a day tidying up and resystemizing before we can start distributing again."

It was within this environment of sadness, resilience, and rage that Kathryn stopped me at the threshold of the container one afternoon, my arms full of trousers. "Guess what?" she said, the look of joy on her face not exactly fitting our circumstances. "I made friends with a mom and her kids in the line. They've invited us to their tent for coffee."

ABU OMAR INSISTED ON GIVING US A TOUR of his home. "Here, kitchen," he said, pointing left. "Here daughter Layla room," he said, pointing right. "Here daughter Nura room. Here Baby Omar room. Here I room. Here wife room. Here salon." With each statement, he moved his hand just a little.

Thirty seconds later, he had completed the tour without moving from his seat on the floor. He spread his arms wide as he grinned slyly. "Welcome we home."

Next to him, his wife, Salma, laughed. The look in her eyes asked, What can you do with this joker?

We were sitting inside the large communal UNHCR tent that sheltered about a hundred people. All of us—mom and dad, three children, guests—took up what he called the "salon," really just floor space covered by a gray blanket and roughly as big as a queen-size bed. The "kitchen" was a conglomeration of stuff: a camping stove the size of a coffee mug, a few eggs in a carton, empty baby food jars now serving as glassware, an orange juice box, some cookies. As for the "bedrooms," those were three wire-frame, canvas-slung bunk beds arranged in a U shape. The beds defined three sides of the family's living space, the fourth being the side of the tent. The family's drying laundry hung on rope strung along the canvas. Their cell phone, battered from wear, sat on Abu Omar's knee.

The Khalils told us that they'd come from Damascus. Seventy days ago—and, yes, they were counting—they'd arrived at Idomeni, only to discover that the border to Macedonia had closed, trapping them in Greece. Their English was rudimentary and our Arabic nonexistent, but their goal was clear: They wanted to go to Germany and start a new life. And their hope was fading.

We drank coffee. Kathryn pulled a deck of UNO cards from her bag, and, despite the language difficulties, the Khalils absorbed the rules almost immediately. Rather than take cards of his own, Abu Omar advised the female members of his family, checking out the hand of one and then another, diagnosing problems and offering solutions. As the play reached its climax, he crouched behind his wife, his chin near her shoulder, his hand on her knee. Gazing at her cards, he murmured in her ear. The girls chattered in Arabic. The baby woke and rubbed his eyes. The discard pile grew taller.

"UNO!" Salma slapped her final card onto the pile on the floor. She was a delicate young woman, shy and demure, her tiny face in a plaid hijab, but capable of thundering triumph. Everyone else moaned in disappointment. Layla rolled onto her back in defeat, then immediately popped back up. "Again! Again!"

Later, Salma pulled the bag of cookies from under the bed and slid them onto a plate. "Hangry?" In English, she was game, although uncertain.

"Hungry," Kathryn said gently.

"Hungry."

"Thank you." I picked up a cookie. Nura sat beside me on the blanket. I was wearing a bracelet of gray, white, and blue yarn that the child had braided, then tied around my wrist as a memento. We were scrutinizing the pictures on a package of face paint I had brought from home. What should she be? A zebra? A fairy? A silly clown?

Nura wanted to be a silly clown. I pulled out the crayons, held her chin in my palm, and drew a line of purple polka dots across her brow.

A few feet away, Baby Omar crawled into his mother's lap and started nursing. Layla leaned into my shoulder and watched me draw on her sister's face.

Despite the language challenges, Abu Omar could make his opinions very clear. "Bashar al-Assad," he said, practically spitting the Syrian president's name. "No good."

"And Daesh?" Kathryn asked. Instead of "ISIS," the Syrians we'd met preferred Daesh, a derogatory acronym that drove the radical group bananas.

I edged green crayon down Nura's nose. The girl closed her eyes, apparently unfazed by discussion of the forces that had helped drive her family from their home.

"Daesh," Abu Omar said. "No good, too." He lifted a finger and slit his throat.

AT THE PARK HOTEL, IBRAHIM KHOURY HAD FINALLY FACED the inevitable and moved to a private room upstairs. He had *too much* money—not more than he could spend, but more than he could manage easily. He used the accounts of friends and acquaintances who offered to help. Sometimes, however, Greek authorities, suspicious of the large number of deposits flowing into those accounts, blocked them. Ibrahim ended up taking a lot of money in cash, which was a risky option for someone sleeping on a sofa in the lobby. Once he moved upstairs, his bedroom also served as an office and an important spot for grassroots meetings.

One day, Jenni James came to the room and made a proposal.

Ever since arriving at Idomeni, Jenni had kept a low profile, focusing her energy on helping out with food distribution, but she wasn't using her skills to their full potential. Greece was charging forward with the plan to empty the makeshift camps and transfer residents to official facilities. Those facilities were not ready. Jenni could improve them, but she needed financing. For a time, she had hesitated to speak with Ibrahim about it. He had a reputation for being gruff, which made Jenni nervous. Though she was fearless in volunteering, she lacked confidence in approaching strangers. And Ibrahim, as Jenni once described him to me, was "a very extremely busy man."

Finally, Jenni gathered her courage and made an appointment. She arrived at the meeting prepared. Tracey had warned her that Ibrahim had no patience for small talk, so she didn't waste his time. "I want to get a van," she told him calmly. "I want to put tools in it." She proposed driving the van to various official camps and making infrastructure improvements wherever she could.

Jenni had prepared a budget, accounting for every expense, from purchasing tools to renting the van to paying for gasoline. "This is what it's going to cost," she said.

Ibrahim listened. He didn't ask many questions. The situation along the border was changing quickly. Lots of people had ideas for helping, but he didn't want to spend precious funds on unrealistic projects. How could he know that Jenni would succeed?

Tracey Myers trusted Jenni, and Ibrahim trusted Tracey Myers. He gave Jenni the money.

When Kathryn and I returned to our guesthouse every night, we posted on Facebook about the situation at the border. Every morning, we found new contributions had been added to our online funds. We were now withdrawing a thousand euros or more from the ATM near our guesthouse before we headed out to volunteer each day, stuffing cash into our money belts to distribute to aid teams later. We felt the weight of people's trust and didn't want to make mistakes. "Thank you!" our friends would write. "You rock!" And "You're awesome!" The comments embarrassed us. We wanted to rock, obviously, but ten days spent handing out soup and money in Greece did not make us heroes. The misplaced praise made us laugh. When I took Kathryn a cup of coffee one morning, she gushed and said, "You're *awesome!*"

Volunteering dragged us through a whole universe of emotions: compassion, indignation, optimism, despair, and, strangely, elation. Once, Barry Fallon, a founder of Hot Food Idomeni, told me that he had worked for years in restaurants in the UK, often complaining about low wages. "If I was getting eight pounds an hour, I'd want to be making twelve," he said; then he started to laugh. "Now I'm making zero pounds an hour, and I'm much happier."

We still had a lot of donation money left and almost anyone we asked for advice offered the same suggestion: Talk to Ibrahim. They usually added a compelling biographical detail: Ibrahim was a Syrian refugee himself.

I'd spent days on the border without ever seeing this famous volunteer, however. Like Tracey and Jenni before me, I hesitated to seek him out, but not for the same reason. He sounded to me like some dodgy guru, the volunteer community's spiritual adviser, seeing acolytes in a private room.

Finally, a few days before Kathryn and I were scheduled to fly home, Tracey led us up to the second floor of the Park Hotel to meet him. The guy who opened the door had the thin face, haggard expression, and slightly disheveled look of a grad student working on his dissertation. We quickly came to understand that, holed up in that room, Ibrahim was managing the allocation and distribution of tens of thousands of euros in aid money. A twin bed shoved against the wall indicated that he in fact lived there, but the space felt more like the cramped headquarters of some start-up firm specializing in shipping and logistics. On the walls hung butcher-paper signs covered with flowcharts, lists, and a message to visitors to PLEASE RESPECT ITS WORKING OFFICE—DO NOT HANG OUT HERE—PLEASE LEAVE IMMEDITLY AFTER THE MEETING/COURSE. THANK YOU! (IBRAHIM).

The guy really was all business. Sitting down with Kathryn, Tracey, and me at a small round table, he opened his computer. "I'll show you what we do," he said, then pulled up a spreadsheet to give us a closer look. The chart demonstrated how, from all over Northern Greece, independent aid teams had sent their funding requests in his direction, and how he, in turn, allocated money out of a pot of donations pouring in from around the world: €11,061 to pay for five hundred "field beds," €10,835 for ten multifamily tents, €1,705 for fire extinguishers. The list went on and on.

Fire extinguishers? The European Union had promised millions of euros in humanitarian aid to Greece, but something was going horribly wrong if the provision of emergency equipment fell to a displaced Syrian living in a hotel room. By now, Kathryn and I had raised nearly twenty thousand dollars in donations. We hoped to make life more pleasant by contributing extras like fresh fruit and coloring books. Instead, our money would go toward basic survival.

"Shouldn't the government or some big international organization be paying for these things?" I asked Ibrahim and Tracey.

It was a question that I would discuss with both of them quite often over the next few years, but that afternoon, neither had the energy to engage. By now, the setting sun was pouring golden light across Ibrahim's butcher-paper admonitions. "This is, of course, a longer discussion," he said, his tone clipped and laced with resignation. "Right now, we try to fill the need."

Kathryn and I unzipped our money belts, pulled out cash.

CHAPTER 17

Rats and Snakes

EVERY DAY, THE LITTLE COORDINATION TEAM at the Park Hotel tried to bring order to a chaotic situation. In a sign of how quickly the border crisis had developed, Idomeni wasn't even listed on UNHCR's "Who's Doing What Where Map" from the summer of 2015. A year later, the map listed fifteen different actors providing aid there. The list included everyone from the Greek police and evangelical church to well-established alphabet NGOs, like UNHCR, MSF, and IOM. The map also listed, as if it were one unit, "Volunteers," but that was an umbrella term for many different grassroots teams providing a wide variety of services, from the meals distributed by Hot Food Idomeni to small, highly targeted operations like Tent Team, whose entire mission was described in its name.

Grassroots workers had a huge amount of energy, but they needed guidance to direct them in a strategic way. Week by week, dozens of new volunteers passed through the hotel lobby, just as Kathryn and I had done. Individuals and small teams communicated through WhatsApp and Messenger, while dedicated Facebook pages served as bulletin boards for the entire movement. The coordinators—Tracey, Ibrahim, Phoebe, and Cyril—couldn't control the entire relief system, but they provided a clearinghouse for information on how volunteers could operate most effectively within it, and they came to play an outsize role in the entire operation. Once, many months after Idomeni Camp closed, I asked Tracey about shouldering so much responsibility for the international aid effort. "Did you ever stop and think to yourself, Wow, I can't believe I'm in the middle of this?"

"Every day, a thousand times," she told me, going on to mention some of the many questions the little team would ask themselves: "What are we doing? Why are we the people making a decision on this? What qualifies us?" Once, after what Tracey called a "shit day" and a bottle of wine in response to it, she received a request at 4:00 A.M. from a UNHCR staffer: "Can you house this Afghan family?" Apparently, that particular emergency went beyond UNHCR's mandate, resulting in Tracey's having the phone to her ear in the middle of the night, wondering why one of the biggest humanitarian agencies on the planet was calling her for help.

Every day, Tracey told me, presented another "serious 'What the fuck?' moment."

And, still, the coordination team remained helpless when it came to solving many very serious problems, such as sexual violence and domestic abuse in the camps. They weren't law enforcement. They could do nothing when they heard that men with access to showers—at one of the gas station camps, for example—demanded sexual favors from refugee women asking to bathe inside. And every day Tracey witnessed unexceptional miseries, like seeing eight people huddled inside a two-person tent. "And people begging you for things for their babies and there being no sense of any fairness or any way to distribute equally."

Tracey also fretted over weaknesses within the grassroots effort. From a security standpoint, the situation had inherent risks. How could you protect people from sexual predators, for instance, when the camps were open to everyone who announced that they wanted to help? "People were doing things that I found scary, dangerous, problematic, and painful," Tracey later told me, adding that volunteers suffered in this environment, as well. Once, for example, at a meeting of grassroots workers, a female volunteer disclosed that she'd been sexually assaulted. One of the leaders responded that she should just accept what had taken place. These kinds of situations led Tracey to consider leaving the movement altogether, but she also knew that the grassroots effort played a vital role in helping needy people. Was it better to quit when things went wrong, or stay and help in whatever way she could?

For now, Tracey stayed because the work felt worthwhile. And she saw improvements, too, including increased coordination between professional aid groups and volunteer teams. The professionals had experience and institutional support. The volunteers had flexibility and energy. When a winter storm made driving conditions hazardous, for example, well-established agencies curtailed operations, even as refugees needed increased help. Volunteers filled the gaps.

But grassroots teams often ended up with responsibilities that were too huge for nonprofessionals to manage. At the Czech Team warehouse in Polykastro, boxes of donated supplies piled up because there weren't enough people to unload and organize so much inventory. As one professional aid worker told me, "How do you run a warehouse? It's not a simple thing." At the same time, however, she pointed out that volunteers "had an amazing way to keep things calm, while most of the big NGOs were just irritating people."

Ibrahim Khoury still wanted to improve conditions in makeshift camps, but he also knew that they would close soon. The new official camps had to become more habitable. His distribution spreadsheets during those last months of spring reflected both efforts. To combat lingering cold, €240 went to firewood for people sleeping in woods and parking lots near a disreputable roadside establishment called Hara Hotel. Other amounts included €1,100 to purchase mosquito repellant and €5,500 paid for rounds of Syrian flatbread handed out in camps. Some of Ibrahim's notes about expenditures—like the €70 listed as "give money to minor" or the €2,600 for "vans/repairs after riots"—read like clues to profoundly complicated human stories. Others—"saop €300"— spoke to the fact that displaced people also need to wash their hands, and that Ibrahim, in his haste, occasionally failed to nail the spelling.

That spring, the grassroots effort received something to smile about. An eighteen-wheeler arrived from Germany with a load of supplies. Ibrahim posted a "thank you" on Facebook for its haul of "beds, sun cream, cooking pots, and many other things we really want!" Amid the other boxes was an item meant to inspire enthusiasm in children. This special package bore a label that said "*Hüpfburg*" and included an English translation: "bouncy castle."

At Cherso Camp, Rima Halabi's five children would have loved to jump in a bouncy castle. They would have loved to have had a solid roof over their heads, a hot meal, and clean toilets. Each day, Rima fought to keep her kids safe and healthy without nutritious food, adequate medical care, electricity, or running water. Her little boys roamed among the tents, using sticks and rocks as toys. Shakira played on Rima's phone or minded the younger ones while Rima washed the family's clothes. All along the perimeter of the camp, people hung their laundry to dry by shoving it through holes in the chain-link fence. Shakira tried to help her mother, but the child was worn down by the dirt, the heat, the boredom. Rima was, too. She cried most nights after she had zipped her family inside two tents, one stuffed inside the other, which was Rima's meager strategy for protecting them from rats and snakes and rapists.

At Cherso, society broke down by nationality and faction. Rima watched as Kurds fought Palestinians and Palestinians fought Syrians. Men attacked one another with metal rods, sometimes going after women, as well. In the line for food, people pushed back at Rima, saying, "It's not your turn!" It seemed impossible to avoid trouble. If one Palestinian got into a fight, someone might retaliate by burning down the tent of another Palestinian with no connection to the original conflict. Camp authorities seemed to do nothing to stop the violence. They'd let a person die, Rima thought.

That spring, Jenni James began driving around Northern Greece in a tricked-out tool van. She wanted to help the thousands of people like Rima Halabi, now stuck in official camps. Jenni had resources to fix toilets, install floors to mitigate flooding, provide lighting so that people could move around more safely at night. Officially, independent volunteers were not allowed inside government-run facilities, but Jenni managed. Arriving at a new camp, she presented her ID and introduced herself. When the gatekeepers saw her nationality, they warmed immediately. "Ah, New Zealand!" they would exclaim, touched that she had come from far away to help. "I want to go to New Zealand."

Jenni always demurred. "Greece is lovely," she'd reply. "I'm lucky to be here."

Before long, Jenni had charmed her way into camps across Northern Greece. It helped, too, that she had a memorable look. On her recent return to New Zealand, she had died her hair electric blue. As she was the only blue-haired Kiwi to show up at the gates, soldiers came to know her, and they began to wave her right through. Occasionally, officials did ask to inspect her vehicle, but they were more curious than suspicious. They liked to see how she'd organized all the chain saws, hammers, and drills inside her van.

Jenni James, independent volunteer, had become Jenni James, founder of an aid team. But how could you run a "team" alone? Eventually, camp residents would also join the effort, but in the early days she had to appeal to Greeks and international volunteers.

Things didn't go smoothly in the beginning. To attract people, Jenni felt she needed a great name. Some of the most successful aid groups—Hot Food Idomeni, Banana Team—had memorable names that made their missions obvious. Jenni wanted a brand that was clear, unforgettable, and maybe even a little cheeky. She chose Pimp That Camp. Then she posted a volunteer sign-up sheet on the wall of the Park Hotel and waited.

Two days passed. Not a single person signed up for Pimp That Camp.

Jenni reconsidered. What was her goal, exactly? What did she really want to accomplish in Greece?

She wanted to get shit done.

Pimp That Camp became Get Shit Done.

The sign-up sheet filled with names.

Into the middle of May, thousands remained at Idomeni. Cool, breezy days had turned hotter. Tempers flared. Residents continued to hope that the border would open, while authorities insisted it would not. At the center of camp, where the north-south rail line crossed the rural dirt road, camp occupants stared down Greek police. Most days, the two sides limited their interaction to glaring at one another, but sometimes the situation devolved into yelling, rock throwing, riots, and tear gas.

The Khalil family's tent lay five minutes' walk from the tense center of the camp. Every day, they passed by to reach the clothing-distribution containers, or the site where the Greek charity Praksis handed out diapers, or the cleanest toilets, which lay on the far side of the camp. Mostly, though, they stuck close to their tent. From here, the girls could make the short walk to the volunteer-run Idomeni Cultural Center for children's activities. Abu Omar could easily reach the MSF clinic for his heart medication, or, on afternoons when they didn't have the money or fortitude to squat over the camp stove and cook, they could stand in line for one of Hot Food Idomeni's bowls of vegan stew. Other than a few brief trips to the hospital—on top of Abu Omar's heart problems, Salma had gone for treatment for a breast infection—the family had spent three months in that field. Over those months, the camp had evolved into a bare-bones but functioning city. Some guys had opened a falafel stand in one part of the camp. A few entre-preneurs sold cigarettes or produce. Mostly, though, it was a City of Waiting. Every resident wanted to go somewhere else.

Though the camp lacked most basic comforts, it did provide one very precious thing—eleven hundred electrical outlets for charging mobile phones, which were residents' sole connection to the outside world. Many large tents had whole panels of plugs, which became gathering spots for anyone waiting for a battery to tick back toward 100 percent. Here, people attempted to register for asylum, even though the system, which operated over Skype, barely functioned at all. On their phones, they passed time playing games, updating their Facebook pages, scroll-ing through the news, and, most important, using free messaging ser-vices to communicate with loved ones far away. Most of Abu Omar's family now lived in Germany, Sweden, or peaceful parts of the Middle East. Almost all of Salma's relatives, however, remained in Syria. Every day, she called from the camp to make sure they were still alive.

The Khalils weren't willing to give up their dream of getting to Ger-many, but the EU-Turkey Deal was now providing money for Greece to set up its own official camps. At the end of May, the Greek gov-ernment brought in bulldozers and began knocking down abandoned tents in an effort to shut down Idomeni. The show of force convinced many makeshift camp occupants to haul their belongings to the buses and move to the official camps. Others refused to move, fearing getting stuck in such places. The Khalils hunkered down, telling themselves that if they left the border, they would lose all chance of getting across. They would not surrender.

Then another riot broke out and authorities used tear gas to break it up. Soon, the foul chemical spread through the camp. Adults pulled scarves around their noses and mouths and covered the faces of their children. Volunteers hurried up and down the paths with bottles of saline solution to soothe burning eyes.

The Khalils ran from their tent and hid in the woods. Abu Omar built a fire. They stayed there all night.

In the morning, they walked back to the camp, gathered their belongings, and boarded a bus.

In the midst of all this turmoil at the border, Ibrahim Khoury had a personal problem to address. As he explained to me in an email once, "im good at planning for my work but for personal life i just don't care." By late May, however, he could no longer ignore it.

The problem was his refugee status. When Ibrahim first arrived in Lesvos the previous autumn, he had been issued documents allowing him to stay in the country for a short time. By the end of that time, he had to have either applied for asylum or left Greece. Ibrahim had done neither. Many months had passed. He was now living in Greece illegally.

Ibrahim had decided to settle in this country. He liked Greece. But he would lose an entire day of work if he were to travel down to Thessaloniki and go through the interview process. He didn't have time for that. Too many people needed food, medicine, rescue from snakes.

He knew the risk. If he went out, immigration authorities could pick him up, throw him into detention, or deport him. Mostly, he tried to keep a low profile, rarely leaving his room at the Park Hotel. He accomplished a lot just sitting in front of his laptop.

Despite all his stress, Ibrahim experienced moments of great satisfaction. Late at night, before he fell asleep, his thoughts ranged over the events of the day and he considered, with some surprise, how he'd become part of a community. Earlier in his life, Ibrahim had thought of the world as divided into two groups—the people you trusted and the people you didn't. Friends and family fell into the first category. Strangers fell into the second. Ibrahim would never have attacked a stranger, but he didn't trust them.

Now, in Greece, he spent all his time with strangers who trusted one another. There were days when people he'd never even met handed him thousands of euros, with full faith in his honesty. He began to trust others, as well. It was easy to see, in a hundred different ways, how he was maturing professionally, but, privately, he considered his growing sense of trust as equally significant. His understanding of human nature had begun to change.

In the end, it was strangers who solved his asylum problem.

Fellow aid workers worried about Ibrahim's immigration status. Again and again, they nudged him about it. One UNHCR staffer became adamant. "You have to apply. Just go apply, for your own sake."

Her compassion touched him, but Ibrahim couldn't see how to focus on his own predicament without ignoring the needs of others. "I'm just busy," he said. "I can't. I don't want to. Just leave me alone."

She persisted. Others did, too. Eventually, the UNHCR staffer presented Ibrahim with a plan. She had contacted colleagues in the Greek asylum service and arranged a meeting. "We understand that you are busy," she said. "You won't have to wait. Just go there. You'll have an interview for one hour and then you'll be finished."

Ibrahim balked. He hated the idea of receiving special treatment when so many others were suffering. But she held firm. "I arranged for everything," she said. "There's no you like or you don't like. You will go over there."

So Ibrahim went down to Thessaloniki for his interview. It took about an hour. The interviewer asked him a set of questions about his past: "Were you in the army? Were you in jail? Do you want to go back?" To his thinking, none of these questions seemed important. At the end of the meeting, he heard the decision: He would receive asylum in Greece.

The issue had weighed on Ibrahim, so he felt pleased to be done with it. For months, he had been unable even to take taxis because drivers refused to pick up someone without proper documentation. One of his first thoughts after he heard the decision was, I can move again. I can take taxis.

BACK HOME IN NORTH CAROLINA, I KEPT IN TOUCH with the Khalil family over WhatsApp. When riots had broken out at Idomeni in late May, Kathryn and I had managed to wire them a few hundred dollars through Western Union, which helped momentarily but didn't change the trajectory of their journey. They still had to leave the border and board a bus for a government-run camp.

On the day of their move in late May, I happened to message Abu Omar just as their bus arrived at the new facility. We had learned to communicate through Google Translate. I'd write in English, then translate it into Arabic before sending it to him. He'd write something in Arabic, translate that into English, then send it to me. Sometimes, Salma wrote to me as well, and I only knew it was her and not him when the tone turned soft and gushy. "I love you and Kathryn" was a typical message from Salma.

"We are in a military camp named Nea Kavala," said Abu Omar.

"I know this camp," I replied. Like so many former volunteers, I now obsessed over events in Greece. In recent days, as the Greek government moved to shut down Idomeni and complete the transfer of its population to official camps, I'd read everything I could about these new facilities scattered around the region. Nea Kavala was a name I'd heard. "It is located close to Polykastro. Is it okay for you?"

"I don't know anything about it because it is middle of the night."

The next day, he had more news, all bad. "It's not suitable for my family to live here," he wrote. "A snake was inside our tent."

He had hacked at the reptile until it lay dead at his feet. He sent pictures of the carcass on the grass.

"The situation is scary for the girls," he said. "I couldn't sleep. There is nothing I can do. Now, we are like prisoners."

I didn't know how to respond to his pain, so I shifted to practical matters. "Do you have showers?" I asked. "Running water? What kind of food? Health care?"

"There are 10 showers (cold water). The food is bad; from 10 a.m. to 2 p.m., there is one doctor."

Our conversation continued for nearly two hours as the father conveyed his anguish and the two of us—one in a tent, one in a comfortable house—painstakingly sent every phrase through translation. "We are fleeing from war and terrorism in Syria!" he wrote. "We came to Europe to ask for protection! Unfortunately, we did not get that, instead we are detained in military camps, which are impossible to live in."

"This breaks my heart," I replied.

While our messages shot back and forth, I searched the internet for snake deterrents, then sent him suggestions. "The cheapest and easiest solution is to throw out some sulfur and it will draw snakes away."

"I will go get a lot of sulfur," he replied.

By the end of May 2016, Idomeni Camp had closed completely. Soon, the only remaining sign of occupation was debris scattered across empty fields. On paper, the change might have marked a positive development because it represented a shift from disorganized temporary camps toward organized humanitarian operations. But the new camps were terrible places. "The reception conditions in Greece . . . are still completely inadequate," MSF asserted in a June "Migration Crisis Update." An official from Save the Children called the situation "deplorable" and "inhumane," while UNHCR spokesperson Melissa Fleming reported that former residents of Idomeni had been moved to "derelict warehouses and factories" and that poor conditions in these facilities "are compounding the already high level of distress of refugee families."

MSF, one of the largest players in refugee response, made a dramatic decision to no longer accept money from European Union member states and institutions. The charity accused the EU of caring more about deterring refugees from traveling to Europe than it did about providing protection once they arrived. "There is nothing remotely humanitarian about these policies," said Jérôme Oberreit, the organization's international secretary-general. "It cannot become the norm and must be challenged."

Some fifty thousand people were now stuck in Greece—men, women, children, and hundreds of unaccompanied minors far from their families. No one knew what lay ahead. They were living in a country that was proving itself unable or unwilling to care for them adequately.

PART III

Volunteers

CHAPTER 18

Taking the Fall

THE CLOSING OF THE MAKESHIFT CAMPS forced the grassroots community to rethink its role in the relief effort. Greece's military ran the new, more restrictive facilities and decided exactly which aid workers would be admitted and which would not. You couldn't just drive in with a truck full of lentil soup and start serving dinner. Many volunteers didn't want to work in this environment and they went home. Others still wanted to help.

Kanwal Malik, back in England, was giving a lot of thought during that time to her role in the effort. She could think of two good reasons to withdraw from volunteering. First, her experience at Idomeni had shaken her confidence in her skill as an aid worker. Second, she knew that she needed to work on her marriage. Practically and personally, it made sense to put Greece behind her. But she could not.

In Nottingham, she and Asad barely spoke. He seemed unable to understand her obsession with refugees, but he didn't discuss it. For six weeks, when they politely sat down for dinner together each night, they refrained from talking of Greece. Day by day, the distance between them grew wider. Sometimes Kanwal thought about the volunteers she'd met who pushed aside all emotion in order to work nonstop. Had she become a robot?

She refused to blame Asad for any of their problems, but she did not blame herself, either. Perhaps each of them had changed too much to succeed as a couple. She could not meet his expectations for what he wanted in a wife. "I was no longer the same person," she told me. During the years they'd been divorced, "I had rebuilt myself up so much that

I now refused for someone to come in and try and mold me back into someone I didn't want to be."

Soon, she came to a conclusion about her marriage: "This is not for me."

Kanwal began to give away her belongings. She told her husband that she was going to Greece for at least three months. They both knew that her choice likely signaled the end of their marriage, but she hesitated to admit it. "I'll make my decision within a month," she told him, "but don't hold out for me." On Facebook, she posted words attributed to Pablo Neruda: "You start dying slowly if you do not travel, if you do not read, if you do not listen to the sounds of life, if you do not appreciate yourself."

To the post, Kanwal appended her own sentiment: "I don't want to start dying!"

AFTER IDOMENI CLOSED, IBRAHIM KHOURY LINGERED at the Park Hotel. Most other volunteers had left the area, but he had distribution reports to complete and financial statements to pass along to donors. Plus, he was also pondering the months ahead. He did not believe the emergency had abated. People who had once slept in tents at makeshift camps now slept in tents in official ones. Meanwhile, the number of aid teams and volunteers had declined significantly—it seemed to him by as much as 80 percent. How would the relief effort adapt?

Eventually, he moved an hour south to Thessaloniki as the grassroots effort relaunched itself in that city. Tracey Myers and Jenni James had found rentals there already. Ibrahim, who liked hotel living, took a room in the center of the city. They really didn't care where they lived. As Jenni later told me, she barely noticed such things. Their accommodations were "just places to drop your head."

By this time, Jenni's Get Shit Done Team was making improvements in camps across the region. A small volunteer crew could not make these facilities pleasant, but a wooden floor inside a tent would at least make life less oppressive.

Ibrahim followed Jenni's progress closely. One day, she posted photos of one of her projects in the camps and thanked Ibrahim for helping out with funds. He responded, "Thank u sis for doing all the hard (shitty) work."

In truth, he preferred to watch Jenni from a distance. He found the blue-haired New Zealander both impressive and exasperating. "Every five minutes, she finished something and then she'd come [to ask for] more things," he told me once. Jenni needed money for projects. She had questions. She required additional volunteers. And she never rested. Some observers might wonder why Ibrahim complained about that, because he never rested, either. He felt enormous affection for Jenni, but he wanted her to take breaks, or at least limit her focus to the construction projects that were her mandate. Once, after returning from a camp, Jenni approached the Syrian and declared, "I went . . . to do construction, but people are in need of food. And you know what? I just bought the food, so give me money for the food." Ibrahim spent his days trying to balance his budgets. This behavior drove him nuts.

"Jenni! You're not doing food."

"I don't care. People needed food. People are getting food. Deal with it."

Ibrahim never once heard Jenni say "This is not my business."

Later, he would look back on those days and remember how sometimes, when he saw her approaching, he felt an urge to "close up my room and run away."

IN THESSALONIKI, TRACEY HAD JOINED two volunteer efforts, a team working on long-term housing and a Greek NGO, InterVolve, which operated at Softex Camp. For the first few weeks after Softex opened, InterVolve, with only four to six volunteers, was the sole active NGO at this facility, whose population soon approached eighteen hundred. During the early weeks, residents didn't even have access to potable water. It was InterVolve, not the government, that paid to bring in water tankers and install pipes.

Tracey had reason to feel some pride, then, when one day she attended a coordination meeting for representatives of large professional NGOs and small volunteer teams. She introduced herself and began describing the successes that InterVolve had achieved. As she continued, however, she noticed hostile silence, like "tumbleweed just rolled across the table."

Tracey hadn't known that large humanitarian actors had taken a stand against conditions in government-run camps. Declaring the facilities unfit for habitation, they had refused to provide anything but emergency aid in them. The decision hadn't reached the volunteers, however. Now Tracey felt rebuked, as if, by working in Softex, she had undermined a moral principle.

At Idomeni, the two different types of aid workers—professionals from large NGOs and grassroots volunteers—had combined their strengths to work together. But the career staffers at this coordination meeting were not the people who had called Tracey for help in the middle of the night. They were more like the aid professionals she'd met on Lesvos Island during her first horrendous months in Greece—the types who conducted studies but seldom made practical contributions. Now, sitting in that tense meeting room, Tracey felt like she was facing the "kind of disrespect that I hadn't experienced since the early days."

The discussion continued, focusing on conditions in the government-run camps. A representative of a large NGO brought up the lack of access to showers, and Tracey replied that her team had already begun working on hygiene and water issues. "We can solve this problem today," she said. "Right now."

A professional cut in. "You're volunteers. You have no resources. You can't fix this problem and it's not sustainable. So, no. Thank you."

Tracey started to laugh, but it was an awkward and irritated laugh. Could these career humanitarians imagine Ibrahim spending every waking hour finding the money to install flooring, provide drinking water, drive away rats and snakes? Ibrahim, for his part, refused to even attend meetings with the large international NGOs. "I could be doing something constructive instead," he'd tell Tracey. Meanwhile, he had directed the distribution of over €120,000 in aid just in the last *month*. That money had paid for many things, including five hundred field beds for new camps, construction supplies, toiletries, and tens of thousands of disks of Arabic bread.

Now, Tracey was surrounded by professional aid workers whose salaries would continue to arrive every month from places like Geneva or New York, while she would remain a volunteer, surviving on the occasional monthly stipend and support from family and friends. But she understood her value. Keeping her voice steady, she said, "I'd just like you to know that we've spent millions in this crisis so far. And we can do this, so please take us seriously."

They did not.

And yet, despite her irritation, Tracey also felt a surge of gratitude toward the professional aid groups for taking a stand. By refusing to work until the Greek government improved conditions, the big NGOs were pushing for necessary change. Volunteer teams didn't have the luxury to insist on anything. They operated within official camps at the pleasure of the government. At any moment, camp managers could deny them access to a site. Lack of power made them meek. Tracey knew some grassroots activists who broke into government camps, documented bleak conditions, then publicized incriminating information. But the activists had nothing to lose. Tracey's team, by contrast, had committed itself to improving conditions. A single complaint could eliminate their access. On social media, Tracey and her colleagues posted happy images—refugee children engaged in art projects, clowns providing entertainment.

This tension between volunteers and activists was actually part of a debate that has, for decades, played out across the world of humanitarian response. Again and again in situations of immense suffering, relief workers find themselves grappling with the question of whether to protest inhumane conditions or say nothing in order to continue the aid effort. In his 2003 book, *A Bed for the Night: Humanitarianism in Crisis,* David Rieff put it bluntly: "Today, for all the talk of human rights, the imperative for most NGOs that want to remain operational is to cooperate with murderers and torturers. They have to do so to help the victims, and, quite rightly, they hate it."

When members of Tracey's team saw abuse, they often kept their mouths shut. "If we [speak out]," they told one another, "[we'll] be kicked out quick." The decision put them in ethical limbo. We pay a blood price, Tracey told herself. We, as a community, [took] this fall. We take this silence.

That's how they stayed in the camps.

CHAPTER 19

The Second School

A S SPRING MOVED TOWARD SUMMER, something significant happened in the life of Rima Halabi. Her infant daughter, Oma, stopped nursing. Rima had given birth to six children and breast-fed each of her five older ones for over a year. Even on the journey from Syria, she kept nursing her baby. But she had never lived in conditions as bad as the ones at Cherso Camp. The baby screamed and screamed. Finally, Rima realized that stress had taken its toll, drying up her milk. On top of every other indignity, now she could no longer even feed her own child. And she'd have to procure infant formula, too.

When Rima described Cherso to me later, she repeatedly said, "This situation was not normal." She had no expertise in humanitarian aid, but she could recognize dysfunction. On days when Musa managed to wire her a bit of money, Rima would skip the camp's food line, walk to the village, and buy supplies in a shop. For a moment, at least, she felt like a normal person.

She also began looking for escape. Greece's official camps were considered closed facilities because outsiders could not just wander through, but residents were free to come and go, or even abandon the place altogether if they liked. In recent weeks, Rima had noticed an increase in people leaving the camp and heading to Athens. No one knew what might happen in the capital, but anything seemed preferable to Cherso. Rima considered the situation, calculating the risks. Then, one day, she made a decision: She would take control of her own life. She called Musa and said, "These are not normal conditions. I'm going to Athens and rent a place there."

Rima looked around her grubby tent. The family had accumulated some donated clothes and shoes, several items of cookware, and the sponges she'd bought at the village market. None of it was important, but it all had value to Rima. Should she haul it to Athens? She could get there and then have to turn around and come back. She hesitated to carry too much up and down the length of Greece.

Rima decided to take half her possessions. She gathered her documents, stuffing everything into a few small bags. Then the family set off for the train station. They left the sponges.

THE KHALIL FAMILY HAD ENDED UP at the government-run Nea Kavala Camp, only twenty miles from Cherso, but they had never met Rima up north. Like her, they suffered many indignities, and they were appalled to discover that Nea Kavala was even worse than Idomeni. At Idomeni, right by the border, they'd maintained hope of crossing. Now they were farther from the border, and their physical situation was worse, as well. At Idomeni, they'd slept in a multifamily shelter, on beds. Now, they slept—if they slept—on the ground in a tent pitched over dirt.

The Greek government had promised that conditions would be better and safer if they left the border. Neither assertion proved correct. At the end of May, tensions between Syrians and Iraqis at Nea Kavala had exploded into violence. Four residents ended up hospitalized with stab wounds.

The Khalils had to get out of this place.

All over Greece, WhatsApp buzzed with refugees' attempts to share information: *How bad is it where you are? Are things better over there?*

The family heard one bit of promising news. In Athens, refugees had found shelter in the classrooms of an abandoned school. Conditions were tough, but it was definitely better than snake-infested tents.

Ten days after arriving at Nea Kavala, the Khalils decided to improve their situation themselves. They collected their belongings, bought bus tickets, and headed to Athens.

GREECE'S SHATTERED ECONOMY MADE IT SEEM like the worst place in Europe to absorb so many refugees, but Greeks knew how to make do with very little. The economic crisis had galvanized the nation's system of mutual support. Citizen-run solidarity groups provided everything from free medical clinics to "without middlemen" grocery stores selling low-cost goods directly from producers. Local anarchists also had a tradition of converting abandoned buildings into squats housing homeless people. Before the border had closed that March, migrants mostly used such accommodations during brief stops on journeys north. Now, with thousands stuck in Greece, the squats began taking in people fleeing camps, and no one knew how long they'd stay.

How do you illegally transform an abandoned building into housing for homeless people? In Greece in 2016, if you knew what you were doing, it wasn't so difficult. First of all, the economic crisis had shuttered thousands of structures, many in fairly good shape and ripe for occupation. Members of the solidarity movement—a mix of people with various sociopolitical perspectives, including leftists, antiracists, and anarchists—chose properties and planned their actions through a decision-making process called "general assemblies." The meetings were often unwieldy, and notoriously long, but early in 2016 they had resulted in the opening of a squat called the Fifth School, a 1920s-era high school building that municipal authorities had closed several years before. The operation to reopen it began simply: Activists broke the locks and went inside. After that, the process resembled a standard renovation. People with knowledge of plumbing connected the pipes to the city line. Those with electrical skills rewired the place to the neighborhood grid. One group installed a kitchen, while others painted, repaired ceilings, and put a new wood floor in a room that would serve as a play area for children. Toilets took more time, so the team set up portable units on the street to use until they got the sewage system working. The Fifth School's first 160 residents had come directly from the makeshift camp at the port of Piraeus, setting up tents in former classrooms that would quicky fill with unrelated people.

Why did local authorities allow such obviously unlawful activity? The need for shelter was acute. Some 46,000 asylum seekers were now stranded in mainland Greece, but the thirty-one official accommodation sites had capacity for only 33,000. Authorities didn't support the squat movement, but they also did little to stop it.

Moving into a squat had plenty of drawbacks, however—most obviously the loss of EU-funded assistance. While occupants of camps received shelter, meal rations, and any available medical care or educational services, occupants of squats had to rely on their own resources, the support of the solidarity community, and the generosity of local people who might drop by with hand-me-down clothing or bags of rice.

When a new individual or family appealed for space in a squat, the leadership committee followed a simple registration system, posing specific questions: "What's your name?" "How's your health?" "What's your profession?"

The questions helped organizers keep track of the population, but they had a practical purpose, too. If a refugee knew how to paint walls, unclog toilets, or run electrical wiring through a building, the squat needed that person's help. Unlike in government-run camps, where residents were mostly passive recipients of aid, this community would succeed or fail based on the active engagement of those who lived inside.

The Fifth School quickly reached full occupancy. Soon the solidarity activists took over another building, the Second School, a mile away. Over the course of the next year, more squats would open, not just in Athens but also in other regions of Greece.

RIMA HALABI AND HER KIDS ARRIVED at the Second School Squat one day that June.

The building sat on a corner of Acharnon Street, a thoroughfare that ran through a lively immigrant neighborhood north of Omonia Square. The former school was actually two connected buildings, an elegant three-story classical structure facing the main road and a modern addition with an open-air breezeway that led from a side street into a large shady courtyard. When Rima arrived, she found the place bustling with activity. Everywhere she looked—in the stairwells, in the classrooms, in the hallways, in the toilet areas—people were mopping floors, scrubbing sinks, washing down walls and windows.

Rima didn't know that she had stepped into the leftist world of the solidarity movement. She only knew that she had escaped the sand, snakes, and violence of the camps. Her family needed a place to sleep, a way to feed themselves, a roof over their heads, electricity and plumbing. Someone gave her some sleeping mats. With her own cash, she bought a tent, then scouted out a space in an upper-floor classroom and moved in.

Something in Rima came alive again. For the first time since arriving in Greece, she could thoroughly wash her children. She filled a plastic tub with warm water and hauled it up the stairs to her room. One after the other, she placed the baby, the toddler, and the two little boys into the tub, scrubbing months of dirt and grime off their bodies. After she finished with the little ones, she and Shakira went downstairs to bathe privately. The school had two types of toilets, Western-style and squat. Shakira and Rima went into a Western-style stall and took turns—one sitting on the toilet seat while the other poured buckets of water over her head. Once her family was finally clean, Rima turned her attention to the next pressing matter: food.

For a time, residents of the squat had subsisted on the honey, butter, or jam sandwiches donated by solidarity activists or other locals who dropped by to help. Eventually, several young male residents proposed an alternative. "You're really paying a lot of money for sandwiches that are prepackaged and don't taste good," they said. "With the same amount of money, why don't you buy us things and we will cook?" The activists agreed, bought some cooking utensils, and began providing food staples. By the time Rima arrived, the young men had converted a courtyard shed into a makeshift kitchen. Every day, they prepared a meal. The only problem was that these guys didn't know how to cook. "It's really bad," Rima told them. Then she offered to cook herself. She would base her meals on dishes she had often served to crowds back home in al-Dana. The young men agreed enthusiastically, but before Rima committed, she made a rule: "I don't want many women with me. If women want to help, they can chop vegetables, but while cooking, I want nobody there."

The young men gave Rima control of the kitchen. Scaling up from twenty to four hundred was no simple task, but she adapted. Every afternoon, she took baby Oma downstairs with her and began to prepare dinner. The shed had a couple of portable burners set on the floor and a spigot nearby that provided water. Rima worked with several enormous pots, each as big as a bathtub for two or three of her kids. She used bushels of onions, eggplants, peppers, and tomatoes, all of which had to be cut up, piled into plastic bins and bowls, then added to the cooking pots and stirred with a ladle the size of a shovel. Some days, she made the Syrian fava bean dish called *ful*. Other days, she made falafel or vegetarian stews. Depending on funds, she served meat twice a week and she prepared a massive amount of rice for every meal. Even if she ran out of the main dish, rice would fill empty bellies.

The past few months had challenged Rima in every way. Her assessment of comfort had radically shifted. She had not forgotten the luxuries of her home in Syria, but she more often thought of her current situation in comparison to the squalor of Cherso. The Second School felt like heaven after the camp. She loved cooking for her community and worked hard to make delicious food. She didn't want anyone to merely subsist; she wanted them to actually enjoy her meals. I cook, she told herself, for the sake of God.

Rima Halabi had joined the volunteer movement.

IN EARLY JUNE, THE KHALIL FAMILY also moved into the Second School. They sent me photos just after they arrived. The tent-filled classrooms looked grim, but the family didn't have to worry about snakes there.

"We are happy now," Abu Omar wrote. "The situation is different from where I was inside the camp, especially Nea Kavala."

But Germany remained their goal. Kathryn and I had been trying to provide information about the asylum system. A few days earlier, she had sent them some links that explained the process of relocation to Germany and what people needed to do to apply. "Was that helpful?" I asked.

"No," Abu Omar replied. "I couldn't register. I try every time to register."

I didn't want them to lose hope. I promised to do more research.

"Okay." Abu Omar changed the subject. "How family members? Are all fine? Peace to all of them."

EVERY DAY, RIMA COOKED FOR FOUR HUNDRED PEOPLE, minus one. Her teenager, Shakira, remained squeamish about germs. Shakira saw the shed where Rima cooked, the gas burner set directly on the crusty floor. She saw the women squatting on the pavement outside, peeling onions and cubing eggplant with their bare hands. When Rima sent a bowl of food upstairs, Shakira carried it back down, untouched.

"I won't eat this," she declared.

Rima tried to reason with her. "I wash all the ingredients with my own hands."

"Other people do the chopping and slicing," Shakira retorted.

The mom could not convince her daughter to touch the food. Every day, grabbing a minute from taking care of her kids and cooking, Rima ran out to a shop nearby and bought Shakira a cheese sandwich.

Rima's days were packed from the moment she woke up until the moment she curled beside her children in the tent at night to sleep. In the morning, before she cooked, she often mopped the floors. Syrians mop by splashing water onto a surface, scrubbing that area with floor cleaner, and then pushing the water toward the next place they want to clean. Rima's ritual began in the room that held her family's tent. She mopped the room, then pushed the water into the hallway, mopped the hallway, then proceeded to the stairs, mopped down the stairs, then began work on the toilets. Once she'd finished the toilets, she was ready to bathe.

One morning, a man approached her while she mopped her room. She recognized him as the husband in one of the families that had recently arrived—big guy, graying crew cut, crooked nose. "I always see you mopping and cleaning," he said. "You have to let others take their turn. It's not your job."

"No, it's okay. I don't mind," she replied.

But it bothered him to see one person work so much harder than others. A lot of people had arrived in the squat in recent days. Many did nothing to help. "Tomorrow, you are forbidden from cleaning," he told her. "Everyone has their turn. They are responsible. They have to do it."

Rima slowed down, but not much.

A few days later, the man approached her again while she was cleaning. "Aren't you the cook?" he asked.

"Yes."

This time, Abu Omar was even more adamant. "You should not be mopping. You cook."

Rima, all alone with her kids, felt touched that someone was looking out for her. Soon, a friendship developed between her family and the Khalils. In the evenings, their children played together in the courtyard downstairs. Layla Khalil joined Shakira Halabi amid the chattering coveys of preteen and teenage girls. Often, the two mothers set their babies' strollers beside each other, and, as the sun swung low in the west, they found shade by the little kitchen shed and talked. Rima and Salma weren't exactly like two neighbors chatting on a stoop back in Syria, but these moments felt closer to that world than anything they'd experienced since leaving home.

CHAPTER 20

Aid Distribution

A s the hot season arrived in Northern Greece, Jenni James was hammering panels of mosquito netting across the open windows of a tent-filled warehouse. After shutting down Idomeni and moving people to official accommodation sites, the government had made promises that now sounded like jokes. "Some will have air-conditioning," a Greek migration official had told *The Guardian*. Some camps did have AC-equipped trailers, but at Softex Camp, which sat in an industrial zone of Thessaloniki, residents slept in sweltering tents. A European Parliament member who visited the site summed up conditions as "no privacy, no fire safety, no light and no ventilation."

The distinguishing feature at Softex, in fact, was the constant presence of mosquitoes—maybe millions of them. Laid out across a flat stretch of land, Softex had a shallow creek running between its two main shelter sites: a decrepit industrial building and an outdoor encampment. Now, in the dry weather, the creek stopped moving and mosquitoes bred in the standing water. Jenni saw children covered in sores. Some ended up in the hospital. Though the industrial building had a roof and walls, it also had huge glassless windows and doorways that were, literally, big enough to drive trucks through. How could you mosquito-proof the whole place? Jenni and her team decided to try.

Relying on funding from "the volunteer penny," as Tracey Myers called it, Jenni's Get Shit Done mobile workshop had already made impressive accomplishments in the region. In one camp, her workers erected a metal-frame community center, despite the fact that the kit arrived without information on how to erect it. "Used google," Jenni told friends on Facebook. "Then instructions were useless anyways. . . . But we got there." With materials cobbled from trash, the team built a private women's prayer space. "I found a tent with no poles," Jenni wrote. "That will do . . . found a pile of poles, they'll do."

Now Jenni and two fellow volunteers stood on ladders fifteen feet off the ground—"not my favorite height," she admitted—trying to attach mosquito netting to every opening in the warehouse.

Not everyone saw promise in this effort. The first day, several residents stood beneath the ladders, watching. They had survived war, made it to Europe, and now found themselves living inside a hot and dusty insect-filled warehouse. They weren't friendly. "What you doing? What you doing?" they yelled from the ground. "No good. No good."

Jenni looked down from her perch. "Good! Good!" she insisted.

"No good! No good!"

The team members hammered away, sweat rolling down their arms and into their eyes, mosquitoes feasting on their skin. They started at the back of the building, covering the openings closest to the stream. One by one, they attached the screens, moving toward the front, window after window. The project faced constant challenges. Children tried to climb the ladders or push them over, so a volunteer stood at the base to keep them away. Kids liked to grab tools and run off with them, so Jenni tied her tools to the ladders. Eventually, to distract the children from the work area, she set up a projector and screen and began showing movies.

Slowly, the atmosphere inside the building began to change. Residents noticed that fewer mosquitoes had invaded their tents. Children scratched at their skin with less savagery. Residents stopped standing below the ladders and yelling "No good!" Now they watched the team in silence. The mosquito population plummeted.

One day, Jenni discovered that an entire pile of chains had disappeared. "Stop," she told her team. "Everyone get down." The volunteers climbed off the ladders and Jenni made an announcement: "Those chains need to be back here in five minutes, or we're out of here. No more mosquito netting." Within seconds, residents took off around the building. They knew who had taken the materials, and five minutes later the chains reappeared, deposited in a pile on the floor right in front of her. The team climbed up the ladders and returned to work.

The border closing had brought migrant journeys to a standstill. Individuals who had once been productive members of society now sat trapped and idle, but that didn't mean they gave up. One day that summer, Jenni noticed that a group of residents had formed their own crew, deciding to attack the mosquito problem at its source. They climbed into the stream and began to clear out dirt and trash to get the creek moving.

In camps, skilled residents began approaching Jenni to join her team as volunteers.

THAT JUNE, KANWAL AND HER FRIEND IRAM returned to Greece. After the implementation of the EU-Turkey Deal, migrant arrivals to the country had dropped from over 26,000 in March to 3,600 in April. Now grassroots teams focused on helping the tens of thousands stranded in the country. Kanwal's and Iram's Lebanese friend Farez had shifted his efforts to Athens, so they joined him. Once again, they had donations from the Muslim community back home.

Ramadan was about to begin. Throughout the holy month, the observant fasted from dawn to dusk. Traditionally, they would consume a light meal, Iftar, at sunset, then a heartier one after evening prayers. Some adherents also liked to wake before dawn and eat something to sustain themselves through the day. To address the change in routine, many volunteer food teams shifted their schedules to offer nighttime distributions. Farez, Kanwal, and Iram began assembling "Ramadan packs," small parcels that included Arabic bread, chunks of cheese, cucumbers, and tomatoes. The Greek government had opened several camps on the outskirts of Athens, so the group planned to distribute rations between 2:00 A.M. and 4:00 A.M., giving camp occupants something to eat before the fast began at sunrise.

Scouring the city for cheap deals, the team ended up in the immigrant neighborhoods around Omonia Square, where North African, South Asian, and Middle Eastern shopkeepers sold inexpensive food. A merchant on Acharnon Street agreed to sell them falafel sandwiches for one euro each. One day, he asked, "Do you know that there's a school opposite us and it needs a lot of help?" He pointed toward a building across the road. "Three or four hundred people have just moved in." He explained that, unlike residents of official camps, these asylum seekers received nothing from the government. "They're desperate."

Kanwal pulled out her phone, conducted some quick internet research, and confirmed that the building was indeed a refugee squat. Curious, the three walked over. In the heat of the day, the courtyard was empty except for a few young men. Farez introduced himself in Arabic, explaining that they were a volunteer team wanting to help during Ramadan. One of the young men, a tall, bearded Syrian, introduced himself as Jabbar and said he was a leader of the community. He called the place "the Second School" and explained that hundreds lived in its former classrooms.

Farez asked about the food situation.

Jabbar said that the refugees were cooking for themselves. They received donations from people in the larger community but could not count on having basic supplies like rice, bread, fresh produce, and meat.

While Kanwal and Iram waited for Farez to translate, they made their own observations. Jabbar looked like a refugee. He wore a torn T-shirt and flip-flops several sizes too small. But he had the eloquence and charisma of an orator. "These are all my mothers," he told them. "These are all my sisters. This is my family."

The women were impressed. "Oh my God," they said to each other. "How *old* is he?"

When the three volunteers discussed the situation among themselves, they all agreed that the residents of the squat needed help. They decided to supply food through Ramadan.

Farez translated the news into Arabic. Jabbar seemed pleased, although not surprised. He seemed to have known that aid would arrive somehow. "God will help us during Ramadan," he responded. "I have full faith."

When the fast ended that night at dusk, residents emerged from their tents in the classrooms and filled the courtyard downstairs. The little volunteer team was ready. Lines formed. Kanwal, Iram, and Farez handed out falafel sandwiches, one after another, stopping only to snap pictures of themselves to post on Facebook for donors back home. In the cool evening, the courtyard became a cheerful place. Children played tag. Adults chatted while they ate their food.

Kanwal didn't notice when Farez stepped away for a moment. She noticed only when he suddenly reappeared with disconcerting news. "This guy just said that we've got to go," he said.

"Who?" Kanwal looked around the courtyard.

Farez motioned toward a man standing some distance away—solidly built, hair in a ponytail, face filled with rage. "That guy."

Farez walked back over and the two men talked in Arabic. The stranger was clearly angry, waving his arms like exclamation points to his fury. Eventually, Farez translated for Kanwal and Iram. "He's just saying that we have to leave."

Now it was the women's turn to get angry. "Well, does the school belong to him?"

The man ignored the question. "You can't take pictures," he told them.

Kanwal found his manner irritating. As an experienced volunteer, she knew the importance of privacy and never posted photos of refugees' faces. "We're not taking pictures of refugees," she said. "We're taking pictures of *us*—handing the food out."

"You need to leave," the man insisted.

A crowd of residents listened as Farez and the stranger talked. Kanwal watched, confused. She knew little about the anarchist movement or the solidarity movement. The squat system was entirely new to her, as well. But she was beginning to realize that this guy was accusing her team of taking money from donors without actually distributing aid.

Now Kanwal reentered the conversation. "You're saying that we're not distributing aid *while* we're distributing aid?"

A moment passed as someone translated. The man replied, "Well, you collected a lot more, so you just come in—"

Kanwal now understood the full implication. The man believed that the three of them collected donations, took pictures to show that they were providing food, then pocketed most of the money. "He accused me of *what*?"

Anyone in the courtyard could have recognized Kanwal's anger then, even if the person didn't speak English. At first glance, the

British-Pakistani social worker came across as gentle and demure. She dressed conservatively, wore flowing tunics and scarves, communicated in a genial way. But she was also Robina's daughter and she could not abide insult. If this man expected her to admit some infraction, he could wait forever. "I am not backing down," she declared.

The little relief team turned around and walked out.

KANWAL AND HER FRIENDS COULDN'T KNOW that this stranger, Souleiman "Castro" Dakdouk, was a prominent leader of the Athens squat movement. He looked like a Beat poet, but he was, in fact, a forty-seven-year-old Syrian émigré who had lived in Greece for decades and was now trying to safely, if illegally, house displaced people.

Castro had a lot going on. He spent most of his time at the Fifth School Squat, about a mile away. There, amid the noise of hammers, the slosh of soapy water, and the squeals of children, there was also, always, the ring of someone calling Castro's phone. Fluent in Greek and Arabic, he had become a link between needy refugees and locals who wanted to help. People called in the morning. They called midday. They called all night. For over a year already, Castro had been at the center of a small-scale disaster-relief network that operated from friend to friend to friend.

Brrr. Somebody had a spare room to offer: "I want a husband and wife and two children."

Brrr. "Families can come over and take a shower here."

Brrr. "I've cooked some meals I want to deliver."

Castro, dealing with constant emergency, made a lot of calls, too, appealing for help in the local community. He had an apartment of his own in Athens, but he rarely made it home. Instead, he spent most nights at the Fifth School, sleeping on a sofa in a former science lab now used as a meeting room and office.

In terms of personality, Castro was reserved, even slightly shy. What he lacked in grand speech, however, he made up for in life experience and commitment. As a teenager in Syria, he'd gotten into trouble for protesting the regime of Hafez al-Assad. By twenty, he'd fled the country and entered exile in Greece. He went to art school and became a painter but never abandoned activism. When increasing numbers of boats began arriving in Greece in 2014 and 2015, he traveled to the Aegean Islands and threw himself into the relief effort. He did what he could for the living and became proficient in arranging burials for those who had drowned.

Castro and his colleagues had opened the Fifth School Squat the previous winter. As the situation grew dire at Idomeni, they had rented buses and traveled north, where they offered displaced people rides to Athens and shelter in the squat. Many of these people already knew Castro, having met him when they'd first arrived on Greece's islands. They trusted him, but few were ready to abandon their dream of continuing north in Europe. Only sixty-four people rode back with him to Athens.

But then the borders closed. People began to see the Athens squats as preferable to camps. The classrooms inside the occupied school buildings filled with tents.

DESPITE THEIR TERRIBLE FIRST MEETING, Kanwal and Castro had a lot in common. Kanwal shared Castro's deep concerns about corruption among volunteers. On Leros Island, she'd seen much worse than financial misconduct. An older Greek volunteer had plied teenage refugee boys with gifts of food, then lured them to his house. "Watch out for him," other Greeks had warned, so Kanwal had contrived a way to expel him from the relief effort. One day, she pulled him aside and said, "We're changing our system. From now on, women will give food to men. Men will feed the women and girls." Denied access to vulnerable boys, the man retreated.

And Castro had enough experience to understand how he had offended Kanwal. He had also been on the receiving end of nasty allegations. As the most prominent figure in the Athens squat movement, he had firmly planted himself on the shady side of the law. It wasn't unusual, in fact, for people—sometimes even fellow members of the solidarity movement—to attach words like *mafia* and *gangster* to his name.

Both eventually saw the need to work together. Not long after the little team marched out of the Second School, Farez's phone rang. It was Jabbar. The community needed food, especially during this holiest month. "Please come back," the young man pleaded.

Kanwal was still fuming. "I don't know who this guy Castro is, but he needs to apologize to me."

Pretty soon, the phone rang again. It was Castro. He asked to meet with them at the Fifth School Squat.

When Kanwal arrived, she was primed for a fight. "How dare you?" she asked Castro. "You have no idea. We've been in Leros. We're completely independent fund-raisers. No one has ever accused us of putting up pictures or keeping the money. You're welcome to look at our Facebook page and see what we do."

Castro seemed contrite. "I was having a really, really bad day," he told them. When he wasn't angry, his features softened considerably. "We could really use your help."

The little group of volunteers returned to the Second School and remained through Ramadan.

CHAPTER 21

A Pampering Session

WHEN KANWAL MET RIMA HALABI, she felt instant affection for the Syrian mom who, alone in Greece with five children, had nonetheless stepped forward to cook for the entire community. Rima provided much more than nutrition at the squat. Her willingness to cook gave other mothers time to tend to their own families. The young men, released from the struggle of preparing meals themselves, felt not only gratitude but also admiration. As Jabbar put it to Kanwal, "She's like our big sister."

Rima and Kanwal were close in age. They shared a sociable nature and a femininity that masked strong wills. It seemed to Kanwal that Rima never stopped working. "She was *always* on the go," Kanwal told me later. "Oh my God. She would cook the evening meal, wash the pots. Then she would clean the kitchen. She would finish at two A.M. Then she would have a bit of a chill-out. Then she would sleep. Then she would be up at nine o'clock again. And she's got these five children, so she'd be washing their clothes. *By hand.*" In time, the Syrian mom invited Kanwal to visit the tent she'd set up for her family upstairs. Kanwal saw that Rima was managing, but her needs remained immense. How could she afford laundry detergent? Toothpaste? With both an infant and a toddler, she always needed diapers, too.

Occasionally, Kanwal's Muslim donors back home offered their *zakat* contributions with stipulations. "I want this money to go for food," someone might say. Or "My donation can be used only to pay rent for a family." One donor had given Kanwal two hundred euros earmarked specifically for a single mom. The donor said that Kanwal should not buy anything for the recipient but should instead give the woman cash to spend herself.

Without hesitation, Kanwal chose Rima to receive the *zakat*. She decided to hand it out in fifty-euro allotments over the course of a month. When she found someone to translate the news, she said, "You cook for four hundred people in a day. I can't think of anyone else I would rather give it to."

Rima nearly burst into tears.

Kanwal made another offer, too. She and Iram had rented an apartment in Athens. "We've got a washing machine," she told Rima. "Give me your clothes and I'll wash them for you."

IT IS ONE OF THE TERRIBLE IRONIES OF THIS STORY that the European Union had authorized €83 million to improve living conditions for displaced people in Greece and yet many fled official camps, taking shelter instead in illegal housing. The rejection of camps testified to their squalor and isolation and the fact that living there made people feel that they'd been warehoused and forgotten.

The camps were also dangerous. Even volunteers, who didn't have to live in them, experienced the threat. Up north, at Softex Camp, someone pulled a knife on Tracey Myers. She had gone to Softex with InterVolve, which was distributing a shipment of flip-flops that day. Tracey, standing at the front of the line, was trying to find shoes that fit each recipient.

Suddenly, her colleague Chloe said, "Come on. We're going."

But Tracey's job demanded close concentration. She didn't pay attention to Chloe. She didn't notice the guy beside her brandishing a knife.

"Come on," Chloe said.

"Two minutes," Tracey muttered.

"No," Chloe told her. "You. Come. Now."

The InterVolve team had been operating in Softex Camp long enough to know that the place had been infiltrated by organized crime, but Tracey wasn't a regular volunteer there. She was a grassroots veteran who had forgotten a basic principle she'd shared with hundreds during orientations in Lesvos and Idomeni: Be aware.

Later, looking back, Tracey saw the knife for what it was, a power play. "They didn't want a flip-flop," she told me. "They wanted me to know that if they wanted a flip-flop, they were getting a flip-flop."

The team exited so quickly that Tracey didn't have time to feel afraid. In fact, she later laughed at her own obliviousness, telling herself to pay better attention next time. But the incident also reminded her of the danger faced by residents of camps. The facilities had the official imprimatur of the Greek government and the European Union, but such labels didn't make them safe.

THE SQUATS WEREN'T IMMUNE TO VIOLENCE, EITHER. One day, passing through the Second School, Kanwal Malik saw two men yelling at each other in Arabic. One of the guys, thickset and graying, was squaring up against the other, almost nose-to-nose. Kanwal couldn't understand his words, but the man's intensity communicated aggression. She kept her distance. Whoa, she thought.

That week, Kanwal began to teach an English class. A young female resident approached her and asked timidly, "Are you the English teacher?" The woman was pushing a baby boy in a stroller and had two daughters by her side.

"Yes."

It didn't take more than a few seconds to realize that the older daughter spoke better English than her mom. Together, the two articulated their next question. "Can I come to your class?"

Within days, the young mother became a fixture in the classroom, always with the little boy in the stroller by her side. Her diligence impressed Kanwal. Despite the responsibilities of caring for her family, she always showed up, eager to absorb new lessons.

And then, on Eid-al-Fitr, the great celebration marking the end of Ramadan, Kanwal spotted her student in the building's courtyard, sitting next to that big aggressive fellow. "Oh!" she said to her student, suddenly understanding the family connection. "So this is your husband?" Kanwal didn't exactly feel pleased.

The three of them talked politely for a few minutes. Though Salma was friendly, Abu Omar seemed cautious and wary. Kanwal assumed that he was trying to figure out who she was and whether or not he could trust her.

As time passed, though, and Kanwal got to know the family better, she realized that there was another reason for Abu Omar's reticence. He felt embarrassed that Kanwal had seen him fighting in the courtyard. One day, he approached her with an apology. "I'm sorry for you seeing me angry," he said.

The courtyard of the Second School served as the social hub of the entire community, the spot where people cooked, ate, bickered, danced, talked, and celebrated. One day, when Kanwal and her friend Iram were sitting there with Rima, they noticed swelling in Rima's legs. Summer had reached its full intensity, making every step a sweaty trudge, but Rima kept preparing meals, cleaning her room, hauling her baby up and down the stairs. Her body began rebelling.

Kanwal and Iram had an idea. Getting an English-speaking resident to translate, they invited Rima to a "pampering session" at their apartment. Would she come?

The Syrian mom had nonstop responsibilities at the school, but she was still the lover of organic cosmetics who had once followed a strict beauty regimen. When the volunteers invited her for an outing, she said, "Yes!" Shakira took charge of the little ones and Rima followed Kanwal and Iram out the door of the squat. Once they reached the apartment, the two Brits gave Rima a massage. They weren't experts, but they tried to relieve the swelling in her legs and soothe her tired feet. When they finished, they handed Rima a towel and showed her to the shower.

More than half a year had passed since Rima left Syria, half a year since her last real shower. Half a year of filth or sponge baths or sitting on a toilet while her daughter dumped buckets of water over her head. Once she stepped inside Kanwal's shower, she stayed. Fifteen minutes passed. Rima scrubbed her skin. Thirty minutes passed. She cleaned her fingernails and toes. Forty-five minutes passed. She stood motionless, just letting the hot water stream over her. An entire hour passed before she emerged, a new person.

Kanwal heard grumbling from other residents when the three returned to the squat. Why was Rima invited for a shower, and not them? "Well, then," Kanwal announced, "whoever cooks for four hundred people can come to [my place] and have a hot shower."

In the Second School's open courtyard, Shakira embraced her mom. "Oh my God!" the girl exclaimed, inhaling the scent of her mother's skin. Soon, other girls approached, laughing and sniffing at Rima, too.

She was thoroughly clean. They'd forgotten the smell of that.

CHAPTER 22

A Rash in a Squat Is a Medical Crisis

A FTER RAMADAN, BOTH FAREZ AND IRAM LEFT ATHENS, Farez to do relief work in Lebanon and Iram to return to England. Kanwal, however, wasn't ready to go home. I'll stay, she told herself. The decision signaled the end of her marriage, but she wasn't really thinking about that. The Second School now absorbed her entire attention.

Over the past month, Kanwal had woven herself in tightly there. She taught English, attended general assemblies, used her donation money to buy supplies. Day by day, she also came to know her fellow volunteers, the local people and foreigners whose practical support and financial assistance helped keep the place running. A team of young Spaniards was dedicating the entire summer to the squat. Others organized activities for the children, taught language lessons, delivered supplies.

One of those visitors was Rando Wagner, a flight attendant for a British airline who regularly volunteered in Greece. Kanwal had never met him in person, but Rando's memorable look—tall, sleekly handsome, and completely bald—was familiar to her from volunteer pages on Facebook. "Hey, Rando!" she exclaimed the first time she saw him at the squat. "I'm Kanwal Malik."

But photographs of Rando were like freeze-frame images of a hummingbird. The guy never stopped moving. He recognized Kanwal, too, but rather than pausing to say hello, he started talking while also shoving the supplies he'd delivered onto shelves in the storeroom.

Among squat residents and volunteers who weren't native English speakers, Kanwal communicated in extremely simple English. When Rando spoke, she struggled to understand him. Was it English? Yes, but

German parents, a childhood in South Africa, and a professional career in Britain had given him a style of speech consisting of a torrent of words laced with adamant opinion, racy asides, and frequent bursts of laughter.

"Whoa. Whoa. Whoa!" she exclaimed. "I can't keep up."

Eventually, she understood that he was making a proposal. Rando spent about ten days a month volunteering in Greece and he raised money online as well. Now he was suggesting that he be the one to purchase and deliver supplies to the squat while he was in Athens, freeing Kanwal from spending her own donation money. "For the next couple of days," he told her, "you don't have to do this."

Kanwal felt a surge of relief. Only a month had passed since she'd first stepped inside the Second School, but she already felt the weight of four hundred lives on her shoulders.

DISPLACEMENT RESHUFFLES THE SOCIAL ORDER. The Second School inspired unlikely friendships. Young Syrian men spent afternoons hanging out with Spanish college students. Rando, who supplied food, and Rima, who cooked it, both occasionally joined the group of residents and volunteers who gathered in the squat to share a hookah.

Salma Khalil observed most of this activity from a distance. Her husband now volunteered on the squat leadership committee. Her daughters engaged in activities for kids. Except for the hours she spent in Kanwal's classroom, however, Salma remained fairly isolated. She was shy, and she also had a baby to care for. Perhaps more than anyone else in the family, Salma grieved for Syria.

One day, returning to the squat after shopping, she saw Rando standing beside his car on the street outside. The two had never spoken, but his bald head, speed, and generosity had made him a celebrity at the Second School. To Salma, he was "Rando who comes in fast and does things fast." He didn't know her, but her head scarf probably suggested that she lived inside. When he motioned to her, Salma walked over. Quickly, he leaned inside the vehicle and pulled something out of a box. Then he turned around and shoved a brand-new hijab into her hands.

A hijab was a high-value commodity. Rando wouldn't have enough for every woman in the squat, and if others noticed his gift to Salma, they'd start pleading for scarves of their own. Salma tucked the scarf into a fold of her stroller. "Thank you," she said. Her hours in Kanwal's English class had paid off.

Salma would remember Rando's kindness. A long time had passed since she'd enjoyed any luxury, and a new scarf was particularly precious. She had never, since fleeing Syria, considered giving up the hijab. She had sacrificed too much to lose her traditions and faith, too. But, practically speaking, the head scarf increased her discomfort in the summer heat. Sometimes, when her skin grew tacky and sour with sweat, she carried the baby upstairs, crawled into the tent, and pulled off the scarf for some minutes of dank relief. From inside the tent, she listened to the sounds of four hundred stranded souls: children skittering up and down the marble staircases, parents yelling for their kids, the swishing broom of whoever was taking a turn at sweeping. For Salma, the hours were like mountains to climb every day. She could steal only a few moments in the tent, sitting with her head uncovered, allowing the sweat around her neck to dry. And then, because babies need to move, she retied her scarf and carried her son back out into the light.

LATER THAT SUMMER, *The New York Times* would publish a devastating piece about the failures of the humanitarian effort in Greece. "Few of the resources pledged by the European Union to assist the asylum seekers and process their applications have actually come through," the author, Liz Alderman, wrote, "leaving the Greek authorities struggling to cope with a daunting humanitarian and logistical challenge that has fallen from view in the rest of Europe." Europe had provided only twenty-seven out of a promised four hundred asylum professionals and only twenty-four out of four hundred interpreters. Though 21,000 migrants had been able to register for asylum, 36,000 had not, and the EU, which had agreed to absorb tens of thousands of displaced people, had, in fact, taken in fewer than 2,300.

Those numbers, of course, only hinted at the particular struggles of thousands of individuals and families. In Athens, Abu Omar and Salma

Khalil put much of their effort into providing stability for their children, despite the fact that they lived in a squat. And they had some success, too. When Salma thought about her baby son, it seemed to her that he had not experienced a happy day in his life, but in truth little Omar didn't know about his own misfortune. Something miraculous had happened that demanded his full attention: He had learned to crawl. Every day, he investigated drying dishes, heaps of blankets, piles of shoes. In addition to the Khalils, their room also sheltered an Afghan family of five, a mother and son from Aleppo, and two young Syrian men. Nothing fascinated little Omar as much as the Afghans' baby. The families could not keep the two kids apart. When the Afghan baby developed a pimply rash, Omar's parents built barriers to separate the two. The Afghan baby climbed right over them.

"What are we going to do?" Abu Omar asked his wife. "You can't kick a kid out of your space."

They knew what would happen, and it did.

A rash in a squat is a medical crisis. Red sores spread over little Omar's face, running down the bridge of his nose, covering his cheeks and lips, swelling his chin with pus-filled blisters. He howled. His misery made his parents frantic. They found a doctor, who referred them to a specialist, who prescribed medicine and told them to bathe the child three times a day.

But the Second School had no bathtub, and washing the baby in a bucket never got him completely clean. All through the squat, people were developing skin conditions, not only rashes but boils and scabies, too. What could the parents do?

In squat leadership meetings, Abu Omar spoke out about the Afghan baby's rash. "This kid will make half the school sick," he declared.

Inside their tent, Omar's sores oozed. Every expression on his face communicated pain. We can't do anything, Abu Omar and Salma told themselves. Layla and Nura watched their little brother suffering. They seemed to expect that their mother and father would solve the problem, which only increased the parents' sense that they were failing.

Finally, Abu Omar came to a conclusion. "We have to leave the school," he told his wife.

"How can we leave?" Salma asked. "We don't have money."

Abu Omar set about finding money and new accommodations, even temporary. At a nearby pizza shop, someone told him about a studio apartment just down the street from the squat. The family could rent it for four hundred euros a month. That was a fortune, but they saw no other option. By borrowing money, and with gifts from a few volunteers, Abu Omar scrounged together the funds he needed.

The Khalils installed themselves in the studio just as Athens slid into summer. Layla, walking barefoot over the cool tile floors, made a video tour of her new home. The footage included the countertop hot plate, the teakettle, the sink, mops, sponges, the water heater in the bathroom, the shower, the mattresses on the floor. During the last few seconds, she lingered lovingly on the air conditioner.

Finally, the family had privacy. The baby's sores healed. Alone inside her home, Salma took off her hijab. Some days, the family invited friends from the squat for a meal. Salma indulged in a beloved Syrian tradition. She baked cakes.

CHAPTER 23

Spoiled Milk

LIKE SO MANY VOLUNTEERS, I RETURNED from Greece determined to remain active in the aid effort. That summer, I held more fundraisers at home. My friend Stephanie Meyers, a mother of five with years of experience in nonprofits, joined in to help. In July, Stephanie and I flew to Athens. We'd raised another twenty thousand dollars to spend on grassroots projects.

Only two months had passed since my first visit, but a lot had changed in Greece. Idomeni had shut down. Boat arrivals from Turkey had decreased. The humanitarian effort now centered on the tens of thousands stuck in the country after borders closed. We found various projects to support, often on the advice of people I'd met up north in May. Through Tracey, we helped fund two initiatives run by Za'atar, a small Athens NGO—the Atlas Project, which supported asylum seekers from the LGBTQ community, and Orange House, which provided shelter for women and children, shower facilities for single men, and educational classes. Through Ibrahim, we paid for fresh produce to supplement the paltry government rations in camps, which were often little more than packets of noodles or rice.

In an email to our donors, I wrote, "You may be wondering why basic necessities are not being supplied by the Greek government, which was promised funding from the European Union. Well, yes, a lot of people are wondering about that, too. Meanwhile, people living in tents need basics, so we buy them."

I wanted to sound practical and upbeat but, in truth, I felt discouraged that our money was going to providing essentials. "It makes me sad," I confessed to Ibrahim. "I was hoping that food needs would be covered and you could be spending money on things like school supplies, mosquito nets, etc."

"U just said the words in my heart," he replied. "Its so sad to keep having emergencies over something like food." But he wanted me to understand the broader effort, too. "Trust me, we are doing much more than food, we have several projects including several schools, mosquito solutions (not only nets)—" his list went on and on, concluding with some words that I suppose were intended to offer hope: "Again trust me as we solved before the food situation we will solve it again it only need time."

STEPHANIE AND I ARRIVED IN ATHENS during the hottest weeks of summer. Greece's capital is known for white stone and cramped spaces, not shade trees or parks. Now it lay gasping, the sun beating down on concrete, asphalt, the roofs of cars, bare heads. The Acropolis, visible for miles, shimmered in the heat.

The Khalil family had finally managed to apply for relocation to Germany. They felt confident that they'd make it there, but they didn't know when. And though they no longer lived in the squat, it remained the center of their world. Abu Omar continued to serve on its leadership committee, and many times during that visit I saw him dash off to meetings like a bureaucrat with huge responsibilities. He complained about the workload, but his complaints looked like joyful bluster. His eyes showed the extreme relief of a man who had drifted, lost for months, then finally found community and purpose.

One day soon after we got there, Abu Omar walked with us to the squat. He introduced us to young, charismatic Jabbar and to Rima Halabi, who was too busy cooking to stop, although she smiled brightly when we peeked inside her kitchen. We met the "security" guys who hovered near the front door, and Harun, the keeper of the storage room, who didn't look old enough to shave.

It was obvious that the squat would benefit from some of the donation money we'd collected back home. "We have euros," Stephanie told

Abu Omar, who had by now learned some basic English. "We can buy food."

He nodded solemnly. "Thank."

I pointed to a child running down a hallway, wearing a single flip-flop. "Shoes," I said. "And soap." I mimed washing my hands.

The big man grinned. "You speak Kanwal." We had heard of the English volunteer who facilitated so many aspects of life in the squat, but we hadn't managed to find her. Now we retraced our steps through the building, Abu Omar repeatedly asking people where she was. One resident pointed down a hallway. Another directed us up a set of stairs. We kept looking. "Kanwal very busy," he said, heading from the third floor back down to the second.

Finally, we spotted a woman standing alone in front of a closed door, searching through a ring of keys. Her dark hair fell nearly to her waist and she was dressed modestly but with vibrant color—an embroidered crimson tunic over a gauzy lemon yellow skirt.

"Hello, Kanwal!" Abu Omar's voice thundered down the hallway.

The woman turned around. "Oh, hello!" Her voice was cheerful, but her shoulders slumped, as if our appearance added to her many burdens.

"This Dana. Stephanie," Abu Omar announced.

Kanwal shoved the keys into a pocket and shook our hands.

"We're volunteers from the United States," I explained.

"We fund-raised," Stephanie added. "We want to help."

Kanwal had large, deeply expressive eyes. The mention of money seemed to ease her anxiety. She said, "We could really use it."

THE NEXT AFTERNOON, WE WENT SHOPPING with a grocery list that Kanwal and Harun, the baby-faced storage keeper, had compiled. Stephanie and I each pushed a cart, which we filled with cooking oil, pasta, rice, crates of apples and tomatoes, large-size containers of shampoo and liquid soap, plus two cases of Happy Barn Milk in single-liter boxes, which we pulled from the store's refrigerated shelves.

It was dusk by the time we returned to the squat, our purchases stuffed inside two taxis. The squat's team of young men filed out to the cars and hauled the supplies to the storage room, where Harun directed sorting and unpacking. By the time we'd finished, the sun had set. Out in the courtyard, it seemed like all four hundred residents had emerged from the building. Rima, by the kitchen shed, had begun dishing out dinner. People stood in convivial clusters, eating stew out of paper bowls with plastic spoons. A toddler ambled through the center of it all, pushing an empty stroller, trailed by his mom. Not far away, Nura Khalil played with other little girls, while her sister, Layla, gravitated toward the teens.

After dinner, the celebration started—nothing special, just another night in the squat. Tall, handsome Jabbar got the music going. He and several other young men had carried out the drums, but he was the one who held everyone's attention, standing in the center of the courtyard with a portable speaker hanging off his shoulder. As soon as he lifted the microphone and began to chant, children swarmed around him. Jabbar hopped. The children hopped. Jabbar clapped. The children clapped. All eyes were on him. He was the planet. They were the moons in his orbit.

The sublime moments never lasted very long. When Stephanie and I arrived at the squat the next morning, Jabbar proudly led us to the storeroom. Harun, sleepy-eyed, jumped up when we appeared, sheepishly rolling up the mat that made this space his bedroom. Even though the boy spoke no English, we could see his pride as he pointed at yesterday's grocery purchases, now neatly arranged on the shelves.

I gave him a thumbs-up. But then something alarming caught my attention. Stacked on a table were the hundreds of euros' worth of Happy Barn Milk that we'd pulled from the grocery store refrigerators the day before. I touched a box. "It's been out all night," I told Stephanie.

Jabbar and Harun stared at us. "What the problem?" asked Jabbar.

"Milk must stay cold," I said.

Stephanie, looking like a mom feeling the brow of a sick child, set her palm against one of the milk boxes. "We can't let anyone drink this."

"Should we pour it down the drain?"

"I don't think we have a choice."

Jabbar, realizing our concern, broke into a wide grin and waved away our worries. "No problem." He walked over and picked up a box of milk. "This okay. No problem. In Syria, no problem."

It took a while for us to untangle the various misunderstandings here, our effort slowed by the fact that we spoke no Arabic and Jabbar had only spotty English. Eventually, though, the cultural differences became clear. Jabbar and Harun came from Syria, where consumers mostly purchased fresh milk to drink immediately. They rarely bothered with refrigeration. If they did need to store milk for any length of time, they purchased boxed brands, which, in Syria, were shelf-stable and needed no refrigeration before they were opened. Fresh, cold milk in a box was totally unknown to them, so they'd left the ones we'd bought on a table.

Stephanie and I, for our part, had made our own assumptions. When we first toured the storeroom the previous day, we saw a refrigerator, so we made our purchases thinking the squat could keep milk cold. The appliance didn't actually work, however. Pulling open its door, I saw that it contained boxes of bandages and cans of tuna. It functioned as a cupboard.

Stephanie started opening the milk and pouring it down the storeroom drain. Jabbar and Harun watched, muttering to each other in Arabic.

"I'm sorry," I told Jabbar. "Children can get sick."

He seemed despondent. He whacked at the old fridge. "This thing no good."

Stephanie looked over at me. "We need to buy them a refrigerator."

THAT AFTERNOON WE SET OFF FOR MEDIAMARKT, an Athens outlet of a large European electronics chain. This time, we went as a team. In addition to me and Stephanie, there were Abu Omar, Kanwal, and Jabbar, each of whom could offer advice. And the Egyptian-Greek trader who supplied produce to the squat came along, as well. An expert haggler, he promised to get us good prices.

I rode in a taxi with Kanwal and Jabbar. Since her arrival at the Second School, she and the young Syrian had developed a good working relationship and a friendly rapport. As our car weaved through Athens traffic, he told me his vision for the squat. Kanwal, sitting between us, gazed toward the road ahead, listening closely, gently helping when he struggled to find an English word.

"We are not just one person, one person, one person," Jabbar said, poking his finger against the air.

"Individuals?" Kanwal suggested. "That's the same as 'one person.'"

"Yes, yes!" Jabbar, in his excitement, seemed too huge for the small car. "We not just individual," he said. "We are—"

"A community?" Kanwal asked.

His hands shot toward the roof of the taxi, then came together as if to embrace the whole world. "A community!"

Kanwal seemed moved by his enthusiasm. Now, she added an opinion of her own. "Nobody should have to live in a place like the Second School. We have to make it better."

Jabbar didn't even use the name Second School. He wanted to rebrand the squat and call it Jasmine School instead. Giving it a new name seemed to be a way of taking ownership and giving agency to the displaced people who lived there. In his mishmash of English, he rattled off many ideas. If the squat had a laptop and projector, he said, they could turn a classroom into a theater and show movies to kids. If they had a "machine of coffee," they could create a small café. Well, not an actual café, he admitted, hesitant to make a promise beyond his reach, but a place where people could congregate and socialize. "With coffee, we talk. We sit. We happy."

Kanwal was laughing now. Jabbar's dreams seemed to fuel her.

That afternoon, we bought a new refrigerator, a deep freeze to hold bulk donations of meat, a laptop that Jabbar could use to create the Jasmine School–Athens Facebook page, and a projector for children's movie nights. Finally, supporting the idea that coffee creates community, we bought an espresso machine, too.

When we returned, we found the squat in mourning. A two-year-old Afghan boy had died from a heart condition. The coordination committee canceled a party they had planned for that evening. "It's not a good night," one of the committee members explained. "You don't want the parents up in their room to have to listen to music." The boy had received free medical treatment, but the services did not include the cost of burial. Kanwal and Castro arranged that.

I HAD ALREADY BEGUN RESEARCH FOR THIS BOOK, and that July I conducted my first in-depth interviews with the Khalil family. Up until then, Google Translate and rudimentary English had worked surprisingly well. Now I hired a professional interpreter, Zakia Aqra, a young Palestinian-Greek academic. The first time I met Zakia, she drove up on a motorcycle, wearing sandals and a summer dress. She was smart, experienced, and committed—all necessary qualities, of course—but it was also her formidable femininity that made her such an excellent partner. People warmed to Zakia instantly. She was kind and sensitive, but she never shied away from difficult subjects.

She charmed the Khalils from the first moment she walked through their door, which was fortunate, because the two of us spent whole days in their tiny apartment. In the mornings, we drank strong coffee out of tiny cups. In the late afternoons, Salma served delicious meals, all of us crowded together on the floor, sharing platters of yogurt and feta, sour pickles, falafel, and hummus. Zakia and Abu Omar gave each other cigarettes. Sometimes she translated while jiggling the baby on her knee.

Finally, small details I'd picked up over months began to come together as a story, and the family's myriad losses became clearer. One day, Abu Omar showed me an online video of their rubble-strewn neighborhood in Damascus, now memorialized through crowdsourcing. Staring at his beloved hometown, he touched the screen with a finger, then touched the finger to his lips, as if the city were some delicious dish for which he suffered constant cravings. "Damascus four seasons," he said as he shifted to a video of an ice-cream parlor in the old part of town. "Beautiful city. Ice cream very good. Now mostly finish." The man made his sadness perfectly clear. We didn't need Zakia to translate.

CHAPTER 24

Paradise

I S IT ETHICAL FOR VOLUNTEERS TO EMBARK on relationships with displaced people? I'm not talking about sexual relationships, which cross an obvious moral line. I'm talking about friendships. Affection and empathy surely increase understanding between people of varied backgrounds, but differences in status—finances, citizenship, the basic stability of having a home—also create power imbalances. Do we want to support a scenario in which the most outgoing, or determined, or proficient in English will enjoy benefits that others don't? The United Nations Office for the Coordination of Humanitarian Affairs promotes a set of core principles that includes *impartiality* ("Humanitarian action must be carried out on the basis of need alone, giving priority to the most urgent cases of distress and making no distinctions on the basis of nationality, race, gender, religious belief, class, or political opinions") and *neutrality* ("Humanitarian actors must not take sides in hostilities or engage in controversies of a political, racial, religious, or ideological nature"). But does that mean volunteers and refugees should not be friends? Do these principles require people to ignore basic human sentiment? Is it unethical to take one refugee out to dinner and not another?

I pondered such questions in regard to my friendship with the Khalil family. Twice I had given them a few hundred dollars of my own money, once when they had to flee the riots at Idomeni and more recently when I'd helped out with the studio apartment's first month's rent. In both cases, I weighed the two competing codes of ethics—the humanitarian principles of neutrality and impartiality versus the human principle that if someone you care about is suffering, you try to help. For me, the second principle won out. I didn't use any donation money to support the Khalils, but I did spend my own.

I wasn't the only one pondering such issues. Some long-term volunteers decided that close relationships with refugees drained them emotionally and compromised their effectiveness. Jenni James made friends with three refugee families during her first months in Greece, and never again after that. Tracey Myers didn't develop any such relationships at all. "There was no room for any individualism that I could do," she once confessed, almost as if she regretted her need to maintain boundaries. "Some of the solidarity volunteers were amazing because they would just get to know people."

In Athens, Kanwal Malik wondered about her friendships, too. She worried that her relationships with Rima Halabi, the Khalils, sweet young Harun in the storage room, and Ayan, a displaced Palestinian barber, made it hard for others to see her as an unbiased presence in the squat. But she was also alone in Greece. She felt emotionally supported by these individuals, which helped her get through her roughest challenges. Often, in the heat of the afternoon, she walked up the street to the Khalils' apartment to join them for lunch or just play with the children in the air-conditioned room. Was she making a complicated situation more difficult by having favorites? Was she contributing to jealousy or compromising people's ability to get along with one another? Perhaps. But she also needed friends.

Up north, Jenni's Get Shit Done Team had outgrown the little mobile van. Ibrahim agreed to her proposal to open a stand-alone workshop, and the two combed the industrial zones of Thessaloniki for space, eventually renting out a large warehouse on the outskirts of town. In one part of the building, Jenni's team set up its workshop. Ibrahim provided the rest of the space to other small aid groups—a food kitchen and a clothing warehouse—and the address was soon operating like a one-stop shop for grassroots relief.

Once Jenni had her workshop, Get Shit Done became a factory for major infrastructure projects in camps. To keep their output on schedule, the team kept three large production tables running full-time. On any given day, between fifteen and thirty volunteers were operating drop saws, hauling timber, framing flooring.

Jenni was pleased with her progress, but the need in camps remained immense. Often, she was trying to run three major projects at the same time—building a community center in one camp, for example, while installing winter insulation in another, and replacing decaying roofs at a third. Though she had both administrative experience and practical skills, Jenni had never managed an operation as large and complicated as Get Shit Done. Now she was overseeing dozens of volunteers, but she had no professional training in project management and wasn't a licensed builder, either.

When possible, Jenni found creative solutions to problems that went beyond her own expertise. In one camp, for example, the electric panel caught fire, leaving only two functioning outlets in the entire facility. Criminal gangs took control and extorted money from people who needed to charge their phones. Jenni was not an electrician, but she saw a solution. First, she met with the military officer who ran the camp. He was as concerned about crime as she was but had no funding to make improvements to the grid. Jenni had some funding, but she wasn't officially allowed inside the camp. Eventually, the two came up with a plan. Jenni's team would tackle the electricity problem and the camp commander would pretend he didn't notice them working on the premises. "Their hands were tied," she later told me, "but they had humanity behind them and basically turned a blind eye."

Jenni hired a licensed electrician to oversee the job, then used her own crew as a team of assistants. Together, they wired the entire camp, installing an electrical panel with a switch inside every tent. Camp residents no longer had to pay off criminals to charge their phones.

THE AMERICAN WRITER REBECCA SOLNIT HAS NOTED how human beings, in the midst of disaster, often experience moments of extreme beauty and joy: "a paradise built in hell," she calls it. During that long, hot summer at the Second School in Athens, Kanwal Malik exhausted herself trying to keep things running smoothly, but she often considered the place a paradise, too. Later, looking back, Kanwal remembered those months as magical. "I really felt that I achieved something," she told me.

"But of course"—she couldn't avoid the truth—"there were issues."

The issues came in various forms. Kanwal's dream of providing a roster of classes, for example, kept banging up against the reality that among prospective students there were vast differences in terms of their previous education. Some had gone to college. Others couldn't read or write but wanted to learn English or German. Some children had missed years of school, which made it hard for volunteer teachers to know how to place them. Backed-up toilets, inadequate food, and oppressive heat presented practical challenges. On top of that, life in a squat disrupted people's sleep cycles. The place came alive in the middle of the night, and many residents didn't emerge from their rooms until afternoon. If Kanwal planned morning classes, students didn't show up.

And there was emotional turmoil, too, which Kanwal saw as "power struggles, rumors, fights, and heated arguments [when] everyone tends to get their cards out and stick them on the table." During her first weeks at the squat, Kanwal had seen Abu Omar fighting. She quickly came to regard such episodes as normal there. Men battled over control of the storeroom. Factions accused each other of receiving more than their fair share. "You're living in a situation where you have many troubles," the storeroom manager, Harun, once told me. "You don't have money. I didn't even have money to buy cigarettes, and there were many people like me. Of course you get bored. You get angry. And you start fighting." One volunteer witnessed moments when male residents grew so furious that they started hurling furniture at one another. The presence of alcohol made everything worse.

Volunteers caused problems, too. Kanwal found most to be dedicated and well-meaning, but not all were helpful. Some ignored basic tenets of volunteering:

- Respect the needs of refugees first.

- Don't post people's photos on social media without permission.

- Don't engage in sexual relationships with people in crisis.

- Don't introduce alcohol into a situation where people's lives are unstable.

Some volunteers liked to drink and shared their liquor with squat residents, which increased fighting and other negative behavior. When grassroots leaders asked these volunteers to stop, they refused, insisting that "no one forces [the refugees]. If they want to drink, they should have freedom."

The Spanish team had dedicated their entire summer to the squat. It seemed to Kanwal that several of these young people regarded the experience as a great travel adventure. Some even slept at the building, curling up among the refugees in tents and eating the food that Rima cooked. It was, Kanwal felt, "like a holiday camp for them." They chose to live like refugees without acknowledging the major difference: They weren't stuck there.

One day, Kanwal walked out of one of the children's classrooms and saw a pool of vomit on the floor—the result, she knew, of one volunteer's excessive drinking. She was also frustrated by the tendency of some female volunteers to wear low-cut tops and short shorts, attire that was perfectly appropriate in Europe but disconcerting to a community of people from the Middle East. Some of the young male residents who were bored, lonely, and anxious about the future competed with one another, even getting into fights over female volunteers' attention.

Kanwal tried to convince the young women to dress more modestly at the squat, wearing less-revealing clothes.

"Well, this is Europe," she was told. "This is what they need to get used to."

Kanwal took such thinking personally, as if it indicated that her own more conservative style—loose-fitting skirts and tunics that often reflected her Pakistani heritage—somehow wasn't fully European. "I was born and bred in England," she told them. "And I don't dress like that."

Nothing changed. The young volunteers continued to appear in their spaghetti straps and miniskirts. The young male refugees continued to drink alcohol and smoke weed with them. A few of the refugee men fell in love with European college students out for a summer of fun. Kanwal felt the tension rise.

Eventually, someone called Castro Dakdouk. By now, Castro and his fellow solidarity activists were managing a system of squats that spread across several neighborhoods in Athens. If trouble started in one of them, residents appealed to Castro to step in. Now, his little clamshell phone rang with a plea for intervention at the Second School. The tired émigré made his way across town and did what solidarians do in moments of crisis: He called a general assembly to bring together the whole community so they could air their differences.

Castro had great respect for general assemblies. He viewed the process as a way to model civilized political discourse for people who came from totalitarian countries. But the meetings lasted hours. Attendees spoke many different languages, and the effort to translate into Arabic, Farsi, Spanish, English, and Greek took so long that people found themselves, at some point, staring at a wall. When Castro held a general assembly, as many as 25 percent of potential attendees never showed up.

"Why don't you come?" Castro would ask.

"I get allergies from the general assembly," one told him.

In the end, Castro had no more success in relieving tension at the Second School than Kanwal did.

THE SITUATION AT THE SQUAT DETERIORATED. It seemed to Kanwal that the hundreds of residents had reached their physical and emotional limits. "They were tired," she told me later. "These people were only supposed to be in Greece for three days." But weeks and months had passed and they remained in limbo. The European Union had, through the United Nations and other NGOs, begun to implement a cash-card system for asylum seekers awaiting decisions about relocation and family reunification. The cards supplied monthly stipends, but they were not available to people living in squats. Residents of the Second School, then, faced constant insecurity about finances in addition to prolonged uncertainty about how long they'd have to remain living in these conditions. The situation created tremendous stress, which, not surprisingly, added strain to relationships. Kanwal spent a lot of time mediating arguments. When conflicts developed between Kurdish and Syrian factions, for example, both sides appealed to her. "They're just trying to use you," one group would say. "Why are you even talking to them?" asked the other.

Kanwal now played a critical role in this community. Residents depended on her presence. Some told her that the atmosphere improved when she arrived in the morning and deteriorated after she went home at night. The responsibility put so much pressure on her that she considered quitting, but then she'd return to the same thought: There are families here that *need food*. She refused to abandon them.

One day, Kanwal received a message via Facebook from another volunteer: "We've heard that aid is being sold at [the squat]." The writer suggested that residents exchanged donated supplies for cash.

"Well," Kanwal responded, "I'm here most of the time and I've never seen evidence of this."

But the accusation made her wonder. She called a meeting with Jabbar and some of the other leaders. "I'm going to be very transparent with you," she said. "I've had a message from someone who says that aid is sold here. For me, at the moment, it's hearsay. But the moment that I see something will be the day that I walk away from here."

The residents denied the charge, but Kanwal became vigilant. She closely watched the Egyptian-Greek produce vendor who had, back in the summer, accompanied us to MediaMarkt to buy appliances. Despite the guy's help that day, Kanwal didn't trust him. She noticed that after his visits a smell of marijuana permeated the squat. She began to suspect that residents procured it from him. She looked closely at receipts, asking, "What am I actually paying for here? How much is a kilo of tomatoes?"

"€1.80," he replied.

Kanwal converted euros to British pounds in her head. "£1.30 for a kilo of tomatoes? That's crazy. Why are you buying such expensive tomatoes?" They weren't even good-quality ones, she thought. "I would be expecting handpicked organic tomatoes for that amount of money." She decided to go to the market and purchase her own bulk produce.

Jabbar attempted to intervene. "I think we should give him another chance." His loyalty to the produce guy made her more suspicious.

From the very first minute that Kanwal had walked into the squat, Jabbar had impressed her. His charisma made him a natural leader, both gregarious and fun. When he pulled out his hand drum in the evenings and began to tap out beats, the whole community coalesced. Now, though, clouds of rumor hovered over him. "No," she said.

CHAPTER 25

Single Men

STEPHANIE AND I WENT HOME TO NORTH CAROLINA even more committed to the aid effort. Two local friends, Jen Maraveyias and Carol Atwood, joined us, too. None of us had a background in the humanitarian sector, but each of us had useful expertise. Stephanie was a veteran fund-raiser. Jen, a former school administrator, had technical and organizational skills. Carol, a lawyer, knew finance. I could write the updates and appeals that explained the problem in Greece and how we could address it. From late summer into fall, we raised thousands of dollars locally, convincing us that our community had the desire and capacity to help. Our plan was fairly straightforward: We'd raise money at home, then take it to Greece and invest it in effective aid teams. Each of us committed, too, to paying her own expenses. We were still months away from filing the legal paperwork, but we were on our way to establishing the nonprofit Humanity Now.

One afternoon that fall, Kanwal sent me a message from Athens over WhatsApp. "I want to speak to you about the situation at the school with regards to bread," she said, adding that she hoped our team could help with funding. Flatbread plays a central role in Middle Eastern cuisine. In a community like the squat, which struggled to provide a nutritious diet, a piece of flatbread would at least fill an empty stomach. A lack of bread would surely increase residents' sense of deprivation.

"Can we speak?" Kanwal asked.

"Sure," I wrote back. I'd been following the squat's new Facebook page, which Jabbar had established with the help of the computer we'd purchased. One post—"Sunday night movie night"—included photos of the laptop rigged to a projector in the courtyard while dozens of people watched *Minions* on a bedsheet pinned to a clothesline. Such updates created an almost visceral connection between the residents of the squat and people like me, who cared about them but lived far away. One video of boys dancing had garnered 2,400 views.

Via Facebook, the community also broadcast bad news. At the end of September, Greek police stopped five boys from the squat as they were walking down a street, then held them on suspicion of being part of an armed group. Their infraction? The children, who were between the ages of twelve and sixteen, were carrying toy guns to use in a performance about their wartime experiences. "Is it a crime for children to dress Up in costumes (General army wear) and carry plastic toy guns in Europe??" the page administrators wondered in a widely shared post. When news of the arrests reached Amnesty International, the human rights group demanded that police investigate, proposing that the authorities ask themselves one pertinent question: "Would this have happened if five Greek children had been found carrying toy guns?"

When Kanwal called me, she was sitting in an Athens café, with Jabbar by her side. Over the next few minutes, she explained that the bakery that provided bread was refusing to deliver because the squat owed too much money. As Kanwal spoke, I heard Jabbar in the background. I couldn't understand his words, but I recognized the urgency in his tone.

Kanwal had called just as Stephanie, Jen, Carol, and I were devising financial and administrative systems to keep our nonprofit running in an organized way. When she asked for money, I couldn't just send it. "I have to talk with the others," I told her. Even though we hadn't yet filed our paperwork with the IRS, we did have a clear mission, which was to raise money at home and *deliver* it to Greece. We wanted to see projects up close and personally observe how the funds were being spent. On occasion, we had indeed wired money for emergencies, but we didn't want to do that often. An overdue bill at a bakery hardly qualified as a crisis.

After I got off the phone, Stephanie, Carol, Jen, and I discussed the Second School's bread predicament. We all agreed that this situation spoke to a larger problem with the squat's financial management. If we bailed them out now, we expected that they'd call in another month with some new request.

Back in Athens, Kanwal and Jabbar awaited my response. I didn't want to imply that I mistrusted their competence, so I put them off with a practical suggestion. "A budget would be really helpful in getting more sustainable help from international friends," I wrote.

Kanwal responded immediately. "I have been trying to get them to work this way for 3 weeks," she wrote, adding that there were "a few ego issues that we are trying to iron out." Reading the message, I laughed at her wry tone. I didn't take it for what it was, a hint that the Second School was disintegrating.

KANWAL DIDN'T SAY SO AT THE TIME, but she later told me that she'd become extremely discouraged. The squat's drinkers and smokers, once sly and surreptitious, now indulged openly, and female residents were suffering regular harassment from drunken men.

These issues came on a wave of other challenges—ethnic tensions, fighting, accusations of corruption, power struggles, "people stabbing each other in the back." Kanwal refused to blame all single men—plenty of them never drank, smoked, or harassed women—but a minority among that group was causing major problems.

Kanwal spent a lot of time at the Khalils' apartment, discussing what to do. The situation upset them, as well. Abu Omar had even stepped away from his precious role on the leadership committee and the family visited the squat much less often. Some days when Kanwal visited, she broke down in tears. Watching her, Abu Omar would mutter to his wife, "These people are sucking everything out of her."

Eventually, Kanwal decided to call the squat's residents together to talk.

"Good. Good." Abu Omar liked the idea.

At the meeting, Kanwal insisted on an open conversation. Acknowledging that she had no power over people's choices to smoke or drink, she proposed a compromise. "I don't want to control you or anyone else. You're free to do whatever you want to do, but don't do it on the school premises." Then she decided to make an additional concession. "Even if you do it in your own room, do it *in your room*. Don't do it so *openly*."

She didn't mention sexual harassment. The victims had asked her not to bring it up. The women had to live in that building, and they feared for their reputations.

The men listened to what Kanwal proposed. She kept her eye on Jabbar, who seemed to be attentive. She knew he smoked hashish. She knew he drank. But he did seem sympathetic to her concerns. "What you're saying," he said, "makes total sense."

They get it, she told herself.

Things improved, but only for a few days. Then, as Kanwal watched, the men slipped right back into their old ways again.

AROUND THIS TIME, KANWAL'S BELLY STARTED HURTING. At the Khalils' apartment, Salma plied her with herbal drinks. The girls huddled close, anxiously offering water. "You don't drink enough water. Maybe it's your kidneys," the children suggested.

Their concern touched her. They're being my full-on nurses, she thought.

One evening, she received a call from Rando Wagner, the fast-talking flight attendant and veteran volunteer. "I need to have a meeting with you." He suggested they have dinner.

"I've got this severe pain in my lower abdomen," she told him.

But Rando didn't immediately register the seriousness of what she was saying. He had something pressing on his mind. "Just come on and we'll eat somewhere." A few minutes later, the two volunteers met in front of the Khalils' apartment.

It wasn't until they had settled in at a restaurant that Rando explained the urgency of this meeting. He believed that food donations to the squat were being sold for cash.

His allegation didn't surprise Kanwal; they just added weight to her own suspicions. The two tried to figure out what to do.

But then Kanwal began gripping her stomach. Rando grew alarmed as she squirmed in pain. "You look really, really pale," he told her.

"This pain is weird. It's been here for two days."

"Appendicitis?"

"No," she insisted, but she had to leave the restaurant.

Kanwal's rental apartment had, over the past few weeks, become a way station for many people. British friends stayed with her when they came to volunteer, as did former residents of the squat, who had fled its toxic atmosphere. Now, Ayan, her Palestinian barber friend, was living in the spare room. When Kanwal got home that night after meeting with Rando, Ayan saw how sick she looked. "Tomorrow, you've got to go to the doctor," he insisted.

Kanwal dismissed the idea. "I've got meetings tomorrow." She had no time to be sick.

The pain kept her awake all night, but the next day she headed out as usual. Kanwal spoke Urdu and sometimes volunteered as a translator for displaced Pakistanis. That morning, she went to translate for a family at a squat near the Second School.

The session started fine, but then her stomach pain increased, until she couldn't bear it. She began to shiver uncontrollably. She broke into a sweat. "Oh my God. I think I need to go to hospital now," she said to the people around her.

A medical team had scheduled vaccinations that morning for children in the building. "Go downstairs," someone suggested. "We might have doctors." But Kanwal flinched at the idea of bothering medical staff. She didn't want to be the anxious volunteer screaming at the doctors, "Hey, can you check out my pain?" So she sat down on the stairs and curled into the fetal position.

And that was when Robina called from England. As soon as Kanwal heard her mother's voice, she burst into tears. "What am I going to do?" she wailed. "I can't afford to go to hospital. They'll charge me and I don't have that money."

Robina responded firmly. "I don't care how much it costs," she said. "Get yourself to the hospital *now*."

Sometimes, it takes an emergency to turn an assortment of acquaintances into a solid support system. Within minutes, two friends showed up—Harun, the young Syrian who had run the storeroom, and Imran, a British volunteer. Seeing Kanwal writhing on the stairway, both men began to cry. Such softies! Kanwal thought. Then they picked her up, carried her to their car, and drove her to the hospital.

At first, the hospital staff suspected appendicitis, as Rando had the night before. "You're showing all the clear symptoms," a doctor told Kanwal. "We might have to operate."

Over the course of the day, they put her through a series of tests and scans, but the results kept coming back normal. Hours passed. Harun and Imran didn't leave her side. Her friend Ayan showed up.

"I told you that you needed to drink more water!" he declared. "You didn't listen to me."

"All right, Mom. Dad. Whatever," Kanwal muttered from her bed.

Word of her predicament also reached the Second School. Worried residents sent her a video message, which she watched from her bed. "Should we all come to the hospital?" they asked.

"No!" she said, staring at the screen of her phone, laughing.

As the day went on, Kanwal's friends devised a plan for her care. Over time, some refugees had managed to secure private apartments administered through the Greek NGO Praksis. Harun and some of the other young men from the squat now lived in one of those apartments, which had enough bunk beds to sleep eight people. "You're coming to our house," they declared. "We've set a bed up for you. We'll keep an eye on you. You'll go straight there." Kanwal would have preferred to go directly home, but the young men would not allow it.

Late in the day, the senior medical practitioner appeared at her bedside. This doctor spoke excellent English. "What are you actually doing here?" he asked.

She was, at that moment, surrounded by worried-looking Middle Eastern men, which may have offered a clue about her life in Athens. When she explained that she was volunteering in the squats, the revelation seemed to solve the medical mystery completely. "Your body is telling you that you need to rest," the doctor said. "You are absolutely burned out. We can't find anything wrong with your X-rays, with your blood count, but clearly there is a problem." He suggested that she stay the night in the hospital on an IV so that the medical team could pump antibiotics into her, just in case she had an infection.

"I don't want to stay here," Kanwal said. She looked at her friends. They had offered her twenty-four-hour care. "They've got everything set up," she said. "I know they will look after me."

So Kanwal went to the single guys' apartment for her convalescence. Later, looking back, she remembered it as a time when one worried young man after another plied her with glasses of a horrible-tasting yogurt and garlic drink. But she recovered.

In October 2016, a young Syrian refugee stepped off a bus in Athens. Sami Malouf had no money. It wasn't a case of having not much money; he didn't have *any* money. He had heard of a place called the Single Men's Squat, where guys could sleep for free, so he found his way there.

The Single Men's Squat, like the Second School and the Fifth School, was an illegal accommodation that solidarity activists had rigged out of an abandoned building, this one a former student commissary. As living quarters, the place was spartan, even for a squat—just a few cavernous unheated rooms, a cramped kitchen area, two toilets, and a single shower, all shared by a sad population of roughly 150 men—older widowers, young guys who had fled Syria to avoid the draft, middle-aged fathers separated from their families. For food, they received a midafternoon "brunch": one boiled egg, one pita round, one banana. At night, if the solidarity groups managed to deliver supplies, the men ate something a bit more substantial.

Sami ended up in a ground-floor room with about thirty men, some too elderly to walk up the stairs. His spot was a thin mat by the front door. Huddled next to seven others, he tried to stay warm beneath a thin, bedbug-infested blanket that he came to think of as "the worst blanket ever." Each time the outside door opened, wind blew across the room, making its occupants even colder. Within a day or two, he'd dragged in an old wooden door he'd found on the street and positioned it to keep out the wind, at least a little.

The Single Men's Squat was a depressing place, but Sami, who was only twenty-six years old, had already experienced much worse.

He came from Latakia, Syria's seafaring region. As a teenager, he'd studied at a prestigious naval academy in Egypt, then later worked on a merchant vessel transporting sheep and camels from Somalia to meat-hungry Saudi Arabia. He loved his career, but he lost it in 2011, when he returned to Syria and was promptly drafted by the Assad regime. He was sent to Idlib; then his battalion ended up in Aleppo. During fighting there, Sami suffered serious injury and saw friends die all around him. As he lay waiting for medical evacuation, he watched Syrian troops toss the bodies of the dead into the bed of a truck. At that moment, he swore to himself that he would never again fight for a government that treated its martyrs like trash. After he recovered, he went into hiding, spending three years living in a secret room in his parents' house. Every day he told himself that the war would end soon. But the news that Sami followed on the internet—Russia bolstering the collapsing Assad regime, factions settling in for a protracted conflict—ate away at his optimism. He finally came to an unavoidable conclusion: This will be a long story. He fled Syria.

In the fall of 2015, Sami reached Greece on board a smuggler's ship from Turkey. Floating offshore, the boat looked like a tourist vessel. Port authorities became enraged when they realized that it was actually carrying 172 refugees and migrants. The officials boarded the boat, determined to arrest the captain, but he had already escaped. Among the remaining passengers, only one seemed capable of sailing this big boat: Sami Malouf, who was carrying his naval academy diploma. They promptly arrested him.

He spent the next year in a maximum-security prison in Central Greece, constantly ruminating on his predicament and the fact that, if found guilty, he could serve a decade. It wasn't until his case finally went to trial that fortune finally turned in his favor. The judge, recognizing that prosecutors had no evidence that he was a human trafficker, threw out the case. A few days later, Sami arrived in Athens.

Now, lying on the floor of the Single Men's Squat, he considered what to do next. Sami carried two official Greek papers, one documenting the date of his original entry into Greece in 2015. The second testified to the fact that he'd been wrongly imprisoned. Sami, like other displaced people in Greece, had three choices available to him. He could stay in this country and apply for asylum immediately. He could choose to apply to another European country for asylum. Or, if he had family somewhere else in Europe, he could apply for family reunification.

The Single Men's Squat was full of people who were desperate to get out of Greece. They dreamed of reuniting with family, or simply ending up in wealthier parts of Europe. But an entirely different impulse drove Sami Malouf. If you added up his three years in hiding in Syria and his one year of actual incarceration in Greece, he had spent four years of his life in one prison or another. Now that he was finally free, he felt desperate to get settled. I can make something of my life right here, he told himself. He chose Greece. But lying there under that disgusting blanket, he did have to wonder how he would get started.

FOR THE FIRST COUPLE OF WEEKS AFTER KANWAL RECOVERED from her stomach ailment, she continued volunteering at the Second School Squat. Even though the place had serious problems, she refused to abandon the residents there. They relied on her.

But then one night in mid-October, she happened to pass through the squat's courtyard alone. It was late, maybe ten or eleven, and she was the only volunteer around. Up ahead were two men whom she immediately recognized as members of the squat's "management"—Jabbar and a middle-aged guy who drank too much and often harassed women. Even from a distance, she could see that they were intoxicated.

The older man reached her first. He took her arm, dragged her close, and set about trying to kiss her. Kanwal shoved him back. Then Jabbar came after her, too. She struggled. Finally, she managed to pull away and flee.

The next day, Kanwal returned to the squat in order to confront the men in public. She felt violated, and she was determined not to let the incident drop. Her own experience underscored the fact that women didn't feel safe in that place. When she arrived, however, she discovered that the entire community already knew about the incident. Very quickly, the meeting devolved into what Kanwal called "a massive blowout."

In many basic ways, a squat exists outside the law. The Second School depended on human beings' commitment to respecting one another—the anarchist model at its most pure. But the squat had veered from that ideal.

The men who had assaulted Kanwal tried to defend themselves. "I was kissing you like a daughter," the older one asserted.

"I think of you as a sister," said the younger.

The men implied that Kanwal had misunderstood, but she stood her ground. "It was not in my head," she declared. "And I know exactly what your intentions were when you approached me."

Of course, the female residents knew the real story. They regularly endured harassment themselves. Now the truth came out, and all the men heard it. Abu Omar, who was also attending the meeting, reacted with rage. Collaring the two men, he said, "This has to stop. There are people's sisters here. There are mothers here. There are wives here." Then he said, "If my daughters were ever treated like that, I would kill you all."

Nothing changed within the squat. Drinking continued. Drug use continued. Harassment of women continued. Or at least Kanwal assumed that it did. She never knew for sure because she left the Second School that day and never went back.

PART IV

Waiting

CHAPTER 26

Girls and Women

THE HUMANITARIAN SITUATION IN GREECE had shifted from acute emergency into a long, slow grind of ongoing suffering. The international media that had once flocked to the islands to report on incoming boats, or filmed the misery and unrest at Idomeni, had turned its attention to different global dramas. Meanwhile, all over Greece, thousands of displaced sat waiting.

After Kanwal left the Second School, the Khalils cut ties to it, as well. The place no longer felt safe to them. It was a sad loss for the family. The Second School had given them community. Their world got even smaller now.

In October 2016, Greece began providing education to displaced children who lived in camps. The fledgling program was meant as a compromise between competing concerns—the children's academic needs versus worry among some Greek parents that their students would suffer if migrant and refugee kids attended their schools. The plan established a second-shift system for camp children, who would arrive for class after the Greek kids went home. This abbreviated instruction had a lot of flaws, but it did provide some access to education.

Layla and Nura didn't live in camps, so they couldn't participate. The girls had fled Syria because they wanted to go to school. Ten months later, they remained far from achieving their goal. In Athens, they had attended informal classes at the Second School. They also participated in programs at the Cube, an Athens start-up incubator. The Cube brought displaced kids together to discuss provocative questions, such as "What makes you and people happy?" and "Why are bees important to us and the environment?" Such programming was simple by both necessity and design. "Our challenge was to provide this with the absolute minimum of resources," the Cube's founder, Stavros Messinis, told a local newspaper. "We have no training material, no target language–speaking teachers— Arabic, Pashto, Farsi, Urdu, etc.—just the will to put our minds to work and provide some mental stimulation for some underserved children."

Layla and Nura both had birthdays that autumn. Layla was twelve now and Nura had just turned nine. Back home, the routine of school had grounded them. But years had passed since they'd enjoyed the luxury—they both considered it a luxury now—of formal education. Like their parents, the girls experienced refugee life as a loss of loved ones, home, and homeland, but in some ways they experienced the loss of education most acutely. In the past, school had given them structure, friendships, a path toward the future. "I feel a little bit lost," Layla told me once. Nura, who regarded their situation as completely unnatural, said, "A child's normal place is to be in school."

Given the chance, the girls jumped at any learning opportunity that Athens offered. Did someone want to hear their opinions about bees? They would eagerly answer. Had a volunteer organized an art class for refugees? The girls would join. Face paint? Yes. Knitting? Yes. Making bracelets from rubber bands? Yes and yes and yes and yes.

Refugee life had turned Layla into an activist, too. Perhaps she was political by nature, absorbing the ideas of the solidarity movement as they filtered down to her. Perhaps she was just a curious girl who listened closely when adults discussed their plight. In any case, when refugees had marched through the streets of Athens the previous summer, Layla had sat on her father's shoulders and, microphone in hand, led the crowd in a chant of "Open the borders!" A month later, a volunteer posted an interview with Layla on Facebook and the girl made a blistering comparison between traditions of hospitality in her own country and those in Europe. "On Syria" she said, in not too bad English, "anybody is coming to my house I open all of the house and I give it to him all the food and everything because this I go to make freedom and I say, 'Open the border. Open the house.' Not like this."

Such experiences provided the Khalil girls plenty of "teachable moments," but nothing took the place of school. In September, an outbreak of chicken pox had shut down programming at the Cube. "Speedy recovery to our awesome students," read the organization's posting on Facebook; "get well real soon!"

The Cube's closing cut off one more chance to learn. Mostly, the Khalil girls sat in the cramped apartment.

UP NORTH, TRACEY MYERS AND JENNI JAMES were well into their second year of volunteering. Their love affair had ended long before, but their friendship had grown stronger. The two women helped each other in practical ways. Tracey was still developing housing for refugees, and Jenni, with her hands-on skills, offered sensible guidance. Similarly, Tracey's experience with human resources meant that she could advise Jenni on managing the Get Shit Done Team's volunteers.

More important, the two women provided each other with emotional support. They were very different—"yin and yang," as Tracey saw it—but they were both alone in Greece, far from friends and family back home. They helped each other through the toughest times. "When things broke down with one of us and the other person was there," Tracey told me, "somehow we muddled through."

In their world of constant work and stress, emotional and professional challenges often became entwined. In Tracey's case, well-funded donors had invested funds to renovate a building for the housing project, but the effort was marred by internal disagreements. Tracey worried about the residents' safety. "If someone turns up to beat up one of these women, how are we going to handle it?" she asked. "How are we going to ensure no one gets abused in this space?" Tracey wanted the team to adopt "best practice" guidelines like those followed by well-established NGOs. Her colleagues, on the other hand, worried that too many rules would slow the process of getting vulnerable families out of camps, which were also unsafe places. It was a classic grassroots/establishment dilemma, and the team couldn't agree. Goodwill deteriorated.

Meanwhile, Jenni faced her own problems. Get Shit Done had committed to providing infrastructure improvements in ten camps. To actually get the shit done, though, Jenni needed a lot more hands.

On Facebook, she posted peppy calls for help—"Come and join us as a self supported volunteer." She had work for any willing person, but she was desperate for professionals from the building trades—electricians, plumbers, carpenters, project managers. The team did attract recruits, but they weren't all a great fit. Sometimes workers claimed to have more experience than they actually possessed, and their deficiencies revealed themselves just when Jenni needed those skills the most. Some had extensive professional experience but, never having worked outside their own country, balked at Greece's unfamiliar regulations or struggled to use tools that were different from ones they used back home. Sometimes, disagreements led to power struggles and Jenni had to say, "I'm sorry. The buck stops with me."

Being in charge didn't mean she had power, however. Jenni's staff was composed completely of volunteers. Some joined only for a few days or a week, and thus had little commitment or impact. Some came for longer but insisted on following their own schedules. Often, Jenni heard some variation of "I will come to work when I want to come to work because I'm a volunteer." She could not meet deadlines if people showed up only when they felt like it.

Thessaloniki was a famously vibrant city. The ancient urban center wrapped around the curve of a bay, then rose into the hills. Sunset brought thousands to the seaside promenade, filling restaurants and cafés with stylish revelers. A night out could easily last until dawn, offering obvious temptations to foreigners spending their vacation time volunteering. Many shared large rental flats that could house a dozen or more people, turning tight quarters into party centrals. Too often after a big night, volunteers slept in and missed work the next day.

Jenni, nearly fifty and considerably older than most of her crew, carried the responsibility for the entire team. She recognized that she had weaknesses as a manager. She tried to listen closely and consider opposing views. Ultimately, though, she had to make final calls herself. Leading a mostly male team, she sometimes wondered if the men resented her role as their supervisor. Her assertions of authority, she once told me, "didn't always go down well because I'm a female, for starters."

Jenni and Tracey both dreamed of a grassroots movement that thrived on flexibility and innovation while also following time-tested models for keeping people productive and safe. Frustrated by setbacks, Jenni finally adopted a code of conduct contract that volunteers had to sign before joining her team, committing themselves to following her schedule and rules. On too many mornings, however, Jenni received calls from volunteers blithely announcing, "I'm not coming in." On those days, Jenni felt her heart sink.

Kanwal Malik had suffered a series of disasters at the Second School. She might have decided at this point simply to return to England. But she wasn't ready to stop volunteering. A U.S.-based nonprofit called the Schoolbox Project had hired her to run a children's education program at Elliniko Camp, on the outskirts of Athens. The job included a small stipend to cover her expenses. Despite all her setbacks, Kanwal felt stirrings of hope when she thought about this new endeavor.

During her months in Greece, Kanwal's thinking about refugees had evolved significantly. On her first stint volunteering, she had felt such profound empathy for displaced people that she defined them simplistically: "These are angels. They're the holy ones. They have to be good because they've been through so much."

Now she considered those views naïve. "They're just like any one of us trying to survive," she told me once. "They have their good. They have their bad. They are just normal people that have been through terrible circumstances and continue to live in terrible circumstances, which actually tests their character."

This conclusion might sound obvious, but Kanwal had actually come to a fundamental truth that escapes many observers of crisis—that refugees are complicated human beings, just like the rest of us. "To accept people's humanity and respect their dignity as individuals should not entail spinning fairy tales about their innate innocence," the writer David Rieff has pointed out.

At the same time, Kanwal now understood, too, the emotional cost of volunteering. Her experiences at the Second School had hurt her deeply and she knew that in the future she'd have to pay better attention to her own mental health. She decided to take a break and go visit her family in England.

She had one important duty to consider before she left. When Kanwal fled the Second School, Rima Halabi and her five kids had fled, as well. The entire family now lived with Kanwal in her little walk-up apartment and they depended on her. Before she left, she doled out an allowance to make sure the family had everything they needed. Then she went home.

Now that Rima no longer lived at the Second School and cooked meals for four hundred people, she devoted all her attention to her family. The squat had been an unruly and sometimes violent place, but Rima and the kids had been part of a rich and vibrant community there. Alone in Kanwal's apartment, they were safer and infinitely more comfortable, but they had very little to do. These days, Rima mostly pondered her life's central question: When would their asylum application be approved and allow them to travel to Germany?

Nothing gave structure to their days. Shakira, the teenager, went through typical moody spells, staying awake at night and sleeping well into the afternoon. The younger children stayed up late, too. It could be one o'clock in the afternoon by the time they opened their eyes and looked up from their sleeping mats. The boys would stand and groggily stretch. Yusuf, the elder of the two, would wash himself in the bathroom, then drag a comb through his now-wet hair, fastidious as his mother already.

Rima spent a lot of time sitting on a mat, cradling Oma, who had turned one by now. Sometimes she'd reach out a hand and try to tame Lina's curls, but that usually ended in failure. At night, before bed, Rima pulled the girl's hair into a ponytail, but Lina always yanked it free. She was a wild child, rocketing after her brothers, turning sleeping mats into stepping-stones, the floor into a slippery slide. Rima instructed her kids to play nicely. If that didn't work, she'd turn disciplinarian and order them to stay apart from one another.

She liked to see them having fun. Their experiences over the last few months had brought too many traumas. Once, when Rima happened to mention their escape from Syria into Turkey, Yusuf reminded her of how their taxi had spun out of control, nearly careening over a cliff. Rima realized that her son had experienced the moment intensely. Even now, there was terror in his eyes when he said, "Mama, remember when we were in the car and it went round and round?"

There was no way to ignore the fact that the past year had affected the kids, even the baby. At the Second School, other adults had often held Oma while Rima cooked, and eventually Oma seemed to need her mother less and less. In that sense, this quiet life in Kanwal's apartment had helped. Oma had definitely reattached. When the baby grew tired and began to fuss, Rima set her on a pillow on her lap and then raised one knee after the other, rocking the pillow like a boat. Oma stared up at Rima's face until finally her eyes closed and she fell asleep.

They were getting by, but Rima yearned for Germany. A year had passed since she'd said good-bye to Musa and Malika. Musa had never seen his baby girl. Malika had never met her youngest sister. The family constantly talked on the phone, but it wasn't the same as holding your dear ones. Rima longed for the day when all the Halabis would occupy the same room. When she spoke to Musa, she called him "my safe place." She called him "my love."

CHAPTER 27

Second Winter

After a short visit home, Kanwal Malik returned to Athens in October. She and her husband had finally and permanently parted ways. She felt ready to take on her new job as site director for the Schoolbox Project, which had set up three small shipping containers at Elliniko Camp in suburban Athens. Arranged in a U shape around an open courtyard, the containers would provide two on-site classrooms and a storage building holding the toys, art supplies, games, musical instruments, and sports equipment that the team would use to program activities for dozens of children.

The Greek government had opened refugee camps in many unconventional (and inappropriate) locations. Elliniko Camp was a particularly odd one. For decades, the Athens airport had occupied this site. That facility had closed in 2001, when Greece opened a new terminal and converted Elliniko into various sports venues, some of which hosted events during the 2004 Summer Olympic Games in Athens. By the time the Schoolbox Project opened at the end of October 2016, the defunct arenas and airport were sheltering some two thousand displaced people, almost all of them Afghan, who slept in tents on playing fields and inside empty airport buildings.

Elliniko Camp was actually three separate camps spread across the site. UNHCR, trying to keep things straight, identified each by its former use: "Elliniko I (Hockey)," "Elliniko II (West/Olympic Arrivals)," and "Elliniko III (Baseball Stadium)." The Schoolbox Project operated outside of Elliniko II, the old domestic arrivals terminal, where planes had once landed from all over Greece. Volunteers at this site didn't bother with its long, official name. They just called the place "Arrivals."

According to UNHCR estimates, Arrivals held some seven hundred displaced people who slept in tents on the second floor of the old concourse. The Danish Refugee Council provided site management and other services, turning the dark and dusty first floor into a location for administration and distribution. Here, boxes of donated clothes sat near the electronic wall unit that had once displayed flight information. Farther back, small rooms that might have once been baggage handlers' offices served as conference areas and counseling spaces.

The children at Arrivals had virtually nothing to do. They entertained themselves by turning puddles into splash pools, fences into climbing gyms, and patches of broken pavement into soccer fields. All this creative play was certainly a triumph of ingenuity, but no one was fooled. UNHCR's assessment of the facility's child-friendly spaces concluded by saying, "Area available, but not appropriate in terms of safety and space." When the Greek Ministry of Education agreed to the Schoolbox proposal to open the container classrooms, the decision seemed to promise a notable improvement at the camp.

Kanwal's new position also marked an improvement in her own life. For the first time since she'd come to Greece, she had an official job that paid a stipend. The money was minimal. Practically speaking, she remained a "volunteer," but the wage would help offset her considerable expenses. She still had the entire Halabi family living in her apartment.

"I am super super excited," Kanwal posted on Facebook just before the container classrooms opened. She described the project as having "an amazing twist." Schoolbox trained its volunteers in a teaching method called "trauma-informed education." Based on the principle that children's experience of trauma affects their ongoing emotional development and ability to learn, the practice aimed to create a calm environment to foster healing. At Schoolbox, Kanwal hoped to provide love and structure. The kids would benefit from developing trust in the adults around them. "We're not going anywhere," she told them on the very first day.

The volunteers painted the containers with cheerful flowers and covered the floors with colorful interlocking foam mats. As days passed, children wandered over to check the place out and join activities. Because the program's educational philosophy centered on trust and structure, Kanwal kept to a regular schedule, offering three one-hour sessions every day, six days a week. During the sessions, children crowded into the shipping containers for board games, art, and music. Soon their Magic Marker drawings covered the walls. Outside, they played tag and skipped rope. One day, a visiting clown troupe entertained them. By creating an atmosphere that was simultaneously stimulating and calm, the program focused on relieving stress and promoting a sense of normalcy.

It wasn't easy. These children had endured war, upheaval, and displacement. Some had lost loved ones. Others lived with drug-addicted parents. Many witnessed domestic violence every day. Emotional problems made them rowdy and sometimes brutal. Watching one boy punch and kick, Kanwal thought, He's *wanting* to do serious harm to other children. But the child also responded well to one-on-one attention. After a volunteer taught him to knit, he sat for long stretches, placidly making a scarf for his sister.

Other children seemed to suffer inconsolable grief. Four-year-old Fatima didn't speak. She communicated instead by kicking, spitting, and screaming. In the open space framed by the containers, the School-box volunteers had installed bright green artificial grass. Here, the children spent hours skipping rope, each child trying to skip longer than the others. During the sessions, the air filled with the sound of children and adults counting together in English: "One, two, three, four," and on and on as long as any single child could skip. Fatima, like the others, became obsessed with these competitions, but she refused to join in. When Kanwal encouraged Fatima to try skipping, the child screamed, "Nooooooooooo!"

THE YEAR 2016 WAS ROLLING TOWARD ITS CLOSE. In Northern Greece, Tracey, Jenni, and Ibrahim all worried as temperatures began to plummet. Thousands of refugees faced another winter in substandard accommodations. In a statement about the situation in early November, Human Rights Watch condemned "Europe's utter failure to respond collectively and compassionately to people seeking protection."

Two weeks later, the cold arrived in full force. On Facebook, Tracey posted:

> Its freezing and snowing in greece. Im wearing every-
> thing I own and am freezing. Last night I had all the
> blankets and an electric blanket and was freezing. People,
> including pregnant women and babies, are sleeping out-
> side on floors in tents. Many have no access to hot water.
> This is the second winter people have been here waiting
> waiting waiting for due legal process and some humanity
> in Europe, having fled the bombs in which we are all
> complicit. As they freeze, people hear aleppo is falling,
> they hear grim news of closed doors across europe. The
> EU and every organisation is failing to do anywhere near
> enough—myself included. . . . [If] our generation does
> not want to go down in history as barbaric we all need to
> do more now.

Many veteran volunteers also experienced a maddening sense of déjà vu. A year earlier, the Greek government, the European Union, and large humanitarian agencies could still claim, with some validity, that the size, speed, and intensity of the situation had left them unprepared. But how could they *remain* unprepared now, after seventeen months? Or, as Tracey put it, "Second winter in a tent. Second year plastic toilets, into second year without basic human rights and with ice cold. Not one person. [T]ens of thousands, not a far-flung place. Greece."

Europe's grassroots community had matured, however, and that helped. The most effective teams managed to marry the expertise and professionalism of large NGOs with the nimbleness and heart of small-scale relief efforts. The Norwegian charity A Drop in the Ocean, for example, had started out by providing emergency aid on Lesvos Island in 2015. By the end of 2016, the organization was sending experienced representatives to international conferences and issuing annual reports. It remained extremely lean, however. The organization had only 1.5 paid positions and relied almost entirely on volunteers. Over two thousand people from thirty-five different countries had served as "Drops" in Greece.

Among these new aid teams, perhaps none grew as quickly or became as influential as the UK-based Help Refugees, which launched in 2015 when a group of British women started collecting money for supplies to migrants in Calais, France. The team set an initial goal of £1,000 but ended up raising £56,000 in their very first week. Their rented storage unit began receiving seven thousand packages a day. As Lliana Bird, one of the founders, later described it, the group arrived in Calais and found that the humanitarian network caring for the six thousand migrants consisted of independent volunteers and a small local charity comprising mostly retired artists and teachers. Given the horrendous conditions there, Bird said, "We thought to ourselves, We cannot just leave." So they stayed.

A year later, this small group of volunteers had transformed themselves into an official British charity, collecting two million pounds in financial donations, plus another one million pounds' worth of goods and services. The founders, as it happened, had a distinct advantage in raising large amounts. Several of them came from the professional worlds of entertainment and promotion, and they were adept on social media. In time, celebrities like Benedict Cumberbatch, Lena Dunham, and Jude Law publicly supported their cause. The playwright Tom Stoppard visited their project at Calais, and the U.S.-based Compassion Collective, led by, among others, authors Elizabeth Gilbert, Cheryl Strayed, and Brené Brown, raised one million dollars for Help Refugees during a single forty-eight-hour fund-raising campaign. By late 2016, the group was funding projects across Europe, many of them in Greece.

Much of the effort in Greece was now aided by Ibrahim Khoury. Just over a year had passed since he'd stepped off a boat himself, and the Syrian asylum seeker had become one of the most trusted aid workers in the country. One of his colleagues at Help Refugees once told me that Ibrahim was "really useful to a group of people who run a charity who have not got that background." The team appreciated Ibrahim not only for his skill but also for his frankness. He had what the colleague called a "very straightforward way of telling you exactly what you're doing wrong."

In those days, some grassroots teams had funds to support their long-term staff, offering basic stipends to cover living expenses in Greece. Money that actor Jude Law brought in through celebrity appearances in Britain, for example, not only allowed Help Refugees to support Jenni James's Get Shit Done projects in camps but also helped Jenni pay her rent in Greece.

Since the previous summer, both Jenni and Tracey had attended meetings that brought together government officials, representatives of large NGOs, and grassroots volunteers. The goal was to discuss preparations for winter. The meetings had not gone well. At one, Jenni found herself begging, "You need to plan now. Do it now. Do it now. Do it *now.*"

Little changed. At Softex Camp, container housing did arrive, a promising step up from tents. But the portable buildings were old damaged models that the government had merely hauled in from another site. Instead of windows and doors, they had empty holes. The volunteers were appalled, but whom should they blame? The aid system was so disorganized that, as Tracey put it, "no one knew whose job was what." In fact, a lack of institutional responsibility was built into the overall system. As the *Guardian*'s Patrick Kingsley put it, "No single actor has overall control of all funding and management decisions in the camps, allowing most parties to distance themselves from blame."

The Get Shit Done team filled the holes with windows and doors.

Meanwhile, many refugees remained in tents inside cavernous warehouses with tin roofs and no insulation. When bad weather came, Jenni observed, a warehouse roof "only stops the rain hitting you. It doesn't stop the cold." And some warehouses were so dilapidated that rain poured through holes in the roofs, soaking tents and causing flooding. Many of these facilities lacked electricity, too, and, in any case, electricity didn't mean heat. "It doesn't matter how many huge heaters you're going to put in that bloody thing," Jenni told me, "all heat would disperse in a place like that and nothing would keep people warm."

Tensions rose among those providing relief, and even the grassroots community split into factions. Tracey described their debate. Activists would say, for example, "Fuck this law that [says] we can't host unaccompanied minors. We're going to put them in a house and look after them." On the other side, the volunteer faction decided to follow the law because otherwise, they said, "we'll get arrested and then we can't help anybody."

Tracey usually identified as a volunteer. Jenni preferred to call herself a "passive activist." The term made Tracey laugh, but Jenni was serious. "I've stood up for my rights. I've been on those first gay marches." But here in Greece, she believed she could be most effective through quiet action. "We all have different talents," she said. "I don't have great words, so there's no point in me trying to be vocal. I get too tongue-tied. But I can do this, and I can do it bloody well. Maybe the activists, if we swapped roles, I'd be shit at that, and they'd be shit at what I'm doing."

Tracey decided to call herself "an activist locked in a volunteer's body."

For Ibrahim, these conversations were academic. He understood the politics as well as anyone, but he refused to let his mind stray from the work at hand. Day after day, he found ways to funnel donation money into practical initiatives, like Jenni's efforts to make shelters warmer by adding insulation and drier by installing floors to lift them off the ground.

None of these efforts solved the overarching problem: a lack of political will to get people into decent long-term housing. When temperatures slipped below freezing, Jenni's floors and insulation reduced the cold only a little. People living in tents bought cheap gas cylinders in a desperate attempt to keep themselves warm. Jenni watched this trend with worry. All you need is a little leak, with the fire already going, she thought. Boom! They're gone.

Down south, in Lesvos, the worst happened that November. In Moria Camp, a gas cylinder exploded, killing a sixty-six-year-old woman and a six-year-old child. Fires soon spread through the facility, destroying dozens of tents. "We are not animals," one camp resident told Reuters after the tragedy. "We are human beings."

MEMBERS OF THE ANARCHIST MOVEMENT had played a major role in setting up Greece's squat system. Because their philosophy rejected mainstream humanitarianism, whenever staff from traditional NGOs showed up at the Single Men's Squat in Athens, residents were expected to shoo them away. Sami Malouf, who slept by the front door and spoke some English, became the gatekeeper.

But Sami had a good brain and four years of pent-up energy. He wanted to contribute more than that. Conditions in the squat were terrible and Sami could not see how the anarchists' rule about NGOs helped achieve the goal of reducing residents' suffering. We need support, he told himself, but these anarchists control our lives. He'd never heard that he wasn't allowed to *talk* to these visitors, so he did. "Sorry. You cannot be inside," Sami would say whenever an NGO staffer showed up. Once he had performed his duty, however, he kept the conversation going. He asked a lot of questions, collecting information about services available for displaced people in Athens.

Other residents of the squat saw Sami standing in the doorway, talking to these visitors. Soon they began to approach with questions of their own. "You talked to the NGO," one man might say. "Can they give me legal advice?"

"Yes," Sami would reply. "Here's the address. Go talk to them. They'll give you support."

Word spread through the squat that Sami had helpful information. More men began coming to him, asking for help on everything from mental health issues to medical complaints to problems related to their claims of asylum. Some had no legal documentation and they were basically hiding in the squat out of fear of being swept up by police and detained or deported. For these men, Sami called his new contacts at the NGOs, who recommended lawyers willing to assist. Then Sami realized that it didn't help to have the name of a doctor or lawyer if the men couldn't communicate with them. He began accompanying fellow squat residents to appointments and translating for them.

The young man threw himself into these new efforts, and he didn't regard himself as selfless, either. The Single Men's Squat was a place of squalor and desperation, where it was easy to lose hope. Some residents turned to alcohol and drugs. When Sami watched them straggle back into the building late at night, he told himself, I cannot do that. I cannot lose it. He had to use his time in a productive way if he was going to survive.

Sami enjoyed being busy. He liked meeting people and learning his way around Athens. After a friend in Germany sent him some money, he finally bought a phone. He felt pleasure every time it rang. Sami had essentially been "sitting," as he put it, for the last four years. He loved being outside in the world, feeling active. I want to do something, he thought.

Sami's presence was already having a significant impact on the life of those in the squat, but some of his fellow residents wanted to take it one step further. "Let's go to the kitchen," they said. The men scavenged wooden boards and nails, then helped Sami build a small table to use as a desk. After that, he spent regular hours in a corner of the kitchen that came to be known as his "office" whenever the kitchen manager didn't need the space to cook. Sami conversed with a succession of men who stopped by to talk about their troubles. He made phone calls on their behalf, gathered helpful information, became their informal caseworker.

It would take time for Sami's own asylum application to go through the process of approval. Until that happened, he was not allowed to take a paying job. But he had found a way to be useful. He volunteered.

Anyone observing the migrant crisis in Greece would notice that there was nothing uniform about the aid system. You could make yourself crazy thinking about unfairness. But who could resist? Was it fair that citizens of some countries lived in peace while war forced citizens of other countries to flee their homes? Was it fair that Europe was more willing to resettle Syrians than Afghans? Was it fair that some refugees shivered in tents while others slept in heated apartments? And why weren't heat and apartments considered baseline human needs? Was that fair?

In the balance between fair and unfair, and in this "everything is relative" world of displacement, the Khalil family now saw their own scale tip toward good fortune. They had managed to retain the studio apartment while their names—along with the names of so many asylum seekers—slowly ticked up some list. By late fall of 2016, they had reached the top, and the family heard news that would transport them from deprivation to stability: Germany had accepted their application for relocation. From now until the date that they traveled, they'd receive free accommodations in Athens.

All this good fortune came just in time, too, because Salma was pregnant.

The Khalils moved into their final residence in Greece. The apartment lay on a once-grand boulevard now dotted with student cafés, cheap clothing stores, and—this was, after all, an immigrant neighborhood—the flashy yellow logos of Western Union storefronts on nearly every block. It was a simple but decent apartment, paid for through the Greek NGO Praksis.

Abu Omar could finally feel secure, even though it wasn't an easy situation. The family of five shared the one-bedroom, one-bath apartment with a Kurdish couple and their two tiny children. The Kurdish family had the inner room. The Khalils had the living room, which doubled as sleeping quarters through the strategic placement of a bunk bed and a couple of twin mattresses that, for socializing, also worked as sofas. Then they waited. Nobody went to school or worked. Little Omar, walking now, zigzagged across the floor.

In the cramped apartment, the Syrian family and the Kurdish family generally kept to themselves. They neither socialized nor considered each other friends, but they lived amicably. Ethnic differences never caused the tension that could flare in camps and the squats. For the first time since fleeing their homeland, they had a decent place to live and no worry that lack of funds would put them back in a squat or, worse, on the street. This sense of security made everyone more generous. When the Khalils received a donation of winter clothes, they shared with their neighbors. When the Kurdish couple came by extra food, they passed it along to the Syrians. These were simple gestures of kindness, but they signified something monumental, too: Day by day, they were reconnecting with the civilized world.

CHAPTER 28

Different Kinds of Crimes

At Elliniko Camp, children showed up for Schoolbox sessions barefoot, even in freezing weather. They often became violent with one another. Kanwal didn't know what happened in the tents upstairs. Some of the kids seemed utterly distraught. They suffered in ways she couldn't begin to address.

But she could also see that her project was making a difference in these kids' lives. One day, she decided to encourage little Fatima to try skipping rope. The team had Farsi-speaking volunteers, so Kanwal paused the other children's skipping long enough to make a gentle announcement. "We're going to give Fatima a chance now."

The other kids quieted down. All attention focused on that one little girl as Kanwal explained the simple mechanics of the activity: "You come in and you start skipping."

"No. No!" the child replied. "Nooooooooooo!"

But Kanwal persisted. The children and volunteers waited. Maybe it was Kanwal's patience, or her quiet determination, or maybe the little girl just needed a tiny nudge. In any case, Fatima finally stepped tentatively out onto the grass. Two adults held the ends of the rope and, slowly, began to turn it. The rope rose into a high arc, then came down on the other side. Fatima leaped into the air and the rope slid beneath her feet.

"One!"

The rope began to climb again. The child braced her legs and made a second jump. The rope came down and she landed right on top of it.

You got one shot at skipping. If you missed, you had to wait in line for another turn. Kanwal wondered what Fatima would do.

The little girl had been observing this activity since Schoolbox first opened. She knew the rules as well as any kid there. Now she followed them like all the other children. She walked to the end of the line and waited quietly for another turn.

On her first try, Fatima skipped the rope once. On her second, she skipped twice.

Some days could renew your faith in humanity.

By December, Tracey Myers had left the troubled housing project and fully joined InterVolve, the small Greek aid team. InterVolve had received funds from the British charity Help Refugees to take children from a dozen camps to an expo called Winter Wonderland in Thessaloniki. The charity had even allocated money to distribute a special gift to each child. Tracey decided to make the project more meaningful—and infinitely more complicated—by making each gift personal. In the weeks leading up to the event, volunteers visited the camps and tramped from tent to tent, laptops in hand, showing parents a catalog of options and letting them pick out items that they thought their kids would love.

Over four days that winter, buses carried hundreds of children and their families from the camps to the expo, where they glided on an ice rink, played games, and spun around on rides. An InterVolve volunteer, dressed as Santa, handed the gift to each child. One day, Greece's prime minister, Alexis Tsipras, showed up at the event, swarmed by paparazzi—"like Beyoncé," according to Tracey. Children from camps presented him with handmade gifts.

As a practical initiative, the Winter Wonderland had questionable benefit. Northern Greece was enduring a horrible winter and thousands were suffering in the cold. Taking kids to the expo did nothing to improve their lives in camps. "It makes no rational sense in terms of need," Tracey admitted, but some efforts had a positive value you couldn't quantify. When she saw the delight on the faces of refugee children riding bumper cars, she thought to herself, It's a super nice thing.

TWO WEEKS INTO 2017, THE GREEK MILITARY announced that it would not permit the Schoolbox Project to continue its work at Elliniko Camp. The team had been operating there for only two and a half months. The reason for the rejection isn't clear. Was the government concerned that a Save the Children project presented a duplication of services? Was it punishment for the fact that a Schoolbox volunteer had brought in a dentist without permission? Whatever the reason, the Schoolbox Project would have to close.

Kanwal learned all this one morning as she prepared to go to camp. By the time she arrived, the children were already waiting in the courtyard, as usual, for the day's activities to begin. Over the past ten weeks, Kanwal had, with difficulty, earned their trust. She believed in full transparency with them, so she refused to hold back the bad news. At the end of the morning's first session, she invited the kids into one of the trailers for a meeting. Realizing that something unusual was taking place, they sat on the floor in uneasy silence.

With a Farsi-speaking volunteer translating, Kanwal used simple language that children could understand. She didn't talk about humanitarian aid strategies, trauma-informed care, or government contracts. She just explained that the authorities had asked Schoolbox to leave the camp. "None of us are happy about the decision," she said, then added her most important point: "I want you to know that you did nothing wrong. You are not the reason that we have to leave."

The children stared at her.

"We love you. We are so proud of you," Kanwal told them.

It took some time for the information to sink in. Then a hum of chatter in Pashto and Dari began to fill the space. All the children talked at once, their voices packed with emotion. The translator, doing the best she could, communicated their random reactions to the English-speaking adults.

"No way!"

"We won't let them!"

"We're going to protest!"

Anticipating their anger, Kanwal had timed her announcement for the moment before a break in sessions so that the children could absorb the news and then regulate themselves during quiet time between activities.

The attempt to maintain calm didn't work. When the volunteers reappeared at the camp an hour later, the children were pushing one another, shoving and biting, pulling hair. Kanwal had seen a good deal of wild behavior among these kids—"They are a right pain in the ass," she would say sometimes. But this scene was different. Some children seemed crazed with fury. Others sobbed. Their lives had been defined by loss and now, once again, they saw it looming up ahead. That day, a coat of snow covered the ground. The children hurled snowballs at Kanwal.

She stood there, head bowed, absorbing the pelting. I get it, she thought. I want to lash out, too.

That night, Kanwal took her sorrow to the Khalils' apartment. Over at her own place, the Halabi children—beloved as they were—created a throbbing mass of activity. Here, Kanwal could curl up on the mattress-cum-sofa and drink cardamom-scented coffee with Salma, or play UNO with Nura and Layla, or patty-cake with the baby. Hope filled the air in that room, and Kanwal needed hope right then. In these cramped quarters in central Athens, you could see it in the way that Salma held her belly, even though her pregnancy had not begun to show yet; and in the fastidiousness with which Abu Omar served oranges to his guest; and in the way that Layla, looking like she didn't have a care in the world, kicked back on the bunk bed and texted with a Syrian buddy on the other side of town, giggling at some moments and muttering "Stupid girl" at others, just like any adolescent who finds a friend mildly galling.

WITHIN THE ATHENS SQUAT COMMUNITY, word had spread about Sami Malouf's success as a volunteer translator. Eventually, Castro Dakdouk, the Syrian émigré and solidarity leader, invited Sami to a meeting in the big squat known as the Fifth School.

Castro recognized that Sami could be useful in the larger operation. The Fifth School served as the administrative center for an entire network of local squats. Castro, a native speaker of Arabic, was also fluent in

Greek, but his English was shaky and he felt bashful about speaking it. He believed that Sami could provide a useful service in the main office by helping him communicate with English-speaking volunteers. With that idea in mind, he made Sami a proposition: "If you want to translate at Fifth School, you can also live here."

Sami quickly packed his meager possessions and moved a few blocks up the road. No one would call Fifth School a nice accommodation. It was still a squat and, therefore, illegal, crowded, chaotic, and full of anxious people. It was practically a palace for Sami, however. Instead of huddling on a mat in a room with 30 people, he now slept in a small room with just a few other men and a door they could lock. Life was much more comfortable, and the work with Castro also allowed Sami to expand his connections in Athens. Suddenly, he got even busier.

One night in January, Castro called a general assembly for the children in the squat. It was 11:00 P.M., but they were all awake, as usual. Taking seats around the conference table, they looked like tiny board members, their faces somber, their bodies fidgety with anticipation. They had never attended a general assembly meant just for them.

Sami stood against a wall, watching the kids get settled. Small clusters were jabbering in Arabic, Farsi, and Dari. Then a Spanish volunteer opened the meeting. Speaking in English, she explained its purpose: The squat was providing academic instruction, but the children failed to attend the lessons. "The German teacher say, 'Why don't you go to class?'"

The kids stared at her, uncomprehending. Sami translated into Arabic, other adults into other languages. Once the kids understood the volunteer's words, they all responded at once.

Mayhem.

Whack-whack-whack! A no-nonsense young woman in hijab rapped a pen against the table. "One by one," she instructed. The translators repeated the phrase in all the different languages. The kids settled down.

One by one, the children introduced themselves in the language each spoke best. Taking turns, they gave their names, their ages, then declared what they would like to study. Most wanted to learn English, some German, some Greek. A twelve-year-old Somali girl announced that she'd been learning Arabic over YouTube and wanted to continue.

The students presented themselves as extremely excited about education. When the Spanish volunteer announced the schedule for lessons, they listened with eager attention. The roster of classes included English, Arabic, Greek, Spanish, Italian, French, and German. Students could study Arabic, for example, on Mondays, Wednesdays, and Fridays at 3:00 P.M. They could learn English on Tuesdays and Thursdays from 3:00 to 4:30.

The system wasn't working well in practice, however, because students didn't go to class. Now the Spanish volunteer looked around the table. "If you say you want to study a language," she told them, "why aren't you showing up?"

The translators translated. The children had no answer.

Castro, wearing an old army green jacket with a black-and-white kaffiyeh around his neck, sat at one end of the conference table. He listened, his expression conveying a mix of fatigue and annoyance.

The Spanish volunteer kept talking. She was an artist who had been painting murals with teens from the squat. The residents knew her well and she usually interacted in a cheerful, relaxed manner. Tonight, though, she looked stern. "You need to come to class, okay?"

The children stared at her, their faces serious. "Okay."

Then one boy piped up. "I didn't go to school," he said, "because I was sitting in the classroom and people made fun of me."

Suddenly, many of the children began articulating excuses. A few blamed parents, saying that they forbade the kids to study.

Castro had been listening closely without saying a word. Day after day, the solidarity leader searched for solutions to practical problems—securing food for a thousand people, organizing dental clinics, unblocking clogged toilets. Every effort took energy. Months earlier, he and Kanwal Malik had clashed over a single food distribution at the Second School. Castro engaged in similar dramas every day. Like so many others who had thrown themselves into the grassroots effort, Castro regularly pushed himself to mental and physical exhaustion.

And yet, injustice still inflamed him. When he finally spoke, every face turned to him. "Your mom is doing you wrong by not letting you go to school," Castro told one of the kids. "That's a crime."

Sami watched the discussion with interest. Before the meeting began, he had scoffed at Castro's plan to bring kids together in a general assembly. "Come on," he'd said. "What do you think they'll say?"

But Castro had shrugged off the skepticism. "Let them say what they want."

Now, Sami began to understand what this aging leftist was after. Castro believed that children should understand the value of education, even if their parents were too stressed or hopeless to pass along that value themselves. Watching the scene from his spot against the wall, Sami suddenly felt moved by the effort. *I don't think he's getting results*, he thought, *but at least he's doing it.*

THE SCHOOLBOX PROJECT CEASED OPERATION at Elliniko Camp, but Kanwal—always hopeful—tried to salvage the initiative. The shipping containers, or "schoolboxes," were portable by design. If she could find a viable new location, she could haul the trailers from Elliniko and start over. These days, in early 2017, a number of refugee camps dotted the outskirts of Athens. Certainly she could find a place that would benefit from a volunteer-run educational program.

One day toward the end of January, Kanwal climbed into a rental van with Rando Wagner, the volunteer and flight attendant. Rando knew all the migrant accommodations in the area and he'd offered to show Kanwal several potential new sites. "We're going to Elefsina," he told her, mentioning one of the day's destinations. "That's a shithole."

They left central Athens and entered industrial Greece. To their right rose a hillside dotted with olive trees and warehouses. To their left, a large tanker moved across the Gulf of Elefsina. Kanwal held on tight. Technically, Rando drove with skill, but seventeen months navigating Greek traffic had made him, like many locals, lax about the law. He made U-turns mid-block, veered around delivery trucks by whipping into oncoming lanes, and occasionally, for fun, raced other motorists down the highway. He did all this while chain-smoking, talking on the phone, and making regular stops at roadside gas stations to get refills of coffee.

"I'm turning into my father," he told Kanwal with an exuberant laugh. "He refuses to wear a seat belt. Now look at me."

Rando laughed a lot. His machine-gun *ha ha ha ha* was as much Rando as his bald head or his witty repartee, but he was dead serious about his work in Greece. Today, while taking Kanwal to search for a potential new Schoolbox location, he also planned to purchase food for distribution, pick up supplies at the airport, and transport a donation of winter duvets from a warehouse to a camp. On the road, Rando's rental vehicle doubled as his office. Now, as they passed the enormous Skaramagas Camp—"Scabbymagas," Rando called it—he was also on the phone, updating a colleague about registering vans brought over from the UK.

As Kanwal listened, it seemed to her that Rando could multitask at a level that would drive most people—herself included—totally insane. But he also seemed impervious to setbacks.

Kanwal was not. Her week had gone from bad to worse. The logistics of closing Schoolbox had demanded regular conversations with the project's founders in California. At the same time, she constantly had to update her team in Greece—international volunteers who had planned to work at Elliniko and now had no idea how to spend their time. Plus, she had to physically shut down the trailers, prepare them to be moved, and figure out what to do with all the supplies.

None of that compared, in terms of sorrow, to what had happened with the children. In the ten weeks after Schoolbox opened, little Fatima had learned to skip rope well enough to jump thirty times. The silent girl had actually entered the social life of children. Schoolbox had become a safe space for her. She had learned to listen and communicate with words instead of spit and screams. She had even formed friendships. But when Fatima heard that Schoolbox would close, she shut down. At first, she showed no reaction. And then, on the program's final day, Kanwal had squatted down beside the child to say good-bye. "I've got to go now. Can you come here?"

"No! NOOOOO!" The girl reverted to screaming that single word.

"Come on," Kanwal urged gently. "I'm going. Do you want to come and say good-bye to me?"

Fatima looked at Kanwal, then spat.

Kanwal and Rando visited two camps that day. She helped stuff a hundred or more duvets into the back of the van, then hauled them out again when they reached the point of distribution. She drank gas station coffee. She raced through a Lidl Market with Rando, stocking up on the crates of apples and bread and chocolate croissants that he would deliver to hundreds of migrants at an abandoned factory the following day. At Oinofyta Camp, she watched as a volunteer medic did an emergency check on Rando's aching tooth.

But neither of the camps would work for Schoolbox. They were too far from central Athens and the public transportation that volunteers relied on to get around.

Rando was right. Elefsina was a shithole. Kanwal would have been fine with a shithole. Elliniko Camp had been a shithole, too.

CHAPTER 29

First, Do No Harm

That January, I was in Athens when the Schoolbox Project shut down. Stephanie, Jen, Carol, and I—now formally calling ourselves Humanity Now—had traveled to Greece to visit grassroots teams and spend the money we had raised back home. For much of our time in Athens, we'd volunteered with Kanwal inside the Schoolbox trailers at Elliniko Camp. We were among the volunteers making paper snowflakes and helping kids skip rope when Kanwal learned that the project would have to shut down.

I wasn't surprised, then, when she told me later on that visit that she had nearly reached the end of her journey in Greece. When we first met the previous summer, she'd seemed exhausted every single day. Her responsibilities made her frantic at times, even physically ill, but I never saw her waver in her belief that she could do good there.

That winter, she wavered. During those cold weeks, Kanwal and I spent hours drinking tea in Athens cafés. For fifteen months, she had tried her best to help. Now, in these blustery days of January, she seemed done.

For volunteers, every day could drag you through a disorienting zigzag of emotion. I know because, even as a short-term visitor, I experienced it myself.

"So, you think you'll leave?" I asked.

Her expression showed both surrender and relief. Over a month would pass before she actually made her move, but she could already see it up ahead. "I'm ready to go home," she replied. "Emotionally, I need to stabilize myself again." She felt worn-out. She missed her life in England.

She missed her mom. "I cut myself away from my world and I need to retie the knots," she told me. "I need to just—" But then she stopped abruptly. She couldn't see what would come next for her.

I MET SAMI MALOUF IN ATHENS THAT JANUARY. Zakia, my translator, happened to chat with him one day when we were visiting Castro at the Fifth School. Later, she suggested that he and I meet. "Sami's a refugee volunteer," she explained. "You could learn a lot from him." So the three of us got together for dinner one night at a bistro a few blocks away.

Sami was the kind of guy who could look perfectly comfortable in almost any setting, whether that be in the crowded halls of a refugee squat or hanging out over dinner in a lively Athens restaurant. Compact and wiry, he had gentle eyes, a laid-back manner, and a scar on his cheek that suggested life had not always been easy.

That night, we drank a lot of beer and Zakia introduced us to some of her favorite dishes, like Cretan cheese and potato with spearmint. When I asked Sami about his resettlement plans, he shared the news that, unlike so many other refugees, he'd decided to settle in Athens. "Germany is boring," he said. "Greece is closer to my country."

A few days earlier, Zakia and I had visited the Single Men's Squat, where Sami had once lived. The men we met there seemed lonely and despondent. Afterward, I kept thinking of their extreme vulnerability, in contrast to Western stereotypes of Middle Eastern men as dangerous threats. I wondered how Sami felt about all that. "You're twenty-six years old, a man alone. People in the West might think you're a terrorist. How do you respond to that?"

At first, he didn't respond at all. He and Zakia went back and forth in Arabic. Eventually, Zakia said, "It's very self-explanatory for them."

I said, "Like, if someone said that I'm a terrorist, I might say, 'Why would you think I'd be a terrorist?'"

"Yeah. It would be so far from reality," Zakia said. "He can't answer the question because he doesn't get the question."

Every culture has its own conspiracy theories. Zakia told me that many in the Arab world believe that the United States and Europe created ISIS. Sami found Western suspicion of guys like himself to be completely baffling, particularly because his homeland had suffered so much bloodshed, often as a result of Islamic extremists. Western volunteers he worked with in the squats sometimes seemed surprised that he was an easygoing, normal person. Their surprise bothered him. "I don't understand why they'd think we'd have claws and big teeth, like monsters," he said.

That night, we spoke about the Single Men's Squat in general terms, but it wasn't until several years later, when Sami and I knew each other better, that he opened up about the psychic toll of living in that place. He and I were having dinner at the same bistro where we always met. Zakia hadn't been able to join us, but Sami's English had gotten so good that we no longer needed her.

"It's miserable," he told me, describing the squat's peculiar humiliations. "We didn't want people to see us living this life."

I realized that he was talking about the residents' reactions when people like me came by to visit. "You didn't want volunteers to see that?" I asked.

Sami nodded. He wanted me to understand how displacement undermines the confidence of people who had previously regarded themselves as respectable members of society. "Everyone's shy about this life," he told me. "Inside Single Men's Squat was nothing. People were sleeping shoulder by shoulder—that's what we say in Arabic, 'shoulder by shoulder'—and they were washing the clothes by hand because we don't have laundry."

Sami told me that squat residents refused to venture into the streets of Athens unless they had washed their clothes and made themselves look clean and neat. But it's difficult to wash clothes if you live among 150 men sharing two bathrooms. And how do you wash your clothes if you don't have another set to change into? Or if you don't have money for soap?

Residents of Single Men's didn't want to be mistaken for beggars in the streets.

"Was it a pride thing?" I asked.

Sami looked stumped. "What do you mean by 'pride,' actually?"

"Pride, like you didn't want to look like you needed help."

"Yes. Yes." He nodded. "We came from different countries where we had support. And we had people who cared about us. Even if it was war . . . we could sleep better than this situation. So, the people they start to get kind of mental issues—pretending we are fine, we are strong. Because they didn't want to look just like poor people and everyone said to them, 'Oh, sorry. I know you are poor people.'"

"They don't want pity."

He stared at me. "Pity."

"Yes. Pity is when people say 'Oh, poor you. Oh, I feel so sorry for you.'"

Sami sighed. "Yes. You find the word I don't know it." He stared out across the crowded restaurant. "We have proud in ourselves. Our ego is, like, big."

ONE DAY THAT JANUARY, I WENT WITH THE KHALIL GIRLS to the central shopping district near Monastiraki Square. The family's living space was now piled with packages of new underwear, nightgowns, and socks, the results of their efforts to stock up on cheap Greek brands before moving to more expensive Germany. I'd decided to buy a new coat for Nura, who'd been wearing a donated one with a broken zipper. After a few hours of strolling through the big chain stores, where the girls proved themselves avid shoppers, we found a cute pink coat at Zara that suited both Nura's taste and my insistence on finding something that would keep her warm through the German winter.

That evening, we walked to a souvlaki joint for dinner. The girls both spoke pretty good English by now, and I listened as they quibbled over details regarding the boat that had carried them from Turkey to Greece. When Nura said the boat was *this* big, pointing from one end of the restaurant to the other, her older sister shook her head and said, "No! *This* big," and proceeded to cut the boat's dimensions by half. In regard to other aspects of their experience, their recollections perfectly aligned: how long the Aegean crossing was supposed to take (two hours), how long it actually took (nine hours), and how scared they were that they would drown.

The girls were sleeping over that night at my hotel, and they wanted to get back so they could finish watching *Barbie: Life in the Dreamhouse* on my computer. When we walked out of the restaurant, however, the drizzle of the early evening had turned to heavy rain. For a while, we managed to stay dry by taking refuge under shop awnings, skittering from one to the next, but we still had blocks to go before we reached our destination. At one intersection, we stopped under a covered portico, assessing our plight. By now, water was rushing like a creek down the side of the road, collecting in deep pools at the corner. There was no way to get to the hotel without soaking ourselves and our feet. I looked down at Layla and Nura. I thought of their parents, back in that little apartment. Abu Omar and Salma had trusted me with their precious daughters and now I had to get them through this storm without delivering them home feverish or coughing. "What should we do?" I asked, looking out at the downpour. "Should we wait? Should we run?"

This question had dictated the girls' lives for years already. Neither of them wavered. They both said, "Run!"

On that winter visit, I flew north to Thessaloniki with Jen Maraveyias, one of my partners from Humanity Now. We took a taxi to Softex Camp, on the city's industrial outskirts, to meet Tracey Myers and Jenni James. Tracey was there when we arrived and stepped out of a warehouse office to greet us. "Hello!" she exclaimed, her manner as warm as I remembered from our days together at the Park Hotel. Eight months had passed since she and I had met at the border. Her hair color had changed from muted apricot to a more outspoken plum.

Greece had suffered through a grim winter. In Athens, we had seen plenty of snow, but that was nothing compared to Thessaloniki, where the January cold seemed almost Scandinavian. Black ice lacquered the sidewalks. Dirty drifts piled along the roadways, and you couldn't escape the bitter winds. Temperatures had stayed below freezing for days, which could mean disaster for people living in the unheated warehouses and tent camps of this region. Here at Softex, everything in sight was gray or brown or white—gray sky, brown buildings, white container housing, and snow everywhere. "Come inside," Tracey said, leading us into the office. She was still working with InterVolve and this small room and storage facility served as its headquarters at the camp. "No heat, unfortunately," she told us, sighing as she glanced at a couple of heaters mounted on the wall. "Those don't work."

From outside, we heard the grind of tires on ice, a groaning engine, someone yelling, "Hey, Tracey!" We walked to the doorway and saw a small blue-haired woman standing beside the open door of a truck. She tugged at some ropes, and three young dogs leaped out of the cab, jumping and barking beside her.

I'd never actually met Jenni in person, but I recognized her from her pictures on Facebook. The previous summer, our group had funded a bike-share project run by the Get Shit Done Team, and she and I had been messaging for months. Now, surrounded by dogs, her face showed the same delight that I found familiar from the many "Thank You, Donors!" videos she posted online.

Jenni led the dogs inside and unclipped their leashes. "Go for it, guys!" she said. The animals tore off across the floor, tumbled into a knot on a blanket, then raced around the table. "Sorry for this added bit of chaos," Jenni said, laughing, as she shook hands with me and Jen. It did make the scene more chaotic, but we were grateful for the dogs. They brought a burst of color to the gray afternoon. Jen squatted on the floor and tickled the black one's belly.

"How do you two have time for three dogs?" I asked.

"They're rescues," Jenni replied, as if the animals' need for a home was explanation enough. Tracey and Jenni had, quite literally, pulled the animals in off the street. They had gone out one day to deliver winter supplies to residents of an unheated camp. On the way back, they spotted a little dog curled under a streetlamp in the snow, taking what warmth it could from the electric light. The women were sharing an apartment at that time and so they scooped him up and took him home. They decided to call him Bear. A few days later, driving past the same spot, they found two more pups—"Bear's siblings," Jenni called them. These days, they were fostering not only Bear but also Raven and Tiger, while trying to find the dogs a permanent home.

Tracey watched Bear cavorting around the room. "I'm in love," she said, and then, as if admitting deficiency, added, "but he probably needs a more responsible mom."

Tracey seemed happy in her new position at InterVolve, whose philosophy aligned better with her own ideas about grassroots relief. The small team had begun to adopt the professional standards of mainstream humanitarianism, in part because larger NGOs refused to work with teams that didn't follow established codes of conduct. "I'm pleased about that," Tracey told us as we sat around the conference table, talking. On Lesvos Island and, later, at Idomeni Camp, unvetted volunteers had access to thousands of vulnerable children, creating what Tracey called "an abuser's playground." She could understand why grassroots teams had failed to screen volunteers during the early days of the crisis. They simply didn't have the resources to do it. "In emergency response," she said, "where you literally have people without shelter in the pouring rain, you're going to take [extra] hands to protect people." But times had changed and now even small organizations had an ethical responsibility to vet their team members. "In longer-term situations, there's no excuse not to do it."

This discussion reminded me of something a man named John Williams had told me back in 2006 while I was conducting research for *The Life We Were Given,* my book about Operation Babylift, the U.S.-sponsored evacuation, and subsequent overseas adoption, of displaced children from Vietnam. The evacuation took place in 1975, during the last few weeks of the war. International adoption agencies, several of which ran orphanages, selected children to airlift out and place with adoptive families overseas. The operation unfolded during a time of utter chaos, and it later became clear that agencies had made terrible mistakes and that some children were not legally eligible for adoption because they had birth families who wanted to raise them. The agencies with the worst records were mostly small grassroots organizations with little experience. In the confusion at the end of the war, they fell into a crisis mentality that led them to violate best-practice protocols, including simple record keeping. Their actions destroyed families.

These stories disturbed me, and I wrote that book in part to document what went wrong. But I also understood that the smaller agencies—run, in many cases, by grassroots volunteers—operated with minimal resources under extraordinarily difficult conditions. John Williams had worked as a professional staffer with a large, well-established agency. When I asked him if the wartime challenge lessened the smaller agencies' responsibility for errors, he told me that it did not. "If you don't have the resources, you shouldn't be doing it," he said.

Here at Softex Camp, Tracey Meyers was essentially saying the same thing. She was like a medical practitioner advocating a primary principle: First, do no harm.

LATE THAT EVENING, JEN AND I MET IBRAHIM KHOURY in a café downtown. It was a dark, crowded spot, full of young people relaxing over cocktails. We found Ibrahim alone at a table in the back, staring at his computer. The Syrian greeted us warmly, if somewhat shyly. This was Jen's first aid trip to Greece, and she had never met Ibrahim. He and I had corresponded occasionally since the previous spring, but I hadn't seen him since that visit at the Park Hotel. To dispel the awkwardness, we did what came most naturally to all of us. We dived into the work. There, in that sociable café, Ibrahim adjusted his laptop so that Jen and I could see it, then proceeded to click through spreadsheets, giving us a tour of Greece's grassroots aid movement, as seen through its financials.

In 2016 alone, grassroots teams had distributed over a million euros to refugee and migrant relief projects all over Greece, and Ibrahim had played a central advisory role in that process. Much of the money came from the British charity Help Refugees, but Ibrahim also helped many small teams like ours.

Tonight, Ibrahim saw reason for optimism. In Britain, *The Guardian* and *The Observer* had named Help Refugees a primary recipient of the newspapers' 2016 Charity Appeal, and the campaign garnered $650,000 for the NGO's relief efforts. Ibrahim was central to that allocation. Yet the grassroots effort rarely had a chance to fund anything beyond the requirements for basic human survival. I knew that Ibrahim, like me, dreamed of a day when grassroots money could fund precious extras, like Farsi-language children's books or sports equipment, but we weren't there yet.

We had not come to vent, though. We had come to give him money. Sometime around midnight, Jen and I trooped down a set of narrow stairs to the empty cellar below the café, sat down on a bench beside the bathroom, and did what we'd been doing all over Greece: With no one else in sight, we pulled piles of cash out of our money belts and counted out seven thousand euros. Then we recounted, and counted again, shoved the stacks into an envelope, walked back upstairs, and slipped it across the table to Ibrahim, looking more criminal than philanthropic.

Ibrahim thanked us, casually pushing the envelope into a pocket. He seemed to find the money infinitely less compelling than the effort to reduce suffering. He didn't try to hide his own frustration, either. "Last year, exactly, we were doing the same thing," he said, clicking through various computer files marked "request from groups," which included things like sleeping bags, flooring, apples, and shampoo. "Sleeping bags?" he muttered, staring at the screen. "Seriously?"

Still, he expressed no doubt that the funds would help. He seemed convinced that every problem had a practical solution, as long as you had the patience to find it. "There is always a way," he murmured, staring at his computer screen. "There is never 'There is no way.'"

It was satisfying to use our funding to improve life in camps, but pure joy was never possible in this business. Our most fervent wish was for camp residents to get off the ground and into beds, out of tents and into apartments, but that was someone else's job, not ours. Ibrahim performed triage, and then triage of the triage. That's why he spent so much time staring at spreadsheets in crowded cafés, crunching numbers, trying to figure out what, among the almost overwhelming deficiencies, he could afford to address.

- *Men Winter Shoes*: 500 size 42, 500 size 43

- *Warm Socks*: 5,000

- *Woolen Hats*: 5,000

- *Men Underpants:* 200 small, 500 medium, 100 large

- *Women Underpants:* 200 medium, 100 large

Which was more pressing, then, warm socks or woolen hats? Was it better to buy three hundred pairs of underpants for women, or eight hundred for men? Maybe half for the men and half for the women? Every single line on the spreadsheet required contemplation and decision.

"Can you think of an example of a mistake you guys made?" I asked.

Ibrahim rolled his eyes. "Plenty," he told me. "I can give you plenty of examples."

"Okay. Give me an example."

He started to laugh. "How *huge* do you want the mistake?"

CHAPTER 30

Lost and Found

K ANWAL MALIK BEGAN PREPARING TO LEAVE GREECE. The demise of the Schoolbox Project had left her angry at the Greek government and mad at herself for failing to keep the program running. Once again, she slipped into the cycle of helplessness and guilt that so many volunteers experience—anguish over her inability to change the situation, then regret that she hadn't done better.

She was ready to go home, but it would take time to untangle the knot of her life in Athens. Rima needed time to find new accommodations before Kanwal gave up the apartment. Kanwal decided, then, to make a quick trip back to Nottingham to see her family, then return to Athens to move out of the apartment and say her final good-byes. She booked a ticket for a 5:00 A.M. flight on a Saturday morning in late January. The night before she left, she joined the Khalil family at their apartment for dinner. Salma and Abu Omar had made a Syrian dish called *mahshi,* which required hollowing out kilos of zucchini and eggplant, stuffing the vegetables with meat and rice, packing them into a pot, and cooking the concoction for hours. It was an elaborate meal, but they all knew that within weeks their community would scatter across Europe. Every day seemed precious.

As they feasted, sitting on the floor in that spartan apartment, Kanwal talked about her return to England. They discussed the timeline for the Khalils to go to Germany. Layla and Nura wondered when they could finally return to school. A new anxiety coursed through the evening, too. They'd heard rumors that in order to get to Germany, they'd have to buy their airline tickets themselves. Where would the family get the hundreds, maybe even thousands, of euros they'd need to cover that cost?

All of which spoke to a more long-term worry: How would they afford Germany when they already struggled so much in Greece? Salma often returned to the apartment with clothes for the baby or sweaters for the girls, all bought at shops near Omonia Square that offered basic goods at prices they could manage.

Abu Omar didn't even have a winter coat.

"Don't buy one," Kanwal told him over dinner. "I'll bring you a good coat from London when I come back."

Kanwal had an early flight to catch, but they lingered for hours. Flu season had arrived and all of them were sniffling and sneezing. Abu Omar brought out a huge bowl of oranges and they loaded up on vitamin C while playing UNO, a game at which they had all become expert by now. Finally, Kanwal had to leave.

They didn't make a big deal out of that good-bye. They expected to see one another again in a week.

KANWAL LEFT FOR ENGLAND ON A SATURDAY. On Monday, January 30, 2017, the Khalils received a phone call from a Greek Asylum Service official who relayed the news. "You are accepted into Germany."

The family had been waiting to hear these words for months. And there was more good news: They didn't have to buy their own tickets.

But the official added an unexpected addendum: "You're leaving in five days."

Five days?

Within hours, open suitcases were scattered across the floor. Packaging for underwear lay in cellophane heaps alongside discarded plastic hangers, slips of receipts, and the foot-shaped paper cards that come inside new pairs of socks. The baby climbed over all of this, crashing into piles of donated coats and hats and scattered shoes as his parents and sisters asked themselves, one more time, the same persistent question: What can we take with us? They knew about baggage limits. They sorted their worldly possessions into stacks: the things to pack, the things to give to their Kurdish neighbors, the things they would pass along to friends remaining in Athens. Theirs was a transient community. Each move shifted stuff from one hand to another.

Abu Omar had yearned for this moment, but he felt no joy once it arrived. His family had tumbled down a deep hole, finally coming to rest in the soft arms of Athens. Here in Greece's capital, the Khalils had begun to feel human again, and they felt distressed about leaving. Five days was not enough time to say good-bye. A parade of friends rushed to the apartment, shook their hands, and hugged the children. The family telephoned Kanwal in England to share the news that they'd be gone when she returned.

Over a year had passed since the Khalils had escaped their homeland. They had hoped and lost hope, trusted and lost trust. They had stood at the border and sobbed. They had panicked. They had fought to keep their children alive. They had given and they had received. They had used their last diaper, spent their last euro, eaten their last disk of bread, then somehow managed to acquire more. It was an extraordinary success story, really, if you chose to look at it like that. Yet they had lost nearly everything in their lives except their family, including their home, their livelihood, their possessions, and their country. Every day now, their hearts breaking, they watched from a distance as their homeland shattered. They had pined for Syria and longed for Europe.

Now they passed their last few days in Greece. They got their papers stamped, underwent their official health assessments. Harried and uncertain, they packed unnecessary items and left behind things that they would later need. At the Athens airport, Salma realized that she had forgotten her prenatal vitamins, so they spent sixty euros for a taxi so that their neighbor could bring the bottle from their apartment. They forgot Salma's pregnancy records, the children's vaccination reports, and their phone chargers, which meant that, once they landed in Germany, they would have dead phones and no way to inform their families that they'd arrived. "Every time we wanted something," they later told me, "we realized we had left it in Greece."

But they got to the Athens airport in time for their departure, Layla's and Nura's heavy backpacks straining against their shoulders. Salma, pregnant, exhausted, and feeling sick, gripped the baby. Abu

Omar huffed and puffed to get six suitcases through the terminal. They barely had time to think. It was a mixed-up, chaotic rush to get on that plane. Maybe the day could have gone more smoothly, but it seemed fitting that it mirrored the mixed-up, chaotic rush of everything that had come before it.

They checked their bags, went through security, and showed the papers that, finally, allowed them to continue on through Europe.

And then, just like that, they flew to Germany.

KANWAL MALIK HAD PROVIDED THE HALABI FAMILY a home for over four months. After Kanwal gave up that apartment and returned to England, Rima got lucky again. A second generous volunteer helped out with rent in a different apartment. It was tiny and barren. Rima and her kids slept on mats on bare floors. But they had a roof over their heads. For that, Rima felt very grateful.

They waited through the rest of that winter and into spring. When she recalled Uncle Kareem's advice back in Syria, it sounded almost ridiculous: Musa and Malika would flee first. Rima would have her baby, then escape with the rest of the kids. Within a few months, they'd all reunite in Germany. So simple!

More than a year and a half had passed since that day in August of 2015 when Musa and Malika left al-Dana, splitting the family in two. Rima and five of the children now waited in Greece. Musa and Malika waited in Germany.

Every day, the couple talked on WhatsApp. The calls kept their spirits up. They discussed their daily dramas, like any other parents raising kids together. Not that Rima shared every detail with her husband. She never told Musa that women were harassed in the squat or that people used illegal drugs and drank alcohol there. Such information, she knew, would only upset him. She focused on other news instead, like the home they'd made in Kanwal's apartment. She described the children's growth, the funny things they said.

Throughout these months, Rima often worried less about the kids in Greece than she did about Malika, who was alone in Germany with her dad. Rima and Musa had been married for a long time. His years working abroad had inured the couple to long separations, but Rima had never been away from Malika. The child, nearly a teenager now, was making the transition from girlhood into adolescence without her mom. In Rima's mind, Malika suffered more than anyone in the family. Without her mother or siblings nearby, she was on her own, adjusting to a new life in a place where she didn't speak the language or understand the culture. Of course, Musa, as a father, cared deeply about his daughter, but his anxiety about the rest of the family made him lash out at her sometimes. Once, while talking with Musa on the phone, Rima heard Malika in the background say something to her dad. "Leave me alone," Musa snapped at her in reply. "I'm thinking of them."

Rima waited. She had a lot of time to think, a lot of time to talk to other worried Syrians and consider the stories spreading through the refugee community. One of those stories worried her most, and that was the rumor that Europe would begin denying applications for family reunification. When Rima thought about this possibility, she became distraught.

SPRING CAME TO ATHENS, WHICH BROUGHT RELIEF from the cold, but the warmer weather also brought scabies and bedbugs to the squats. At the Second School, the situation got very bad. Up and down the building's hallways, in their tents, and out in the courtyard, children scratched at red, blistered sores that covered the insides of their elbows, their genitals, and the skin between their fingers and toes. Adults suffered, too, but they tried not to claw themselves in public.

The solidarity leadership team dispatched a doctor, who asked Sami Malouf to come along to translate. Sami had never lived at the Second School himself, but he was intimately familiar with the life of squats, first from sleeping on the floor at Single Men's and, more recently, at the Fifth School. The move to better accommodations had improved Sami's physical comforts considerably, but he felt more isolated, too. Because the Fifth School mostly housed families, a young man like Sami couldn't easily find companionship there. People mostly sought him out for help or information. Without many friends, Sami staved off loneliness through volunteering.

The Second School that Sami's little medical team entered that day wasn't all that different from the one that Kanwal Malik had walked out of a few months before. Tents filled the classrooms upstairs. Children played in the courtyard with foreign and Greek volunteers who came by to skip rope or do art activities or teach classes. To a large extent, these were different residents, different volunteers, different children from the ones that Kanwal had known, but the needs remained as overwhelming as ever.

Sami and the doctor explained to the residents the reason for their visit. The mention of scabies and bedbugs, however, immediately made people hostile.

"Do you think we don't shower?" one asked, clearly offended. "Do you think we're dirty?"

Sami responded with public health information. "This is not about showers. This is about insect eggs that get under your skin." He pulled out pictures of scabies mites and bedbugs. He explained that these situations easily occurred in places where people lived in close proximity to one another.

Factual information did not appease the residents' suspicion. The outbreak humiliated them, and they refused to admit to a problem. Someone yelled, "Get out of here!"

The little medical team kept trying. "This has nothing to do with showering," the doctor said. "You need cream to deal with it. You'll need to throw everything out." The two men walked into the building and began making the rounds from floor to floor. They talked to people in the hallways, in the classrooms. Whenever they saw anyone, they shared basic information. To combat the epidemic, they explained, people should do two things. First, they had to treat themselves with a topical cream to kill the mites and their eggs. Second, they should throw out all their bedding so as not to infect themselves again.

Resistance continued. In one room, a woman began yelling. "Who are you to come in here? Do you think we're dirty people?"

Sami stayed calm. "I think you might have scabies. This can happen in sensitive areas of your body. It will make you itch."

The woman heard him, but she remained adamant. "It's not your job," she said. "Get out of here."

Sami felt discouraged. How could they help if people refused assistance? The little team continued through the building, speaking with anyone they could find. After they visited every room, they descended the school's grand marble staircase and emerged into the courtyard below. Then they looked up. In all the tent-filled classrooms, people had shoved open the large windows and begun to toss out their bedding. Sheets, blankets, sleeping bags, and towels were now toppling out the windows, landing in heaps on the asphalt below. Sami and the doctor looked at each other. People had listened after all.

The cleanup continued. Downstairs, the medical team opened their clinic. A line formed quickly. The first person in line was the woman who had yelled at Sami upstairs. Her manner had softened considerably. "Thank you," she told him. "I just felt embarrassed. I was itching, but I thought I had allergies or something. I didn't know it could be scabies."

"I'm not judging you," Sami told her. "I'm just trying to give you information."

The day ended successfully. The doctor handed out scabies cream and treatment for bedbugs, too. When Sami wasn't translating for patients, he helped haul the mounds of debris to the trash.

The doctor, watching Sami, offered a warning. "You're going to get it, too."

Sami wasn't concerned. "I'll be fine."

The doctor laughed. "Now you're sounding like them. You'll see."

And, indeed, later that day Sami started itching. By the time he returned to his own room at the Fifth School, he was carrying scabies cream to rub on the blistery rash that had broken out all over his body.

Sami's job as a translator threw him into the middle of everything. If there was an infection or virus going around the squats, he caught it. Scabies was hardly the worst. One day, he translated at a medical appointment while holding two sick kids on his lap. Soon he began feeling weak and achy, then developed a fever. He lay in his bed at the Fifth

School, miserable. One of the volunteer doctors, a British woman, came in to see him.

"This is really bad," she said. He'd caught chicken pox, a disease that's usually mild in children but capable of causing serious problems in adults, including pneumonia, sepsis, and encephalitis. Sami looked at the doctor. His body was covered in itchy red welts. "Just shoot me," he told her.

The next day, when she checked on him again, he felt even worse. "This is really hell," he said.

Now the doctor grew worried. To avoid serious complications, Sami needed more medical attention than she could provide at the squat. She took him to a local clinic for treatment. The bill came to three hundred euros, which Sami—who couldn't even buy himself a cup of coffee—didn't have. The British doctor paid the bill herself, gathered the medicine for him, then took him back to the squat. "You just need to rest," she told him. To protect others from infection, he had to stay in his room.

Sami's illness caused a change in the way people regarded him at the squat. Suddenly, he wasn't just the guy who spoke English anymore. Residents began to see him as someone who needed help. People who'd had chicken pox as children, and therefore had developed immunity to the disease, began to appear at his room, bringing food and tea. They played cards with him, or just stopped by to visit. One day, a Greek volunteer came by the room and sat with him, rubbing cream onto his sores. Suddenly, Sami couldn't help himself. He started to cry. He had never asked anyone for help, and now, when he found himself in need, people came through for him. Tears running down his face, he thought, I'm not alone.

After Sami finally recovered, he decided to leave the relatively cushy digs at the Fifth School and return to the Single Men's Squat. He would continue translating for the entire squat community, but he wanted to live with his closest friends, men like him. Within the world of refugee relief, single men were often the last to receive assistance, and their isolation had grave consequences. Sami felt that by living among these particularly vulnerable people he could have a positive impact that went beyond translation.

So Sami carried his things back down the hill to the Single Men's

Squat. Before he could settle in, he went out scavenging and found wood pallets to keep himself off the dirty, mildew-covered floor. That night, he settled into his old spot on the ground near the door, surrounded once more by seven other men. Lying there, he breathed the same stale air. He listened to the old men's familiar coughing and wheezing. He thought about everything he'd experienced in the months of his absence and about how little had changed right here. One thing was different, however. He had a better blanket now.

CHAPTER 31

All Else Failed

I N MAY 2017, SEVERAL MONTHS after Kanwal returned to England, I traveled to the UK for work and had a chance to visit her. In Nottingham and the surrounding area, she played tour guide, shepherding me to the grand old Chatsworth House, through landscape that looked like a setting for *Robin Hood,* and out for a ploughman's lunch at Ye Olde Trip to Jerusalem, purported to be the oldest pub in Britain. Meeting each other far away from the refugee communities of Greece, we realized that we shared a weakness for storybook versions of England.

But this place was home for Kanwal, too. I stayed with her in the pretty brick house that she'd bought after her first split from Asad. We shopped at her favorite South Asian market and spent an evening with her mom, the formidable Robina, who cooked us a Pakistani feast. I won't say that Kanwal seemed entirely different from the woman I'd come to know in Athens, but she seemed grounded in a way that is difficult to achieve far from home, and almost impossible if you are also trying to provide humanitarian relief to displaced people.

One morning, sitting in the sunny parlor of her house, I asked Kanwal if she felt that her time in Greece had been worthwhile.

"Yeah," she said, "I think it's invaluable. I don't think I could ever, ever . . ." She stopped and, gazing out toward her back garden, her thoughts seemed to shift. "There's some things that I think, Should I have done that differently? Should I have formed such close relationships?"

I thought of Kanwal's sparsely furnished Athens apartment, the mats on the floor where Rima and her children had slept. Kanwal said, "I didn't want it to be a relationship of dependency. It should always be about empowerment." And then she looked at me and smiled grimly. "That's me questioning myself."

Kanwal treasured the friendships she'd made. She hoped they'd last for life. But the intensity of these relationships—and perhaps the experience of living in tight quarters with so many kids—had deepened her sense of her own needs. "One of the things that hit me is that I do want a family of my own," she said. "I'd like to have children. [In Athens] I felt as though I needed companionship. Sometimes it got very, very lonely."

In Nottingham, she had started to look for work and reconnect with local friends. I could tell that her attention had shifted from Greece to her own hometown.

"If I had the means to continue, to go back [to Greece], I would," she said at one point. Then she added an amendment that didn't sound so certain: "I possibly would."

"You're not sure," I suggested.

Kanwal shrugged. "I'm not sure. Yeah."

WORKING WITH HUMANITY NOW, I spent most of my time among volunteers. On my visits to Greece, however, I also sought out government officials and humanitarian professionals. I wanted to understand the aid system as a whole and I knew that I could learn from them. After all, money from grassroots teams would always be supplemental. We could make effective targeted investments with the contributions of fifty or one hundred dollars sent by our donors, but it was nothing compared with the money spent by the large international actors. Between 2015 and the end of 2020, the European Union would have provided Greece with €2.81 billion.

That was a mind-boggling amount of money, and, from the perspective of many volunteers, these larger actors had largely failed to spend it effectively. But I wondered how professionals gauged the response. Did they consider their efforts to be more successful than volunteers did? Sometimes, their answers surprised me.

One of the most interesting conversations I had on this subject had taken place earlier in 2017, on my January visit to Thessaloniki. An aid professional from a large international NGO agreed to meet me for a drink one evening at around 6:00 P.M. The first thing that struck me when I arrived at the restaurant was that she was already there, sitting at a table, finishing up a big meal. As an American, I'd trained myself to follow Greece's later hours. People seldom broke for lunch before 3:00 P.M. At night, crowds started filling restaurants around nine or ten.

"Early dinner?" I asked, pulling up a chair.

She shook her head. "Late lunch." She hadn't taken a break all day.

Volunteers—whose work earned them, at most, a stipend—sometimes imagined that professional aid workers spent their time in fancy office suites, taking long lunches. This professional—a young Greek woman—seemed as overextended as any volunteer. In fact, the major difference between her and grassroots aid workers was the fact that she needed permission from her organization to speak to me on the record. Because she didn't have it, she asked that I not use her name.

The professional had an extraordinarily broad understanding of the situation in Greece and expressed as much anger over the official response as the most furious volunteers. "NGOs' intervention, it's more than a year. It's almost two years now," she said, summarizing the history of the effort: "Sorry, it's crap."

"Are you seeing self-reflection in the system?"

She started to laugh. "I can't find many NGOs that did this 'self-reflecting.' I haven't seen any contemplating 'What are we doing wrong here?' Most of them are very . . . How do you say this?" She paused, then hit on the English word. "Defensive."

"Defensive?"

"Yes. 'We are trying our best.'"

She launched into failures and their accompanying excuses:

Vulnerable people in camps lacked secure housing. "Oh! We cannot find any hotels. We cannot find apartments."

But volunteer teams were finding alternative housing. "But they don't need to follow [standard procedures]."

Finally, exasperated, she pretended to lecture her own colleagues: "Then *collaborate* with them," she sputtered.

To some degree, the humanitarian predicament in Greece wasn't a conflict between professionals and amateurs. It resulted, rather, from the fact that several systems—each with its own strengths and weaknesses—lacked a mechanism for moving forward together. A hundred different generals were each fighting a separate battle. Together, they were losing this war.

Back in Greece the following summer, I spoke with other officials. One day, I visited Gelly Aroni at the Greek Ministry of Education in Athens. Aroni served as the administrator charged with setting up a system for displaced children to go to school. I didn't get the sense that she took lunch breaks, either. In her dim office on an upper floor of the ministry building, she described a wide range of hurdles, from the challenge of registering children who were continuously on the move to the need to address the concerns of Greek parents, some of whom balked at the idea of having their children attend the same schools as refugee kids. "We had no idea," she told me, "how humongous the task would be."

At UNHCR headquarters in Athens, I met with two officials, Boris Cheshirkov and Leo Dobbs. Their assessment of the migration situation in Greece over the past few years echoed what I'd heard from everyone else, professionals and nonprofessionals alike: The international community had been slow to respond to the growing emergency, and, especially in the summer of 2015, much of the relief burden had fallen to the "goodwill and selflessness," as Cheshirkov put it, of volunteers. Looking back on that period, he said, "There's no debate. In the summer of 2015, volunteers were the response."

Dobbs said, "It was all a bit of a mess early on, really."

In the minds of these UNHCR professionals, the rise of volunteerism indicated failure, not success. They were less interested in how the small-scale grassroots movement presented new, flexible models for aid and more interested in how the situation in Greece revealed shortcomings within larger institutions. Speaking of the international community's slow response to the influx of refugees, Dobbs asked, "Why wouldn't they think that this could happen? Because Turkey, Lebanon—they're not very far away, really. . . . When you look back, you think they should have tried to boost that capacity years earlier." The two men seemed gratified that volunteers had stepped forward to take up the slack, but they didn't draw many lessons from it. For one thing, how would volunteerism scale up? The people who set up soup kitchens on Greek islands were unlikely to provide a similar response in, say, South Sudan. "If anything," Cheshirkov told me, the drama in Greece "has reaffirmed the need for strong humanitarian structures." By that, he meant large international organizations, like UNHCR.

But in Greece, the international organizations had not met the challenge. It was true that the grassroots model could not be replicated all over the world. Here in Europe, though, when all else failed, it was volunteers who made the difference.

I HADN'T SEEN TRACEY MYERS AND JENNI JAMES since earlier that year, on that bitterly cold January day when we talked at Softex Camp while three zany pups raced around our feet. When I saw them again that July, the pups had new homes and summer had arrived in full force. After touring camps in the north, we took an afternoon off and went swimming at my hotel.

Even then, on a sunny patio overlooking the sea, our conversation kept tracking back to the misery of the camps and the responsibility that volunteer teams had taken to improve conditions. By this point, nearly two years had passed since the spike in arrivals in Greece. Jenni, as a volunteer, kept hoping that the government would improve basic infrastructure, allowing her Get Shit Done Team to focus on quality-of-life projects, such as building small libraries or community centers. That rarely happened.

"We were asked to put in the gravel for the Nea Kavala camp," Jenni said, offering an example of a project that she considered the responsibility of the Greek government. "Should we be doing this? Why should we have to be putting in drainage?"

We were lounging on sofas by the pool. Jenni took a sip of water, then looked at me, a plaintive expression on her face. "Why should we have to be doing toilets to make them work properly?"

Tracey, sitting beside her friend, muttered, "Why?"

Jenni had a whole list of projects that, in retrospect, seemed totally ridiculous for her to have taken on. "Why should we have to be making taps so water can come out of them properly? Why should we have to be stopping the flooding? Why?"

"The accountability in this whole mess," Tracey said, "is just totally absent."

Both women seemed shaken by the failures of mainstream humanitarianism, but while Jenni reacted with frustration and distress, Tracey sounded more prosecutorial. "And this is on the physical, infrastructure side," she told me. "On the other side, like, Chloe, our director at InterVolve, why is she responsible for burying people? And having big NGOs phoning her up, going, 'Can you set up this funeral? We can't.'"

THE HALABI FAMILY WAITED IN ATHENS that summer. Day after day, the little ones chased each other through the empty apartment. Mischievous Lina tugged at her baby sister's hair. Shakira slept through the morning and much of the afternoon, then sat in a corner, texting with other teens she knew in Athens. Sometimes, fellow refugees came by to visit. Sometimes, Rima took her family out for a neighborhood stroll, but they lived on an upper floor. It took a lot of effort to get all of them, including two toddlers and a stroller, down to the street and then back upstairs. Many days, they didn't leave at all. To bring a bit of breeze into the hot apartment, Rima opened the door to the balcony. The little ones stood there, leaning on the railing, barefoot and in their pajamas, staring down at the street below.

Toward the end of summer in 2017, the family received the news that Rima had prayed for: Germany had approved her reunification application. Finally, she would see Musa and Malika again. For the Halabis, *reunification* wasn't even the correct word. Germany's decision would unite this family—including baby Oma—for the very first time.

Rima could not let this moment pass unobserved. A less social being might have quietly celebrated alone in that apartment, but Rima needed other people to share her joy. On the day she got the news, Rima gathered the children together, hauled the stroller down the stairs, bundled the baby inside, and went to a nearby bakery. For the past few months, she'd been surviving on a cash-card stipend allotted to asylum seekers by the European Union. Now she spent some of her meager funds on sweets. The family then marched to the Second School, the only community they had known in this country. When Rima and her children arrived with their news and all the treats, the place erupted in celebration.

On the first morning in August, Rima woke early and nudged her children out of bed. For over a year and a half, the consummate Syrian homemaker had been forced to lower her standards in every way. Today, however, she would make her family beautiful. One by one, she bathed the younger ones, scrubbing the grit from around their necks and under their arms, ignoring their complaints and squeals. Both of the little girls had fine, curly hair that easily tangled. After she gave them each a shampoo, she combed out the knots, then pulled their hair into neat ponytails. Next, she turned to the boys, gripping their chins in her hands and brushing their unruly bangs across their foreheads. She dressed them in their nicest clothes, touched up the girls' faces with eyeliner and lipstick, then admired pretty Shakira, the girl's hijab now neatly tucked around her head. They all looked good. They smelled good. They were ready. When the moment came to leave, Rima corralled her family together, zipped closed her five suitcases, and set off for the airport. Because they had so much luggage, they left the stroller behind. Throughout the journey, Rima held little Oma in her arms, handing the child to Shakira only when they arrived at the airport and had to check in. It was a complicated, fussy effort to get the children and all their belongings onto the plane, but Rima sailed through. Every single moment she felt calm, infused with joy.

Hours later, after their plane touched down in Germany, Rima and the children stepped out of the security zone and found Musa and Malika waiting. Lina and the boys, in their excitement, practically knocked their father over. Shakira, a demure teenager now, gave Musa a shy hug. Rima took Malika into her arms and felt how time had transformed her scrawny daughter. The girl had grown tall, gained weight. She was nearly a woman now.

A few feet away, Musa held Oma, who was nearly two. An airport arrival hall is, almost by nature, a place of reunion and jubilation. Passing strangers might not have realized that something spectacular was happening here. In that busy lobby, a father finally met his little girl.

WEEK BY WEEK, SAMI MALOUF PIECED TOGETHER a life out of the bits of opportunity he found in Athens. After three years in hiding in Syria and one year incarcerated in Greece, he felt the rapture of freedom every day. He applied for asylum, and the government seemed willing to expedite his application as a sort of reparation—if not apology—for the time he'd spent in prison. While he waited, he ruminated about the future. Sami had prepared for a professional life at sea, but the world had changed and he sensed that he would struggle, as a refugee, if he tried to have a career that required that kind of travel. He decided, then, to concentrate on his blooming English skills. He prepared a résumé and began sending it around to NGOs. None would hire him without a work permit. "If you have papers, you're human," he told me. "Without paper, you're not human." He continued to volunteer, biding his time until the day when he could become human again.

That day arrived in the summer of 2017, when Greece approved Sami's request for asylum. Now he could look for paying jobs. One small social service agency agreed to consider his application. They had an opening for a counselor to work with displaced teens and young adults. The position was still considered "volunteer," but it came with a stipend. More important, it provided staff with free accommodations. If he got the job, Sami could move out of the Single Men's Squat and into a real apartment.

But then he saw the application. Instead of requiring him to fill out detailed forms, it merely requested, in an email, that Sami respond to three questions.

He read through them. These are three stupid questions, he thought. But he had nothing to lose, so he answered them.

1. *What is the meaning of society?*
   Come to the Single Men's Squat. We have 12 different cultures there.

2. *What would you do with young people ages 16 to 21?*
   Teach them something educational.

3. *What would you do if you couldn't achieve your goal?*
   I'm a refugee. My life was destroyed. I know how to deal with this.

Sami got the job.

PART V

When the Sun Rises

CHAPTER 32

Help Shouldn't Be a Brain Thing

In the fall of 2017, Humanity Now funded a playground that Get Shit Done was building at Sinatex, a small camp near Thessaloniki that sheltered about a hundred Kurds. At one point, Jenni sent us a photo of the work in progress. It looked wild and ambitious: a single interconnected climbing structure, all built from salvaged lumber, tires, rope, and plywood. She called it the "Dinosaur Playground," and, though we didn't actually know what that meant yet, a "sneak preview" photo showed a bright green cartoon brontosaurus painted across three plywood panels.

I later learned that the Dinosaur Playground represented a single bright spot during a period when the Get Shit Done Team had become mired in challenges. Donations had declined and the crew now mostly supplied labor to other teams who had funds but lacked the expertise to complete their projects. In some sense, these collaborations demonstrated the value of combining resources, but it also meant that Jenni's team wasn't mapping its own future. With sufficient financing, they could continue taking on infrastructure projects while also providing quality-of-life enhancements for residents of camps—supersize wooden chess sets, kid-height Jenga towers, handmade wooden scooters. Even in a funding crunch, Jenni's volunteers never ran out of discarded wood to repurpose creatively, but they lacked money to do much more.

And then a new manager took over the warehouse where Jenni ran her shop. He was a Greek guy, the only nonvolunteer in the building, and he immediately moved to exert control over the small NGOs housed there. From Jenni's perspective, "it was very clear he had a problem with women." He clashed not only with Jenni but also with the female leaders of a neighboring aid team. Soon he and Jenni were barely on speaking terms. Even an attempt at mediation did nothing to help. One day in late fall, he gave Jenni a week to clear her workshop out of the warehouse.

For over a year now, Jenni's team had been beating the odds in this country. A million mosquitoes? They got rid of them. Housing with holes in it? They installed doors and windows. Rainwater flooding people's tents? They built wood floors. But now Jenni faced a problem she didn't know how to fix.

The year was rolling to a close. Soon she would be heading back to New Zealand for her annual break. When the warehouse manager ordered Get Shit Done off the premises, Jenni made up her mind to shut down her team entirely.

Jenni had one more project she wanted her crew to finish, though. Over those remaining days, the team threw everything they had into the Dinosaur Playground. Her carpenters completed the process of turning a pile of leftover lumber into a multitiered climbing structure. Painters put the last touch-ups on the brontosaurus panels, attaching bright green ones to one side of the structure and a hot pink set to the other. They built a sand pit. They fastened old tires together to form a climbing wall and attached another tire to a length of chain to make a swing that hung from the dinosaur's mouth. Just before Christmas, the volunteers hosted a party for the families of Sinatex Camp. Each child received a gift, but the greatest excitement came from the playground itself. Soon kids were jumping into the sand pit, scrambling up the tire ladder, flying through the air on the swing.

And with that, the Get Shit Done Team ceased operation. The crew pulled down the bulletin boards that they had used for scheduling, disassembled worktables and boxed up the saws, swept the last piles of sawdust off the floor, and hauled out the final load of trash. Before leaving Greece, Jenni made one last drive across the region. She followed the same rural routes to far-flung camps that she had taken so many times already, but now she wasn't visiting to make improvements. She was saying good-bye and distributing her team's remaining machines and tools to small workshops now operating within the facilities themselves. Nothing got wasted.

Two and a half years had passed since Jenni flew to Lesvos for a stint of volunteering. Now that period of her life had ended in the span of a few short weeks. When Jenni spoke with me later about the demise of Get Shit Done, she made no effort to hide her anger and sorrow. "It was a horrible way to finish," she said.

THE YEAR 2018 BEGAN MUCH LIKE 2017 HAD, with cold weather and thousands living in precarious accommodations and squalid camps. One gray afternoon that winter, not long after Jenni returned to New Zealand, I wandered through downtown Thessaloniki with Tracey Myers and my partner Jen from Humanity Now. Tracey was still working with the small Greece-based aid team InterVolve, which was about to launch its biggest venture yet. For an organization born out of humanitarian crisis, this project signaled a major shift in strategy—from responding to emergency to addressing chronic, long-term need. A few weeks earlier, the team had opened the Irida Women's Center, a permanent facility that occupied several floors of a downtown office building. Open to any woman but specifically geared toward the city's rapidly expanding immigrant population, the center offered a wide range of activities, including language classes, legal aid, psychosocial support, creative and culinary activities, and even yoga.

That afternoon, Tracey had given Jen and me a tour of the new facility. Even though it had only just opened, it already had a homey, lived-in appearance. Children's watercolors covered walls. In one hallway, dozens of artfully decorated "leaves," all cut in the shape of people's hands, filled the branches of a cardboard tree. The sewing room featured a display of repurposed secondhand clothes—a shimmery green pantsuit, a black sheath embellished with sequins, a child's dress with a new waistband, collar, and cuffs. More than simply providing an outlet for creativity, these activities had therapeutic value for clients, many of whom had suffered acute trauma. In the sewing room, we found a small group of Kurdish women embroidering cross-stitch squares. In recent weeks, Turkey had been bombing Kurdish regions along its border. Within the Kurdish diaspora, Afrin, the name of one of the most heavily hit towns, had become, like Dresden or Hiroshima, a one-word expression of suffering. In Irida's little art room, one grim-faced woman had cross-stitched the green and red of the Kurdish flag and was now adding a small heart and a single word: Afrin.

Tracey was, by then, only a few weeks away from returning to England for good. I felt lucky to see her before she left. Nearly two years after she and I had first met, I was also grateful for her continuing guidance on funding projects in Greece. Humanity Now had decided to help furnish Irida's nursery, so Tracey, Jen, and I went searching for toys. We started out at the superstore Moustakas, three floors of Toys "R" Us–style cheaply made imported plastic. "I know there's something better," Tracey said. Many of the children who visited Irida had fled war and lost everything. Even now, settled into long-term housing in Greece, their families lived on very little. Tracey was determined to fill Irida's nursery with well-made toys that could ignite the imagination. The three of us walked out of Moustakas. Tracey had an idea. "I remember a little shop I've seen not too many blocks from here." She led us north through the old city center.

On that cold February day, Thessaloniki felt considerably grimmer than the festive metropolis we'd strolled in the previous summer. Tracey herself added welcome color. She still looked like the leader of a punk band, with her maroon boots and black miniskirt; plus, she'd tied a vibrant scarf in a bow around her (now cherry-colored) hair. But her manner was glum, which I took as a sign of her determination to find great toys. Eventually, we entered a quiet neighborhood of cobbled streets and twisted lanes, then found the place Tracey remembered: a tiny gem of a toy store, piled high with puzzles and games, things that fly and things that float, sequined costumes, tambourines, fluttery birds hanging on strings. Over the next hour, we picked out wooden puzzles, sets of stacking blocks, and a stand-alone puppet theater with a red satin curtain. Jen and I were thrilled. Tracey looked pleased but not much happier. By now, the sun had set. We had to hurry to a nearby café, where we were meeting some other volunteers for dinner.

Few volunteers could stay in Greece indefinitely, and the loss of veteran relief workers added strain to a situation that was not improving. Week by week, many asylum applicants were accepted to countries of their choice in other parts of Europe. Others were rejected and stayed in Greece. As the relocation program ended in September 2017 and newcomers continued to arrive, the number of displaced people in the country climbed from 44,000 in August 2017 to 51,000 in February 2018; by the summer of 2018, it would reach nearly 60,000. Those numbers were undercounts, too, reflecting only the people whom authorities managed to tally.

Ibrahim Khoury had no plan to leave Greece. He had received asylum and planned to continue with the aid effort. Though he had slowed his pace somewhat, he still worked day and night, still experienced the same guilt about letting others down. Ibrahim was Humanity Now's most reliable adviser, the one with the most comprehensive understanding of the needs and funding opportunities in Greece, but he was very hard on himself. Back home, I regularly received messages from Ibrahim, who apologized for being rude or late with information.

In 2018, the Aegean Islands became, once again, a focal point of human suffering. The largest number of boats were arriving here and conditions deteriorated. The 2016 EU-Turkey Deal had turned the islands into registration centers, which forbade asylum seekers from even proceeding to the mainland until they received official approval. The wait could last months or even years, and some applicants would never receive approval. With so few moving on, island camps became fetid holding areas. The largest, Moria, had a capacity for 2,000 people, but UNHCR's data for the end of January showed that 5,113 actually lived there, with over a thousand in tents. UNHCR documented so many deficiencies that even its bureaucratic accounting made Moria sound like something out of Dickens:

- *Provision of hot water*: Yes—inadequate

- *Showers available in a separate area for women*: Yes—insufficient number

- *Sewage system in place*: Yes—inefficient

- *Fire safety for the site insured*: Yes—partially

- *Provision of electricity*: Yes—insufficient

- *Toilets available in a separate area for women*: No

- *Laundry facilities*: No

- *Children also attend Greek formal education*: No

For over two years now, Ibrahim had focused his efforts on the needs in Northern Greece. But with conditions on the islands becoming increasingly desperate, he began spending more of his time on Lesvos. The move wasn't hard for him. For someone who preferred living in hotels, it was a simple-enough maneuver to check out of one establishment, fly south, and check into another. By the time the four of us from Humanity Now arrived in Greece that winter of 2018, Ibrahim had taken up residence at a hotel in the island's central town of Mitilini.

We were looking for successful projects that would be more effective with an infusion of our funding, so he introduced us to leaders of some of the island's most successful teams, among them One Happy Family Community Center and Refugee 4 Refugees. One Happy Family offered activities, meals, and classes to hundreds of Moria residents. Refugee 4 Refugees operated a clothing-distribution center a few minutes' walk from the camp. Though he still called himself an independent volunteer, Ibrahim continued working closely with the British aid group Help Refugees to identify needs and distribute funds. Sometimes, following Ibrahim along a path in Moria or up the stairs of a migrant community center in the town of Mitilini, I felt as if he were carrying the burden of the relief effort on the laptop he kept in a backpack slung across his shoulder. At this point, the grassroots NGOs—both international and local—held even greater responsibility because larger organizations, like UNHCR, were starting to scale back their work in Greece. As we toured grassroots projects, we saw how some offered quality-of-life improvements, like children's spaces and language instruction, but many still focused on baseline needs. That winter, for example, Ibrahim distributed thousands of euros to pay for extra trash removal because the government's limited garbage pickup had resulted in a public health menace—mountains of debris scattered around the camp.

By this time, I'd grown used to Ibrahim's gruff but kindly manner. In Lesvos, he often joined the four of us from Humanity Now for dinner at a restaurant overlooking Mitilini's harbor. I don't know if he had changed since we first met at the Park Hotel, or if we just knew each other better, but he was more relaxed these days, more easygoing and silly. One evening, a soccer game on the flat-screen TV happened to catch his attention and he picked up his napkin and waved it like a flag above the floor. "You'd call this stupid if you did it with a cat, right?"

The four of us, confused, looked at him, vaguely nodding.

Then he tipped his head toward the athletes on TV and asked, with a glint in his eye, "Why do you not call it stupid, then, when you watch those people running after a ball?"

On the subject of refugee relief, I could pose difficult questions to Ibrahim and hear honest answers. I often ruminated about the role that volunteers played in Europe's humanitarian system. By rushing forward to fill gaps in aid, I wondered, was the grassroots movement inadvertently letting larger actors off the hook and helping perpetuate a failing system? In fact, Tracey Myers had once suggested to me that it might be better if, instead of spending their time in Greece, volunteers became activists and camped out for a year in front of the European Union headquarters in Brussels. Maybe, Tracey surmised, "we could have impacted greater change."

One afternoon, I raised this issue with Ibrahim. "If the small grassroots aid groups didn't do these things, do you think the larger actors would step in and take more of that responsibility themselves?"

He responded immediately. "No," he replied, bristling at the suggestion that refugees and migrants might benefit if the small NGOs pulled back on their efforts. "There is nothing wrong with the volunteers doing anything. What you said—'It's their responsibility'—I completely disagree. It's not one responsibility. It's everyone's responsibility."

I had often heard Ibrahim condemn the sluggish response of the Greek government, the European Union, and mainstream charitable organizations. He certainly wasn't praising them now, but he had something else on his mind. "If you were walking in the States," he said, "and an old woman falls down, we wouldn't say, 'Oh, someone from the government have to take this responsibility and help her.' You go and help her. That doesn't mean to take the burden off the state. It just means it's more help for the people."

Ibrahim was talking about a human compulsion that we don't discuss very often—the basic desire to lend a hand. "Help shouldn't be a brain thing," he told me. "If someone is in need, you can't say, 'Oh, it's not my responsibility.'" As he saw it, we weren't paying for trash removal because larger actors had failed; we were paying for trash removal because people were suffering and we had the power to help.

CHAPTER 33

The Dinosaur Playground

THAT FEBRUARY OF 2018, AFTER HUMANITY NOW finished its funding trip in Greece, Zakia and I flew to Frankfurt, Germany. From there, we took a high-speed train to Würzburg, changed for the local line, and got off at a small town, where Abu Omar Khalil was waiting. More than a year had passed since I'd seen him, and the two of us greeted each other shyly. Zakia, never shy, let loose in an exuberant stream of Arabic and English: "It's so cold! I'm freezing! I need a cigarette!" After we found a taxi, Abu Omar got into the front seat, and, demonstrating that he could be a translator, too, began talking with the driver in hesitant but surprisingly serviceable German.

Things had certainly changed. When I met the Khalil family at Idomeni, they lived in a tent. Now, nearly two years later, they lived in a subsidized two-bedroom apartment in bucolic Bavaria. The girls and Abu Omar, who was taking an intensive language course, spent weekdays at school. Salma stayed home with the little ones—their number plural. A year earlier, she'd given birth to their fourth child, Zahra, a little girl.

For three days, the eight of us hung out in their apartment. That week, a cold front that meteorologists dubbed "the Beast from the East" was blasting across Europe, and none of us wanted to go outside. In the mornings, after Zakia and I arrived from our hotel, Layla or Nura would switch on the TV, which doubled as a stereo, and we listened to the haunting voice of Fairuz, the beloved Lebanese songstress, while drinking coffee. As always, we ate practically all day long. After coffee came platters of hummus, pickled vegetables, and *labneh* cheese. Later, from a kitchen that was just a galley off the main room, they managed to produce *kabseh,* a cashew-dotted pilaf, and *imsahab,* a broiled chicken and potato dish that required big Abu Omar to sit cross-legged on the kitchen floor, staring into the oven to make sure it browned just right. One afternoon, while the girls and I played maybe our twentieth round of Rummikub, he emerged from the kitchen with a sweet called *madluqa,* layers of cream-and-pistachio-covered semolina, which we devoured before returning to our game.

Mostly, we talked. Salma could speak a few words of English. Abu Omar knew more, but his brain was so saturated with German that every time he tried to say "thank you," it came out as "*danke.*" I could sense his frustration with starting all over at the age of forty-one, but he never complained. The man had a family to support. "The key to this society is language," he told me. He glanced at Zakia, who made it possible for us to converse. "It's not like I'll get a job and they'll assign me a translator."

Their relocation to Germany brought joy and sorrow, both. They had reunited with Abu Omar's war-wounded brother, Anwar, who lived nearby, but their extended family now formed part of the Syrian diaspora scattered across Europe and the Middle East. New life brought new challenges. A staffer at a large humanitarian aid organization once shared with me the disconcerting observation that some asylum seekers become *more depressed* when they reach their final destination. Up until that moment, displaced people endure the hardship of their situation by continually repeating a simple mantra: "This is temporary, this is temporary, this is temporary." Once they receive asylum, she said, "the dream stops." Suddenly, they face two painful realities at the same time: losing their homeland and beginning again in an alien culture, separated, perhaps permanently, from loved ones far away. These two realizations, experienced simultaneously, can send people into a tailspin.

On the surface, the Khalils were adapting well. Or maybe I should say that they were determined to adapt well, but they faced struggles both small and large. Their village in Germany, for example, lacked the dynamism of urban Damascus. "The neighbors go out and walk their dogs," Layla told me, "and then they go back inside." The family missed the streetscapes of home. They also missed the lively refugee enclaves of Athens. The difference between vibrant urban neighborhoods and quiet country villages might have seemed mostly atmospheric, but it also spoke to their isolation here. At school and in the village, the girls had begun to socialize with other children. They'd even gone on a ski trip with their class. But the parents had not made friends or, as Abu Omar adamantly put it, they had not made friends *yet*.

They dreamed of having a car. With a car, Abu Omar could run a taxi service. With a car, he said, the family could get out of the apartment, instead of sitting around "looking at each other until our eyes hurt." But that dream remained a dream. Meanwhile, they kept in close touch with family back home.

I had, since our first meeting at Idomeni, played a role in their lives. Much of it was friendly, like the time I took them bowling in Athens or played all those sessions of UNO with the girls in their apartment. And some of it was financial—the few hundred dollars I'd given them during emergencies. The money helped, but, like the volunteer movement in general, it offered only a temporary solution to a larger problem. In regard to their most serious needs—to get to safety, to receive asylum, and to see peace, finally, restored in their homeland—I could do nothing for them. Grassroots volunteers were like the support teams that ride on the boats trailing long-distance swimmers: We offered supplies and encouragement, but refugees were alone down there in the water.

If the war ends, Abu Omar told me one day, "we will go back." He described displacement as a long, harrowing night. Things would get better, he said. "At some point, the sun will rise."

"And what then?" I asked. "What will happen to you?"

"When the sun rises, it will be our turn to help people."

AFTER TRACEY MYERS RETURNED TO ENGLAND, she felt pleased about the grassroots accomplishments in Greece, but she also experienced something like grief over the failures of the volunteer effort. Lack of experience had impeded success and sometimes even caused harm. Volunteer teams didn't do a good enough job of sharing hard-earned lessons, which hindered their ability to grow from their mistakes. She also considered it a missed opportunity that international and Greek volunteers had not collaborated better; they could have learned from one another. She had thought it valid, back in 2015, to excuse the movement's inexperience and lack of knowledge because almost everyone was completely new to the effort. On Lesvos, she remembered, volunteers found their own incompetence amusing. "It's like volunteers are determined to learn lessons the hard way," they would joke with one another.

But after nearly three years of volunteering, Tracey wanted to see a movement that was growing stronger. "I'm not taking myself out of this equation," she told me. "I made a ton of stupid mistakes." She believed they could all do better, that you couldn't build a successful response if you were continually starting from scratch. She didn't want grassroots teams to lose their nimbleness and creativity, but she yearned to see practices that made organizations more resilient. Maintaining official hours of operation, for example, compelled downtime and helped preserve volunteers' physical and mental health. Likewise, the time-consuming process of interviewing prospective volunteers—rather than simply welcoming anyone who showed up—helped keep dangerous individuals from joining teams. Tracey was advocating for something more organized than the makeshift system she had come to know so well, a system that didn't leave volunteers feeling they'd been used up and thrown away.

Ultimately, she had left Greece feeling that way herself. As early as Lesvos, she told me, she suspected that the work would take a toll on her psyche. "I knew it was going to physically and emotionally hurt me. From that first week, I knew it," she said. "And I decided that that was okay. So there was consent here for this, really."

Hearing those words from Tracey, I felt surprised by her distressed tone, and by the suggestion that the experience had been traumatic. "It's like getting involved in a relationship that you know is going to be bad for you," I mused.

"I guess so," she said; then she was quiet for a moment before adding, "but with a better outcome. In a negative relationship, there's no positive. But, in this case, it was actually 'I am willing to lose this in order to gain that.' And gaining was actually contributing something."

ONE DAY, I CALLED JENNI JAMES, who'd been back in New Zealand for some time. She lived in Auckland now, and she hadn't had an easy time transitioning out of the crisis-to-crisis intensity of the grassroots relief movement. In an effort to maintain a connection to refugee issues, she had joined the Refugee Council of New Zealand as a volunteer, but the group focused on policy and had little need for her practical expertise.

The Jenni who returned to New Zealand was a profoundly different person from the one who had first gone to Lesvos to volunteer. She felt that her values had changed completely. She lived extremely simply now. "My life's not ruled around having things," she told me. "I find I haven't got any will to find a nine-to-five job. . . . And yet I can work eighteen-hour days and seven days a week for nothing and live on the bare bones of my ass."

I asked if, given the opportunity, she would go back to Greece.

"In a heartbeat," she told me.

Jenni had given years of her life to volunteering. As a means of addressing human suffering, she still considered the grassroots effort to be a completely inadequate response. "There has to be a better way," she told me. "But if it wasn't for the volunteer movement, there'd be nowhere near the care for people."

Jenni knew I was writing this book, and before we got off the phone, she made a request: "Don't forget the Dinosaur Playground." When she thought back on her efforts in Greece, she liked to recall that cold December day when the structure opened and Sinatex Camp's youngest inhabitants spent their first giddy moments exploring it. "It was my final bow-out," she told me. "That's how I finished."

Sinatex closed a few months after Jenni left Greece. The government transferred its residents to another facility, Lagadakia, which wasn't much better. Jenni James was back in New Zealand, but other Good Samaritans remained in Greece. Somebody took apart the play structure, loaded it into a truck, hauled it to a different camp, and reassembled it there for other children to play on.

CHAPTER 34

Alhamdulillah

ONE AFTERNOON IN ATHENS IN 2019, Zakia and I propped my computer on a pillow in my hotel room and called Rima Halabi over Skype. As soon as her image appeared on the screen, I noticed something unfamiliar in her expression. Rima had always seemed cheerful and confident, even during hardships. But now, in Germany, she seemed altered in a way I couldn't pinpoint.

That afternoon, Rima talked while sitting at her kitchen table, children flashing past and her husband, Musa, intermittently calling out to her from another room. Little by little, she caught us up on her life. During their first year in Germany, the family had lived in a refugee dormitory. The government eventually helped them move into a house of their own. About this house, Rima bubbled with enthusiasm. She described it as "really big, really comfortable," with a roomy kitchen, a nice bathroom, and bedrooms on the second floor. Though the government provided the accommodations, Musa, who worked as a carpenter now, could manage the remainder of his family's expenses. "And imagine this," Rima added. "In the other places we were living, before we moved here, we didn't even open our luggage and unpack our clothes." The family had endured displacement for years already. Rima, the fastidious housekeeper, had refused to get organized until they settled into a permanent home.

The Halabis had faced challenges, of course. It had taken time to readjust as a family once they reunited. During their two-year separation, Malika had learned to live without her mom. After Rima stepped back into her life, the girl resisted maternal affection. But time passed and nature assisted. When Malika reached puberty, she developed acne, and, desperate, she allowed Rima to smear a homemade yogurt mask across her face. The rose water–scented concoction did its job in several ways. The girl's skin cleared. Mother and daughter grew closer.

Having a home of their own had a profound effect on the family. "Everything is different now," Rima told us. "When you shop, you don't think, Is this necessary? You just shop because it's your house and you've established yourself and you don't keep on saying, 'I'll do this later.' No. This is your house. You buy it now."

That's when I realized what had changed in Rima. She looked *satisfied*. I'd never seen that emotion in her before. "It's like you're back in a real life again," I noted.

"Yes. I feel like I've come back to life," Rima said. She began to laugh, touching her fingertips to her cheeks. "Don't you see my face? I'm all *fresh*!"

I had first come to know her as the Second School cook who, almost single-handedly, provided daily nutrition for four hundred people. But before I knew her, of course, she had pulled her children out of a war zone, herded them through Turkey, gotten them safely across the Aegean, endured nights on the floor of a gas station and then months in a tent, traumatized by snakes. But to understand Rima's sense of identity, you had to trace her route all the way back to Syria and a house with a modern kitchen and good doors, the last address where her family had led a stable, peaceful life. "Refugee" was only a temporary state. It didn't define her.

"*Alhamdulillah*," Rima said via Skype. I understood that word. It meant "Praise God."

And then Zakia translated the rest: "She hopes it stays like this forever."

THAT AFTERNOON, ZAKIA AND I ALSO CALLED THE KHALILS. Two years into their life in Germany, they occupied the same apartment that Zakia and I had visited the previous winter. Over Skype, we saw Salma, without her hijab, thirty-three years old and still looking like a teenager. Abu

Omar sat beside her, wry and weary as ever. Little Zahra, on her mother's lap, could talk now and said, "Hi! Hi! Hi!" to us on the screen. Her brother, Omar, almost four, kept a curious eye on us while leaning into his father's knees. Next to their parents sat Layla and Nura, now fourteen and eleven, respectively. Layla had fully blossomed into a teenager, but Nura still had some little girl in her serious features. In the years since we'd met, I'd come to love these girls deeply. Perhaps more than with anyone else in this story, I felt pained by the upheaval of their lives.

"We have a car now," Abu Omar announced, glancing archly at his wife and kids. "Now I'm a chauffeur for my family. They don't pay me. I do it for free."

Salma laughed, refusing to show any particular appreciation for his efforts. "On the Day of Judgment," she said blithely, "he'll have his reward."

The two parents spoke in Arabic, letting Zakia translate, but Layla, exuberant as ever, chattered in English. "We can now be late," she told me, explaining how the car had changed their lives. "Every day we have to wake up early for school and I say to my Dad, 'Oh, I'm sorry, I'm late now. You have to go with me with the car.'"

This car was no small thing. Because the family lived far from an urban center, the vehicle dramatically reduced their isolation. More than that, it symbolized their rehabilitation. One day at Idomeni in 2016, Abu Omar had patted the roof of our rental car, then said in his fill-in-the-blanks English, "Me. Syria. Car." He didn't have the vocabulary to explain how, for many years, he had driven professionally, but he could communicate that he had not always lived in a tent and that, back home, he had played a productive role in his society. The purchase of a car in Germany helped the family feel whole again.

Salma said something that made Zakia laugh. "She was so happy when they got the car, that she started—" Zakia looked at me. "What is that vocal thing we do when we're extremely happy, like at weddings?"

I barely knew the word myself. "Ululating?"

Zakia nodded. "She started ululating."

In fact, the once-timid Salma had been the force that propelled the Khalils into the world of independent transportation. The family bought the vehicle before Abu Omar actually acquired a license to operate it, and he had planned to keep it parked until he had the permit. "We can't use the car without the license," he'd explained to his wife.

Salma objected. "Hell no," she'd told him. "We're using it. I need to go to the pharmacy." She won that battle and looked triumphant as she described it to me now.

The story of displacement can't have a happy ending. It chronicles too much loss for that. But there is something more necessary and durable than happiness, and that's resilience. Sometimes, in the crush of bad news about global migration, we focus so much on people's reasons for flight that we forget how much strength they muster to get away. They pull themselves out of war zones, escape poverty and violence, recognize when they have reached the end of one path, and with determination set off on another.

Several times in the years since I'd known her, I'd watched Salma sob over all that she'd lost. I had no illusions that she had moved beyond her grief, but she was clearly finding her way forward. This was not the life that any of them had expected. It wasn't even the life they wanted. But they would take it.

Epilogue

In November of 2019, the four of us from Humanity Now visited Moria Camp, the largest migrant reception center on the Continent. Conditions in the camp were so notorious that Moria had become a symbol of humanitarian failure in Europe. Each time we visited, in fact, the place seemed worse than before. Moria's official capacity had increased to three thousand, but by the time of our visit, the population had soared to seventeen thousand. People were living inside its fenced enclosure and in the makeshift "jungle" camp that stretched across the hills outside. Walking through Moria felt like walking through a crowded subway station at rush hour, except that people had to live in this place. Only a few had shelter in official housing—containers that had been subdivided, then subdivided again. The vast majority squatted in tents or in handmade sheds. Crafted from scavenged debris and topped with tarps, these hovels sat in the gaps between buildings, on damp ground near public latrines, and even on a narrow slice of land that someone had briefly conceived of as a playground.

Moria's occupants spent their days waiting. They waited for food, basic supplies, and habitable accommodations. They waited to transfer to the mainland, and they waited for the results of their asylum applications. Each day, crowds converged at central locations to receive rations—orange juice and a packaged croissant in the morning, a hot meal in a small plastic box in the afternoon. Combined, these distributions provided what one volunteer leader told us amounted to eight hundred calories per person. For additional nutrition and other needs, UNHCR administered an EU-funded finance system, which allocated individuals ninety euros in monthly cash assistance; people used this money for everything from refilling the cards on their cell phones to buying toothpaste, dish soap, and rice. Of course, cash assistance did nothing to relieve the camp's rampant social problems—drug abuse, crime, violence, and all kinds of mental health emergencies. Late that year, UNHCR spokesperson Liz Throssell called on Greek authorities to reduce crowding by transferring vulnerable residents to the mainland. "Keeping people on the islands in these inadequate and insecure conditions is inhumane and must come to an end," she said. Such calls to action had almost no effect at all.

On that visit, the Humanity Now group toured Moria with Jonathan Turner, one of the founders of the German aid organization Watershed, which deployed plumbers, electricians, and engineers to improve water, sanitation, and shelter facilities. These volunteers did dirty work, like flushing out blocked drains, replacing moldy showers, and installing toilets. Day after day, sometimes in freezing cold and other times in withering heat, Watershed's technicians used a little money and a lot of ingenuity to shore up Moria's fragile infrastructure. Jonathan showed us a refurbished shipping container, for example, that now provided six individual toilet/shower cubicles for vulnerable single women. Each stall had a squat toilet, a detachable showerhead, and a sink. Jonathan, a bespectacled British engineer, pointed to a shelf attached to the wall of one of the cubicles and explained, "We put in the shelf so women could keep their belongings off the wet floor as they showered." The women slept in shared quarters, often with strangers, and they likely held their valuables close at all times. The shelf was nothing but a simple enhancement to an otherwise spartan setup, but it addressed a real need.

A year after our visit, in September 2020, a fire raced through Moria, annihilating the camp. Fortunately, no one died in the blaze, but it displaced the camp's entire population, which was then twelve thousand. Some particularly vulnerable former residents were quickly transferred off the island, but the vast majority spent subsequent days living and sleeping in the rough on the surrounding hills and along nearby country roads. The fire rendered the camp uninhabitable, wrecking the tents, the hovels, and those clever showers with their convenient shelves.

After the fire, the Greek government and large international relief agencies located an empty piece of land for a new camp, only a few miles from the former site. Officials named it Mavrovouni, but many people just called it Moria 2.0. Not surprisingly, given the history of the aid effort, problems became obvious from the start. A portion of the land had formerly been used as a military firing range, which raised concerns about lead contamination. On top of that, the place needed virtually everything to make it habitable. And winter was fast approaching, which meant that frigid weather would soon become a challenge—again.

The fire did not destroy the grassroots aid network. While large international actors brought in tents and installed drainage, it fell to volunteer teams, as usual, to fill the gaps. A coalition of small NGOs created sandbag bunds to reduce the threat of flooding. Watershed helped install "bucket shower" cubicles, where people could dump cold water over their heads. Over the next few months, these teams worked continually to improve conditions. By March, six months after the fire, people in the camps had access to hot water for bathing. A team of some ninety camp residents—known as "community volunteers"— oversaw five shower areas.

The participation of displaced people, in the end, reflects a major strength of the grassroots effort and also an important indication of its evolution since the days when Greek villagers, tourists, and volunteers from stable countries handed out bottled water on Aegean beaches. Many of these displaced staffers now play leadership roles in relief operations. "If we are serious about not exploiting the most vulnerable, we have to empower them," British psychiatrist and humanitarian professional Lynne Jones has said. Sometimes the most astute and pragmatic humanitarians are the ones who have moved through the system themselves.

A CRISIS ON THE SCALE OF THE ONE IN GREECE leads to myriad smaller crises: A baby's rash drives a displaced family from its shelter; a young refugee, mistaken for a human trafficker, spends a year in jail; a woman decides to volunteer with the aid effort and ends up destroying her marriage. Occasionally, however, a small-scale calamity has an effect that spreads far beyond the lives of the people most directly involved.

In early 2020, one such situation unfolded in Greece, and it rocked the grassroots movement.

That winter, a female former volunteer accused Ibrahim Khoury of rape. The two had served together with the British charity Help Refugees, which now went by the name Choose Love. Both Ibrahim and his accuser agreed on several basic facts: Three years earlier, in 2017, the two had dinner together in Thessaloniki and sexual intercourse occurred later that night. He says that they both got drunk and that the sex was consensual. She says he drugged and raped her.

After the woman came forward, Ibrahim stopped working with Choose Love, and the charity launched an investigation into the rape allegation. In the UK, the organization operates under the auspices of a larger British charity, Prism the Gift Fund, and Prism sent investigators to Greece to conduct an inquiry. The team interviewed Ibrahim, his accuser, and others with knowledge of the situation. While the final report has not been publicized, Choose Love later called the findings 'inconclusive.'

The situation had remained private, but in 2021 the alleged victim went public with her accusation. She not only condemned Ibrahim, whom she did not identify by name, but she also slammed Choose Love, saying that the NGO had failed to both protect her initially and respond appropriately after she came forward with her allegation. "I found," she wrote on a website she'd created, "that the worst and most painful part of my trauma has been the manner in which [Choose Love] handled it, by claiming 'we are taking this situation very seriously.'"

After she accused him of rape, Ibrahim sued her for defamation of character. She responded by filing a counter-complaint against him. As the cases wound through Greece's judicial system, Choose Love embarked on an organizational restructuring that established formal protection measures for aid recipients, staff, and volunteers. By then, however, many in the grassroots community had divided into camps that either supported Choose Love or aligned with Ibrahim's accuser. Of these two camps, the NGO's critics were by far the loudest, filling social media forums with complaints, some of which proved constructive, like the assertion that the charity needed to put in place strong protection measures. Other assertions, however, were opinion-based or unsubstantiated. Critics blasted the charity for funding aid teams they didn't like, withholding funds from ones they did, associating with the "establishment," raising money with the help of celebrity endorsements, and acting like a "business." As often happens during such firestorms, respectful discussion became impossible, and any hope that the criticism might help Choose Love improve its services to refugees was lost in the vitriol enabled by social media. Those who attacked the NGO castigated people who disagreed with them, questioning their morals and intentions. Supporters of Choose Love mostly refrained from the debate for fear, I suspect, of being attacked themselves. None of the claims provided credible evidence that the organization had misspent funds.

The scandal had a disastrous effect. Since 2015, Choose Love had raised more than sixty million dollars for refugee relief efforts, helping support dozens of small NGOs in countries around the world. The situation provided an opportunity for the organization to recognize its weaknesses and grow stronger and more competent, but public debate marred that process by focusing on anger and recrimination, not constructive criticism. By late 2021, Choose Love, reeling under a funding shortfall, pulled support from seven relief teams in Calais, France, and cut funding to many teams in Greece as well. Together, these teams had relied on the charity for hundreds of thousands of British pounds in aid. "This year," Choose Love announced, "we have had to make some difficult decisions."

I first learned about the situation in 2020, when Ibrahim called to let Humanity Now know about the rape allegation and to inform us that he would no longer advise our funding efforts in Greece. He told us that he had also ended his collaboration with Choose Love and was withdrawing from the aid movement because he didn't want the scandal to damage refugee relief efforts. Eventually, the highest criminal court in Greece would examine the allegations against Ibrahim and, in 2022, rule in his favor, freeing him of all charges. But the situation underscored the fragility of a relief movement that relies heavily on the goodwill and energy of volunteers. As a result of the scandal, by late 2021, Choose Love, the largest funder of grassroots aid in Greece, seemed to be fighting for its very existence. This singular event had devastating consequences for an aid ecosystem that lacked a stable institutional infrastructure to help it survive emergencies like this one. The grass-roots attitude that makes these volunteer aid groups so agile in the face of quickly changing conditions also makes them vulnerable to the kinds of events that larger institutions can weather through formal systems of crisis management.

I want to note, however, that the grassroots effort did not collapse.

When hundreds of thousands of displaced people arrived on Greece's Aegean Islands in 2015, they turned the country into a laboratory for small-scale humanitarianism. That movement has generated both aston-ishing successes and dramatic failure. Its most vital attribute, however, is its ability to endure. Against sometimes overwhelming odds, vol-unteers have continued to offer aid even while dealing with scandals, shipwrecks, fires, bureaucratic ineptitude, bigotry, and countless crises and tragedies. When the COVID-19 pandemic threatened the lives of thousands sleeping in tents on Samos Island, teams of volunteers—most of them camp residents—helped slow the spread of the virus by attach-ing hand sanitizer dispensers to the trunks of trees. Their contributions have been essential. Yet I find myself returning to a version of the same question that I asked myself the first time I visited Idomeni: Why did so much of the responsibility for protecting migrants from COVID-19 fall to volunteers? The answer is unchanging and still shocking: Because the international community has failed to provide a comprehensive response to human displacement.

War, instability, climate change, and bigotry have forced the world into an era of migration unlike any we have seen in generations, and the problems grow more urgent. These days, few communities in the world remain untouched by it. The question is not "How do we stop it?" Rather, it is "How do we adapt?" The drama unfolding in Greece over the last few years provides one practical answer, which is that individuals can play an important role in the effort. It's not necessary to travel to Greece and stand in the surf as a sea rescue volunteer. All around the world, newcomers need language instruction, beds, tables, chairs, and jobs. They need friends, too, and a sense of community. We have seen this fact play out more recently as millions have fled Afghanistan and Ukraine: Volunteers can help no matter where they live.

The Greeks have a word for the desire to help people in need. They call it *philoxenia,* or "love of strangers." The term helps explain the generosity that Greeks have shown the tens of thousands of migrants in their midst, but it also speaks to the broader ideals of the grassroots effort. I often think of Jenni James standing on that ladder at Softex Camp, mosquito-proofing a derelict warehouse. Or Sami Malouf helping fellow residents of the Single Men's Squat communicate with their doctors. Or Rima Halabi, hovering over a pot in a shed, cooking dinner for four hundred. Or Tracey Myers pulling a drowning man from the surf. Any one of them, seeing despair, might have left the problem to those in charge of handling it. They might have turned away, but they didn't.

Acknowledgments

MANY PEOPLE GAVE ME SUPPORT as I researched and wrote this book. First, I want to thank the individuals and families who so generously told me their stories. It takes courage to share the details of your life with someone who plans to write about it. Thank you for your trust. I tried my best to do justice to your experience.

I have traveled back and forth to Greece many times since 2016, and four individuals have been my most treasured companions. The first three—Stephanie Meyers, Jen Maraveyias, and Carol Atwood—joined with me to create Humanity Now. Working with them has been one of the great joys of my life. Similarly, I first contacted Zakia Aqra back in 2016 to translate a few interviews. Our collaboration has ended up stretching over six years and she has been an essential partner, not only translating Arabic and Greek but also helping me to better understand a complex and deeply challenging situation. I've been very fortunate to have these four as colleagues, travel companions, and friends.

I am grateful not only to the people whose names appear in this book but also to many others who provided insight on the volunteer effort specifically and the migrant situation in general. These include Nikos Agapakis, Artur Cipllaka, Barry Fallon, Celine Gagne, Ingrid Kantarova, Chloe Kousoula, Stephanie Larson, Mary Beth Bride Leland, Marina Liaki, Penny Mylona, Josie Naughton, Zora O'Neill, Holly Penalver, Phoebe Ramsay, Ariel Ricker, Cyril Romann, Nico Sanders, Carolin Senby, Sumita Shah, and Matthew Sheppard. Thanks also to Abdullah, Ahmad, Ali, Salwah, and Rami for sharing your stories.

I want to extend a special thanks to Meg Storey, who read numerous drafts and helped me figure out what I needed to say and how to say it. Thanks also to Karen Bender, George Bishop, Jenna Butler, Amy

Damutz, Nina de Gramont, Sara Frankel, Joe Gannon, David Gessner, Judy Goldman, Laura Goodman-Bryan, Laura Hart, Rosalind Hudis, Bill Irvine, Eileen Kelly, Rebecca Lee, Sheri Malman, Hope Mitnick, Celia Rivenbark, Adam Sachs, Ira Sachs, Lynne Sachs, Susan Salzer, Kathy Steuer, Angela Stilley, and Mark Street for kindnesses large and small. Kathryn Winogura inspired me to go to Greece and write a book about it, and Paula Whyman, of *Scoundrel Time,* published some of the earliest essays that grew from the experiences I had there. I am forever grateful to my agent, Doug Stewart, for believing in the value of this story, and to my editor, Erika Goldman, for her dedication to the plight of the displaced and for so wisely and kindly guiding the book to completion.

I'd like to add thanks here to the journalists who worked so hard to report on what was unfolding daily in Greece, and for the media outlets that saw the value in financially supporting their efforts. They have created an essential record of what happened, which helped me immeasurably, laying the groundwork for this book.

Several arts institutions helped me in important ways as I researched and wrote *All Else Failed.* The Hawthornden Literary Retreat for Creative Writers and the Weymouth Center for the Arts and Humanities gave me residencies in the most gorgeous, splendid places. A grant from the North Carolina Arts Council provided financial assistance.

Finally, the word *thanks* seems insubstantial when I think of the debt I owe to my large and loving family. They have given me the things I value most in my life. My husband, Todd Berliner; my sons, Jesse and Sam Berliner-Sachs; my parents, Diane Sachs and Ira Sachs; and my siblings, stepparents, in-laws, and nieces and nephews have all given me love and enormous support during the best times and during painful ones, too. There is nothing like writing a book about displacement to make a person recognize her own good fortune in having a home.

Author's Note

I FOLLOWED SEVERAL DIFFERENT AVENUES in researching this story. The core material in the book grew from interviews with the seven individuals (or, in two cases, families) whose experiences I've woven together to create the central narrative. Because I wanted the book to reflect how their lives and perspectives changed over time, I spoke with each of them repeatedly over a period of years. Most of these interviews took place in Greece, but we also met in other parts of Europe and via Skype. To communicate with people who were most comfortable speaking in Arabic or Greek, I relied on Zakia Aqra for translations.

In addition to these core interviews, I also learned from numerous individuals who shared knowledge and expertise about the humanitarian crisis in Greece. Among these were Greek representatives of government and civil society, career professionals from mainstream aid organizations, United Nations staffers, Greek political activists, displaced adults and unaccompanied minors, and many grassroots volunteers. My research also benefited from numerous primary documents and scholarly studies, both published and unpublished, including NGO, European Union, and Greek government reports; media coverage; discussions on volunteer-group Facebook pages; the social media posts of volunteers and displaced people; and books about humanitarianism and Middle Eastern culture and history. Finally, I relied on my own experience as a journalist and a volunteer aid worker in Greece.

As I've noted at the beginning of the book, I have changed some identifying details in order to protect people's safety and privacy. To simplify a complicated narrative, I occasionally omitted people who might have been present at a given time but who were incidental to the book. I have also sometimes changed the order of events to help maintain clarity and the flow of the narrative.

THE JOSEF AND ANNI ALBERS FOUNDATION is proud to support this publication by Bellevue Literary Press of *All Else Failed: The Unlikely Volunteers at the Heart of the Migrant Aid Crisis* by Dana Sachs. The chance for people to escape tyranny and live in freedom mattered more to Anni and Josef than their own individual pasts, issues of nationalism or race, or artistic doctrine, and we feel that this book is true to that spirit.

In 2006, the Albers Foundation created Le Korsa, a nonprofit organization devoted to improving human lives in Senegal. In Pulaar, a predominant language in the Tambacounda region where we do most of our work, "korsa" means "love from respect." In the past decade, we have partnered with teachers determined to see children in rural villages gain the education that will enable them to realize their potential; with doctors who labor under taxing conditions to provide health care to everyone who comes to their clinics and hospitals; with women who have established agricultural cooperatives to improve their families' nutrition and develop their own income source; and with artists wanting to expand their scope and explore their similarities with, as well as their differences from, people of various backgrounds. In the course of our work, we have become deeply involved with the issues of migration from sub-Saharan Africa to Europe and elsewhere, and the issues raised in Dana Sachs's compelling book, as well as her understanding of effective action to combat a humanitarian crisis, are dear to us.

Josef spoke of achieving maximum effect from minimal means; Anni spoke of the human needs for encouragement and beauty. After 1933, when the Alberses found refuge from Nazi Germany in the United States, they held to these beliefs while successfully achieving racial integration of the faculty at Black Mountain College in North Carolina and managing to get Anni's parents, other family members, and friends out of Germany even once ships with refugees were denied entry into the United States. *All Else Failed* is a major achievement in the ongoing struggle to enable migrants to survive and thrive. We are honored to support Dana Sachs's fine book because we know that the real legacy of Anni and Josef is their wish for people everywhere to savor existence.

Bellevue Literary Press is devoted to publishing literary fiction and nonfiction at the intersection of the arts and sciences because we believe that science and the humanities are natural companions for understanding the human experience. We feature exceptional literature that explores the nature of consciousness, embodiment, and the underpinnings of the social contract. With each book we publish, our goal is to foster a rich, interdisciplinary dialogue that will forge new tools for thinking and engaging with the world.

To support our press and its mission, and for our full catalogue of published titles, please visit us at blpress.org.

Bellevue Literary Press
New York